WOMEN AND PAID WORK

Women and Paid Work

Issues of Equality

Edited by
Audrey Hunt

Foreword by Robert M. Lindley

St. Martin's Press New York

Scholarly & Reference Division,
St. Martin's Press, Inc., 175 Fifth Avenue, New York, NY 10010

First published in the United States of America in 1988

Printed in Hong Kong

ISBN 0–312–01200–4

Library of Congress Cataloging-in-Publication Data
Women and paid work.
Bibliography: p.
Includes index.
1. Equal pay for equal work—Great Britain.
2. Women—Employment—Great Britain. I. Hunt, Audrey.
HD6061.2.G7W66 1988 331.2'1 87–23477
ISBN 0–312–01200–4

Contents

List of Figures

List of Tables

Notes on the Contributors

Shirley Dex is a Lecturer in Economics in the Department of Economics, University of Keele.

Peter Elias is a Principal Research Fellow at the Institute for Employment Research, University of Warwick.

Audrey Hunt is a freelance social researcher. She formerly worked at the Office of Population Censuses and Surveys.

Brian G. M. Main is Professor of Economics at the University of St Andrews

Kate Purcell is a Research Fellow at the Institute for Employment Research, University of Warwick.

Ed Puttick is a Senior Research Officer at the Equal Opportunities Commission.

Lesley Rimmer was formerly the Deputy Director of the Family Policy Studies Centre.

Lois B. Shaw was formerly a Senior Research Associate of the Center for Human Resource Research, Ohio State University.

Foreword

The present labour force position of women has not been reached through a continuous process which simply sped up during the last twenty or thirty years. During the twentieth century alone, the relative importance of paid employment in women's lives has fluctuated markedly. Any belief that the work of women during the First World War would quickly alter social attitudes and begin the march of progress towards greater labour market equality was soon belied by the experience of the inter-war years. Nor did their Second World War contribution produce a radical rethinking of the position of women. The exigencies of war rather than the possibilities of peace seemed to dominate: the married women in Beveridge's welfare state were expected to return to motherhood with only a small minority pursuing gainful employment. What rescued women from a regression to the past was not a cultural change born of war-time experience but the rising demand for labour in the post-war boom. By the time the British economy again experienced unemployment on the scale of the inter-war years, the position of women had altered and a ratchet of changed social attitudes and economic convenience appeared to be in place to defend it.

The present labour force position of women may not, of course, be irreversible. But the fear that high unemployment will nurture negative attitudes towards equality has been less important than the focus on whether or not what has been achieved amounts to as much as it seems. One of the main aims of this book is to deal with this central issue by replacing the rather static pictures of female labour force participation by dynamic ones which capture the patterns of education, paid and unpaid work undertaken by women over their life cycles. Comparison of these life cycle representations from cohort to cohort yields much richer insight into the place of paid work in women's lives. This does, however, create methodological difficulties requiring quite complex manipulation of individual work history information. It involves the creation of new summary statistics to capture the main features of women's activity. It requires a careful attention to cohort effects in order to extract the maximum information from cross-sectional surveys when much-needed longitudinal surveys are not available. It calls for a reinterpretation of familiar aggregate labour force statistics in terms of underlying decision-making processes and the preferences and constraints which govern the observed outcomes.

Through this subtler treatment of the female life cycle in statistical and econometric analysis, this book pursues a second objective: to create a wider area of common quantitative ground on which economists and sociologists might seek a more productive synthesis of their different perspectives.

Finally, *Women and Paid Work* considers the main policy issues which arise from studying the current position of women in the labour market and changes which have taken place since the Second World War. The prospects for greater equality in preparation for, access to and experience of the labour market give little room for complacency. The need for government to create a stronger legislative framework within which greater equality can be achieved is given particular stress. It remains to be seen whether this will be forthcoming. Nor can we be sure that it will be enough in a period of increasing pressure on labour force flexibility and the minimisation of labour costs. Meanwhile, however, the contributors to this book have provided new evidence and interpretations on the developing position of women in the labour market and the place of work in women's lives.

The research programme which provided the main basis for this book was co-ordinated by Peter Elias and funded by the Equal Opportunities Commission. On behalf of the Institute I should like to acknowledge the key role played by Peter Elias in undertaking this collaborative initiative and thank the authors and Audrey Hunt, as editor, for participating in the programme.

ROBERT M. LINDLEY

Preface and Acknowledgements

It is often easier to comprehend the purpose underlying an edited collection of research material in a book if the reader knows something about the process which drew together the authors of the various chapters and determined the issues which they sought to explore. This preface is intended to give the reader this perspective and to acknowledge the tremendous help that we have received from many individuals and institutions during the course of undertaking the research projects and preparing this book for publication.

The earliest common thread for this work goes back about fifteen years when, ironically perhaps, the three male contributors to this publication met during a period of study and teaching at the University of California, Berkeley. There was, at that time, an evident contrast between the status of women in paid employment in Britain and California. Many more women held top jobs in industry, commerce, state and federal government than was the case in Britain, and women had moved into occupations in the USA which were completely male 'territory' in Britain (e.g. heavy goods vehicle driving, telecommunications, mining). The concept of equality of opportunity had been grasped by women and men in the USA by the early 1970s and, with active litigation, had made a substantial impact on the male-dominated occupational and industrial hierarchies.

By the late 1970s the three of us had made our separate ways back to Britain; Brian Main to a lectureship at the Department of Economics, Edinburgh University: Ed Puttick to a post in research administration at the recently formed Equal Opportunities Commission (modelled on its US counterpart); and I had moved into full-time research in the Manpower Research Group, later to be the Institute for Employment Research, at the University of Warwick. In 1979 our interests once again converged. The EOC had a need for research information on the transitions made by women between full-time and part-time working over the period of family formation, and the consequent effect with respect to their occupational status. Ed Puttick had identified the 1975 National Training Survey as a possible source of information because of the work history data it held. I had been developing access to large-scale survey data at Warwick and had acquired the National Training Survey. Brian Main had been working on the methodology of handling complex work history data bases. This convergence of interests led to a small research project in this area being funded by the EOC. The published findings from the project (Elias and Main, 1982) showed the extent to which part-time jobs in Great Britain were low in status and pay, were most often held by women at a particular point in their life-cycle, namely when their children were young, and there was evidence to suggest that a considerable number of well-qualified women were working in unskilled part-time jobs. Above all else, though, this re-analysis of survey data indicated how useful it was to explore work history information to gain an insight into the life-cycle aspects of occupational mobility and the role of part-time work in women's working lives.

Around the same time that this research was being conducted, the Department of Employment had initiated a programme of research on women in the labour market, the largest single project within which was a national survey of women of working age. This survey, the 'Women and Employment Survey' (Martin and Roberts, 1984a) was carried out in 1980. Apart from a wealth of attitudinal information on paid and non-paid work, the survey collected detailed work histories covering the whole of the female respondents' working lives. The intention of this survey was 'to establish the place of employment in women's lives' (Martin and Roberts, 1984a, p. 3). This survey was planned at a time when unemployment was rising rapidly, in marked contrast to an earlier detailed survey of women's employment, carried out on behalf of the (then) Ministry of Labour by Audrey Hunt at the Government Social Survey (now the Office of Population Censuses and Surveys) in 1965. In her summary of general findings, Audrey Hunt had commented upon the urgent need to expand the labour force and had forecasted with accuracy that 'more and more women will regard it as natural to continue work after marriage at least until the birth of the first child, and to return to work when their children are old enough' (Hunt, 1968, p. 8).

The impetus for the project which culminated in the publication of this book came from Ed Puttick. Initially, ideas focused on the possibility of applying the research techniques developed for analysis of women's work histories in the 1975 National Training Survey to the more detailed and more up-to-date work history information in the 1980 Women and Employment Survey, then to extend the work which Brian Main and I had begun on the relationship between family formation, occupational mobility and part-time work. Brian Main expressed an interest in using the information in the Women and Employment Survey to investigate the possible relationships between a woman's current earnings and her history of full- or part-time work. Further discussion widened the scope of the project to embrace a broader analysis of the survey data sets held at the Institute for Employment Research, thereby contextualising the analysis of the Women and Employment Survey and providing a picture of the changing nature of women's employment over the period 1965–81. It was decided that a group of researchers should undertake this project. Lesley Rimmer, well-known for her work on family employment issues, was commissioned to provide a synthesis of recent research on female employment in a family context and to explore the Family Expenditure Survey for further information on recent trends. Audrey Hunt, now retired from OPCS, has prepared an historical overview of women's changing employment patterns in the period leading up to the early 1960s and, in a separate chapter, has examined the effect of caring for elderly and infirm relatives on female employment. Shirley Dex at Keele University agreed to provide a summary of her recently published research with Lois Shaw from the Center for Human Resource Research, Ohio State University, contrasting two similarly aged groups of women from the 1980 Women and Employment Survey in Great Britain and the Women's National Longitudinal Surveys in the USA. Shirley Dex and Ed Puttick investigated the changing employment status of parents at and around the time of family formation. Finally, Kate Purcell, a sociologist at the Institute for Employment Research, currently working on a major investigation of social and economic change in six British towns, has worked with me in the drafting stages of this publication and with the writing of the final, prescriptive chapter.

We greatly underestimated the task we set ourselves. First, we had to acquire a copy of the data tapes for the Women and Employment Survey and establish a system for interrogating these data. Second, for Lesley Rimmer's chapter, special analyses of the Family Expenditure Survey tapes were called for. For the chapter prepared by Shirley Dex and Ed Puttick some tricky programming of the 1981 Labour

Force Survey data was required to reconstruct household-based information from this enormous data set. Finally, for Audrey Hunt's work on carers, special tabulations were required from her 1965 Survey of Women's Employment. All of these tasks posed unique problems, both administrative and technical, but we have been most fortunate in terms of the assistance we received from many individuals. First, our thanks must go to Ceridwen Roberts at the Department of Employment for ensuring that the Women and Employment Survey data were made available to us at the earliest possible date. As it turned out, we were in the unique position of having access to these data for a project funded from outside the Department of Employment well before publication of the official report from this survey. Eric Roughley and Marcia Taylor at the University of Essex Data Archive had the thankless task of unscrambling this survey from its statistical packaging, sorting out the documentation and forwarding the data and documentation to us in a most expeditious manner. Eric has also done much work to make the Family Expenditure Surveys and Labour Force Surveys available to us. Tim Clark at the University of Warwick Computing Services designed an extremely efficient system giving access to all of the Women and Employment Survey data files. Audrey Hunt did a marvellous piece of detective work by tracking down an entire set of punched cards containing her 1965 survey, in the basement of St Catherine's House. Roger Thomas of OPCS very kindly arranged to have these cards transferred to magnetic tape. Phil Spruce at the University of Warwick Computing Services gave me a lot of help with programs to unscramble the information on these cards. Mike Bradley at OPCS assisted with the reconstruction of household information from the Labour Force Surveys.

Co-ordinating this work was not without its problems, mainly because of the conflicting short-term demands placed upon researchers nowadays. For this reason, and because large-scale social survey data consume much time to collect and analyse, there is a time lag between the information from which we draw our conclusions and the date of publication of this book. The latest major survey referenced in this book is the 1981 Labour Force Survey. For this reason, we have spent some time in the final chapter considering recent trends and developments in women's employment, including the debate on the taxation of husband and wife, the amendment of the Equal Pay Act, and proposed changes in the social security system.

Our thanks go to all those individuals who, at various stages, have commented upon our work. Particular thanks are due to Ron Barrowclough, formerly at the EOC who, with remarkable patience, has maintained an interest in the project since its inception in 1982 and has given valuable guidance to us all. Karen Clarke, also at the EOC, provided many useful comments on earlier drafts of these chapters. Thanks are also due to: Linda Ammon, Barbara Ballard, Heather Joshi, Robert Lindley, Jean Martin, Robert McNabb, Thea Sinclair and Roger Vickermann.

Throughout the lifetime of this project, Christine Jones has given much valuable assistance with the data analysis and the production of draft tables and figures for this book. Clive Edwards has done an excellent job in preparing the artwork for us. Maureen Garcia, Rosalie Edkins and Janet Burnell typed many of the drafts of the chapters. Margaret Birch gave much organisational help to us all.

Finally, all of the other authors to this publication join with me in expressing our thanks to our editor, Audrey Hunt, for maintaining her level-headed approach throughout our meetings, discussions about the issues and our analysis of complex data. I know she will not tolerate such sentiments, but were she not the editor, we would dedicate this book to her.

PETER ELIAS

1 Women and Paid Work: Issues of Equality. An Overview

Audrey Hunt

INTRODUCTION

The twentieth century has seen many changes in the role of women in society in most Western countries. Probably the trend which has had the greatest effect on women's lives in Great Britain over the past fifty years has been the increasing participation of married women in paid employment. The contributions to this book examine the relationship between women's paid work and their domestic experiences from different aspects: marriage, childbirth, bringing up children, unemployment in the home, and caring for the elderly and infirm. The information in this book is mainly derived from a number of surveys carried out between 1965 and 1981. Between them these surveys cover the lifetime of women born between 1901 and the late 1960s but the authors for the most part concentrate on the post-war period.

Since the end of the Second World War there has been a growth in interest in matters affecting women, but the seeds of this growth were sown much earlier in the century. The experiences of women described in this book have been influenced by earlier events. This overview seeks to give an outline of events in the recent past which have affected women's work to date and are likely to have a bearing on the future.

Women workers in many occupations have been, and still are, regarded as an inferior substitute for men (Braybon, 1981; Hunt, 1975). The engagement of married women in most areas of paid work has been a subject of controversy since the later years of the nineteenth century. Because of these attitudes women's work has been, even more than men's, subject to the effects of two world wars. Many people born since 1930 are unaware of the virtual exclusion of married women from the labour market during the inter-war years in Great Britain. Many born earlier in the century think that the work of married women for pay is a comparatively recent development. While the latter may be true of the wives of the upper and professional classes, it is certainly not true of the wives of manual workers. Indeed, as far back as 1351 the famous (or infamous) Statute of Labourers decreed: 'Every man and woman, free or bond, whatever his or her condition, able of body and within the age of three score shall be bound to serve the employer which shall require him or her to do so and shall take only the wages which were accustomed to be taken.' The employment of married women in paid work was an important part of the economy before and throughout the Industrial Revolution.

Some of the surveys used as source material for the contributions to this book cover women's employment as only one of a number of topics. Two, however, are concerned solely with aspects of women's work. The first (Hunt, 1968) was carried out in 1965, at a time of full employment. Ironically, the main object of this survey was to elicit information about 'the factors which were preventing some married women from working outside their homes, given that the long-term interests of the economy demand an increase in the productive labour force which, for the most part, will have to come from married women who are not working at present'. When the second (Martin and Roberts, 1984a) was carried out in 1980, the overall focus or objective of the survey was 'to establish the place of employment in women's lives'. This overview gives a brief account of some of the developments which have taken place during the lifetime of the women interviewed in these two surveys and of events which have affected their work histories.

In order to achieve a coherent structure and also to demonstrate how various aspects of women's employment have changed over time, we take four main periods: from the turn of the century to the end of the First World War, the inter-war years, the Second World War and the post-war years. Within each period we examine, as far as possible, demographic factors, the employment of women, family relationships, attitudes to women's work, legislation, and economic conditions. Sometimes it is not feasible to deal with these separately because their development is interlinked and they need to be examined together.

It is only in comparatively recent years that detailed statistical information about the backgrounds of working women has been available. The collection of statistics as part of the administrative process has developed alongside legislative measures (such as those relating to national insurance and pensions) which have required factual information for their planning and implementation. Sample surveys of population groups as we know them today have only been undertaken since the 1930s. Consequently our information about the earlier part of this century is less detailed than that relating to more recent times. Nevertheless, the qualitative material available enables us to build up a picture of working women from the start of the century to the present day.

One factor which must be taken into account is the change in the minimum age at which marriage could take place. Since the Age of Marriage Act of 1929 this has been 16 years for both sexes, but prior to that it was 14 years for males and 12 years for females. Statistics for the first quarter of the century often refer to married women *over 12 years of age*, which affects comparisons with more recent figures.

FROM 1901 TO THE END OF THE FIRST WORLD WAR

Our most detailed source of information about the family backgrounds of married women workers in the early years of the century is *Married Women's Work*, a report of several small surveys carried out in 1909 and 1910 (Black, 1915). Though not conducted in accordance with modern statistical methods, these studies were very thorough and provide some interesting comparisons with recent findings. For example, among 560 families in Leicester, 43 per cent of married women were earning wages, a figure identical to that for the East Midlands in 1965 (Hunt, 1968). The studies were mostly confined to married women in what would be called today the lower socio-economic groups. The conditions of these married women were a cause of much concern. Some of the women interviewed in 1965 would have grown up in homes described by Black. A striking difference between these homes and those of the latter part of the century is the number of children, particularly the number of children who had died. To take one example only, of the families of 127

London charwomen, there were averages of 2.6 living children and 1.8 children who had died. Black concluded that there was no connection between mothers' working and child mortality, the latter being mainly due to appalling living conditions and poverty. One can only speculate on the effects on labour force participation which Main in Chapter 2 and Elias in Chapter 4 might have found had the number of children remained at the level of those days. In 1965 the average number of dependent children in the homes of working mothers was 1.7 (Hunt, 1968) and in 1980 it was 1.6 (Martin and Roberts, 1984a). Fortunately infant mortality has now fallen to a level where it is no longer considered a necessary part of a social study of women's work to include questions about children who have died.

Titmuss (1958) estimated that in 1900 a woman aged 20 could expect to live another 46 years, of which about one-third would be spent in bearing and rearing children. Such a woman in 1960 could expect to live to 75 years of age and would spend only 7 per cent of that time exclusively devoted to childbearing and rearing. Main in Chapter 2 shows that this tendency has continued up to 1980. Roberts (1984) says of women growing up in the early years of the century: 'Inhibitions about talking of their own experience were reinforced by a widespread belief that artificially limiting one's family was not respectable.' In the present writer's experience such attitudes were still prevalent in the 1920s and early 1930s.

The 1901 census showed that 32 per cent of all women over 10 years of age, 52 per cent of single and 13 per cent of married or widowed women were in paid employment. Married or widowed women accounted for 22 per cent of the female labour force. In making comparisons with more recent figures it must be remembered that the lowest age of marriage for females was 12 and that, although the statutory school-leaving age was 14, it was possible to obtain an exemption in many areas from the age of 11 onwards, provided an adequate educational standard had been reached and the employment was deemed 'beneficial' to the family. Criteria varied in different local authority areas. Exemptions were not abolished until 1918. As was found to be the case in 1965 (Hunt, 1968), there were wide regional variations in the percentage of married women who were in paid employment, the percentages being particularly high in textile areas. Nearly one-third of women workers were employed in domestic service, one-seventh in textiles, and one-tenth in clothing trades.

The 1911 census showed that 34 per cent of women over the age of 12 years were working. There had been some growth in the numbers of women in non-manual occupations, which then accounted for about one-fifth of the female labour force. However, most of these were in what would now be classed as 'junior non-manual'. Only 3 per cent were teachers and 1 per cent nurses. Some local studies pertaining to this same period give insights into the relative earnings of married couples. An example from Black (1915) provides an interesting comparison with Rimmer's findings in Chapter 3. Rimmer shows that, in 1981, 11 per cent of working married women without children and 4 per cent of those with children earned more than their husbands. In 1909, among working wives in Leicester, 18 per cent earned more than their husbands. Some further details of family incomes in 1909–10 show that, although absolute magnitudes have changed, relativities may not be much altered. For example, among 103 families of working wives in Manchester, the average weekly wage of the wife was 10 shillings and 8 pence (53p) compared with 28 shillings and 11 pence (£1.45) for the whole family, including the wife. Among 59 families in London the mean income per head of the family was increased from 4 shillings (20p) to 5 shillings and 5 pence (27p) when the wife's income was included. Unlike Rimmer's findings the Black studies (although unquantified) seem to provide evidence that many married women were more likely to work for pay if their husbands were sick or unemployed, or drinkers or gamblers. At that time there was no sickness or unemployment benefit, nor any child benefit, so there was every inducement for married women to work under these circumstances. (The first National Insurance Act was passed in 1911. It was opposed by some women's organisations, who felt that the employees' contribution would bear hard on low-paid women workers.) Black also indicates that some husbands, particularly if unemployed, were prepared to do household tasks and look after children while their wives were at work.

While there was no formal marriage bar in existence, many employers dismissed women on marriage. Many women, particularly in the middle classes, were constrained by the mores of society to leave paid work voluntarily. To have a working wife constituted a social stigma for many a husband. Married women who wanted or were compelled to work had perforce to take ill-paid, arduous and filthy jobs, often as home-workers. Black's studies give many examples of these. Attitudes to married women's work were largely hostile, mainly because it was felt that work outside the home was harmful to women's natural primary role as wife and mother. Braybon (1981) analyses some of the arguments. Undoubtedly much of the work done by women was harmful to health, but so too were constant pregnancies and heavy work in ill-equipped homes, as pointed out by Black (1915) in her introduction. She herself opposed the banning of married women's paid work and goes on to say:

> the wage-earning wife needs to be relieved not of the work which she frequently does well but of that which she does either ill or at quite disproportionate cost to herself ... The grave drawback of much of the work done for money by married women is not that it is injurious in itself but that it is scandalously ill-paid.

Among the legislative measures of the pre-war period, of particular relevance today is the Trade Boards Act of 1909. This was the first of a number of legislative measures which sought to alleviate the evils of sweated labour. The boards (now called wages councils) were intended to set minimum wages in trades which were notoriously ill-paid. The present government has taken action to weaken the powers of these councils and, in some cases, to abolish them.

The outbreak of the First World War in August 1914 did not immediately result in an influx of women into war industry or into jobs previously done by men who had gone into the armed forces. However, by the spring of 1915, appeals were launched to all women, married or single, to enter war work, with some employers giving preference to soldiers' wives (Braybon, 1981). Some of the women who entered war work saw a brief upgrading of jobs. Women did jobs in factories, transport and on the land which would nowadays be regarded as 'men's work'. As has often been the case, many ingenious methods were used to avoid giving women equal pay. Braybon (1981) and Lewenhak (1977) describe some of the manoeuvres. Some trade unions were less than whole-hearted in their support for women.

At the peak of the war effort in 1918 Marwick (1977) estimates that 946 000 women were working in munitions factories and that 7.3 million women (37 per cent of the female population over 10 years of age) were in paid jobs, compared with 6 million (31 per cent) in 1914. Braybon (1981) estimates that married women accounted for 40 per cent of the female labour force. Many women who went to work in factories saw 'the development of welfare measures designed to help women war workers and their families' (Marwick, 1977). Although nurseries were not unknown before 1914 (some of the studies in Black, 1915, give examples of their use) the First World War saw a considerable expansion, and by 1919, 174 officially sponsored nurseries were functioning. There were others run privately by philanthropic individuals.

Attitudes to women's work were divided. There was patriotic approval for their contribution to the war effort on the one hand. On the other, employers then (as now) tended to regard women as inferior substitutes for men. Male trade unionists, concerned with protecting their own jobs and rates of pay, resisted the introduction of women into male-dominated spheres. Only under the pressure of acute shortages of manpower did bodies such as medical schools admit women as students in place of men in the forces. Lewenhak (1977) and Braybon (1981) give detailed accounts of the controversies that raged. One can see throughout the predominant idea that women's real function was to produce and raise children and that paid work, though possibly necessary in times of crisis, would interfere with this function.

THE INTER-WAR YEARS

Many women hoped that, as a consequence of their contributions to the war effort, their role in society and as workers would have radically changed and that they would be accepted as equals by men. These hopes were for the most part unfulfilled. In particular, their position as workers deteriorated, as we shall describe.

With the end of the war the upgrading of women's occupations ceased. Women in skilled jobs were dismissed as soon as hostilities ended to make way for returning servicemen, and they were expected to return to the home. Although the Sex Disqualification (Removal) Act of 1919 permitted women 'to carry on any civil profession or vocation', it contained many loopholes and lacked means of enforcement. For example, most medical schools were able once again to close their doors to women until 1948, when the University Grants Committee compelled them to include at least 15 per cent of women among their entrants.

The number of economically active women fell from an estimated 7 million or more in 1918 to just over 5 million (32 per cent of all women) at the 1921 census. This was a lower percentage than in 1911. Married women accounted for 14 per cent of working women, and 9 per cent of married women were working. In 1931, 5.6 million women were in paid jobs, of whom 16 per cent were married; 10 per cent of married women were working. However, census data underestimated the numbers of working married women, both because of the intermittent nature of women's work and because some married women would not admit to working for fear of losing their jobs.

A number of factors contributed to the worsening of women's position as workers during the inter-war years. Unemployment was endemic until the late 1930s. The rules for drawing unemployment benefit were operated more strictly in the case of women, particularly married women. The heavy casualties of the First World War, together with the differential mortality rates among male and female infants, led to an excess of women over men in all age groups in the inter-war period (in 1931 the ratio was 111 to 100). These were often offensively described as 'surplus women'. This situation undoubtedly influenced attitudes towards married women working: the view was widely held that a married woman ought not to hold a job which otherwise might be held by a single woman or man. The effects of this prevailing climate of opinion can still be seen in the attitudes of some of the women interviewed in the two main surveys which provide material for this book (Hunt, 1968; Martin and Roberts 1984a). Today's high level of unemployment makes women in employment particularly vulnerable to such attitudes, as will be discussed by Elias and Purcell in Chapter 9.

A marriage bar existed throughout public and private industry apart from a few firms and the British Broadcasting Corporation. The London County Council abolished the marriage bar for certain qualified staff in 1935. The marriage bar operated to the advantage of employers in that women who were compelled to leave upon marriage often did so at a time when they were becoming entitled to higher pay. They could be replaced by younger, cheaper labour. Enforcement of the bar became stronger as unemployment increased, and was probably at its most rigid in the mid-1930s.

Direct comparisons of pre-war unemployment figures with those of today cannot be made because of the difference in the principles of national insurance. Before the 1948 Act, unemployment and health insurance applied only to certain occupations and to those earning less than a certain amount (which increased from time to time). Given that the figures for size of workforce and number of unemployed were both byproducts of the insurance system, it is quite probable that both were understated. Most professional workers (including, for example, teachers and nurses), many white-collar workers and domestic servants were ineligible for benefit and therefore had no source of income when out of work. In 1935, out of an insured workforce of

10.4 million, there were 2 million unemployed (approximately 300 000 of whom were female). This level is on a par with that of today, but it involved considerably greater hardship. To say this is not to belittle the problems faced by today's unemployed but rather to emphasise the severity of unemployment in the 1930s. At that time, when the meagre unemployment benefit ran out, the Unemployment Assistance Board provided support. This was accompanied by a means test so severe that not only the unemployed person but all his or her family had to prove that they had no savings or assets whatsoever. Although many wives could obtain domestic work or other ill-paid jobs, it was not worth their while to do so because their husbands and children would lose their unemployment assistance. Rimmer in Chapter 3 draws on recent evidence to show that a similar situation may exist at present.

We have no detailed statistics about the domestic responsibilities of women workers during this period. In the experience of the writer, many women would not admit to family commitments for fear of losing their jobs. There was not at that time even the limited job security afforded by the 1975 Employment Protection Act. Pregnancy was considered a reasonable ground for dismissal even by firms which regularly employed married women. Although women constituted nearly one-third of the workforce, little attention was paid to their situation. Internationally there was none of the interest in women's rights as employees that has been shown since the Second World War. To many women who grew up during the inter-war years there was an atmosphere of hopelessness, accentuated by the ever-present threat of war.

THE SECOND WORLD WAR

More detailed statistics are available about the role of women during the Second World War than about earlier years. In addition to statistics collected as part of the administrative process, sample surveys had become accepted as a means of obtaining reliable information about population groups.

The First World War had depended initially on volunteers from both men and women. Conscription for men was introduced in 1916, but not at all for women. At the start of the Second World War conscription for young men had already been in force for a year. This, coupled with rearmament, had reduced the number of unemployed to

1.3 million (HMSO, 1944). Women, too, were conscripted during the Second World War. Compulsory registration for employment was introduced by the Registration for Employment Order 1941. By mid-1944 10 million men born in the years 1892–1926 and 11.6 million women born in the years 1893–1926 had been registered for either military service or essential industry (HMSO, 1944). Young single women could be directed into the armed forces or into essential work away from home. Married women without children could be directed into essential work within daily travelling distance of home. This was the first experience for many married couples of both partners going out to work. A contemporary survey (Thomas, 1944) showed that 50 per cent of married women workers complained about the difficulty of coping with domestic tasks because of their work. The problems they faced were to some extent recognised by official welfare measures. These were primarily designed to help women working in industry, but men also benefited. Canteens which provided good meals at a reasonable price not only ensured adequate nutrition for essential workers but also relieved women of the burdens of shopping for foods in short supply. School dinners and free milk maintained children's health. The Wartime Food Survey (a continuous detailed study of food purchases and consumption by households which continues to this day in a modified form) monitored the intake of essential nutrients. Its findings had much influence on food policy throughout the war and early post-war years.

Women with children at home were exempt from call-up, but many inducements to work were offered to them. Perhaps the most important of these were the provision of nurseries for the care of very young children and the expansion of nursery classes for those just below school age. The peak of nursery development was reached in the summer of 1944. At that time more than 112 000 young children in Great Britain were receiving care outside their homes in various types of nursery. About 35 000 children were in nursery schools or classes and 103 000 children under 5 were in reception at public elementary schools. It was argued that 'nurseries were partly an expression of the *right* of mothers willing to contribute to the war effort to this sort of service ... The nursery was a contribution towards the feeling of mutual responsibility between Government and the family' (Ferguson and Fitzgerald, 1954). There was some criticism of nurseries for medical reasons but not on psychological grounds (Riley, 1983).

Thomas (1944) found that one-third of married women workers (most of whom worked full-time) had dependent children. This is higher than the 23 per cent of full-time workers who had children living with them in 1980 (Martin and Roberts, 1984a). It might be assumed that welfare provisions made it easier for mothers to work; on the other hand, the low rates of pay of men in the armed forces may have compelled their wives to work.

In the summer of 1944 the workforce (including armed forces) totalled nearly 15 million males (of whom 71 000 were unemployed) and over 7 million females (of whom 31 000 were unemployed). About 900 000 women were doing part-time work (HMSO, 1944). Like many statistics produced before part-time work acquired its present importance, this source counted two part-time workers as one full-time worker, making exact comparison with present statistics difficult. It can be calculated that roughly 50 per cent of the female population aged 15–59 were working (5 per cent of them part-time) compared with 54 per cent (18 per cent part-time) in 1965 and 60 per cent (26 per cent part-time) in 1980 (Hunt, 1968; Martin and Roberts, 1984a). The 1944 figures did not include women working less than eight hours a week in private domestic service or certain kinds of homeworkers, so it appears that the 50 per cent recorded in that year understates the proportion of women working by at least 5 per cent. However, it is apparent that when women have freedom of choice a much higher percentage choose to work part-time.

In 1943 26 per cent of women worked in the metal and chemical industries (HMSO, 1944), compared with 11 per cent in 1965 and 8 per cent in 1980. They accounted for 37 per cent of the labour force in this industrial group. Many of these women were doing work traditionally regarded as men's work: many women 'dilutees' (as they were called) acquired a degree of skill equal to, if not surpassing, that of men who had served a full craft apprenticeship, but not for equal pay. Male dilutees, that is unskilled men who received the same training as female dilutees, received the full craftsmen's rates by agreement with the trade unions, but the women (also by agreement with the unions) received about 75 per cent to 80 per cent of these rates. Women in non-manual occupations were similarly paid less. In 1944 a move to secure equal pay for women teachers by means of an amendment to the Education Bill was frustrated by the Prime Minister, Winston Churchill, who made the issue a vote of confidence.

Attitudes to women's work, and to married women's work in particular, were for the most part approving, if perhaps a little patronising. It was, however, widely felt that married women's paid work was a temporary wartime phenomenon which would vanish when peace was declared, in the same way as it did after the First World War. This attitude was typified by the Beveridge Report (HMSO, 1942) which, in the view of many people, laid the foundations of the welfare state. It is worth quoting some paragraphs of this report, as they show the attitudes prevalent among comparatively progressive people less than forty-five years ago and explain some of today's discriminatory attitudes towards women in paid work:

> In any measure of social policy in which regard is had to facts the great majority of married women must be regarded as occupied on work which is vital though unpaid, without which their husbands could not do their paid work and without which the nation could not continue. In accord with the facts the Plan for Social Security treats married women as a special insurance class of occupied persons and treats man and wife as a team.
>
> During marriage most women will not be gainfully employed. The small minority of women who undertake paid employment or other gainful occupations after marriage require special treatment differing from that of a single woman. Since such paid work will in many cases be intermittent, it should be open to any married woman to undertake it as an exempt person, paying no contribution of her own and acquiring no claim to benefit in unemployment or sickness. If she prefers to contribute and to re-qualify for unemployment and disability benefit she may do so but will receive benefits at a reduced rate.
>
> The attitude of the housewife to gainful employment outside the home is not and should not be the same as that of the single woman. She has other duties . . . Taken as a whole the Plan for Social Security puts a premium on marriage in place of penalising it . . . In the next thirty years housewives as mothers have vital work to do in ensuring the adequate continuance of the British race and British ideals in the world.

In quoting these and other parts of the Beveridge Report, Wilson (1977) comments: 'The married woman was to be treated as befitted her legal status: as the dependant of a man . . . Not only did Beveridge want to get women back into the home so they could breed, he also wished to discourage immorality.'

THE POST-WAR YEARS

The individual chapters of this book provide detailed statistical evidence of the development of women's paid employment since the end of the Second World War. This section gives some background information to help set these developments in a wider context.

We have already shown that in the earlier years of the century the number of women exceeded that of men in the population of working age. This has changed dramatically in recent years. At mid-1983 the ratios for younger age groups were 105 males to 100 females for 0–14 year olds and 102 males to 100 females for 15–44 year olds. Thus, given the decrease in infant mortality and the fact that proportionately more male children are born than females, men today outnumber women in the marriageable age groups and are likely to do so for the foreseeable future. Almost any woman who wants to will be able to marry, and it seems likely that the proportion of working women who are married will increase. About eight out of ten married women will have children if present trends in fertility are realised. The effects on labour force participation and on types of work and earnings of having children are described in several chapters, and these effects are likely to continue if population trends follow the pattern described.

Events after the Second World War did not follow the same course as after the First World War. The latter was followed almost immediately by a slump which continued with only small temporary improvements until the Second World War. An apparently easy way of alleviating unemployment was to dismiss women from their war jobs and to introduce a marriage bar. Braybon (1981) describes the effects on women's aspirations of these and other measures. After the Second World War post-war reconstruction initiated a boom which continued well into the 1960s, the era of 'you've never had it so good!' This was followed by the slump of the mid 1970s which has continued to the present day.

The post-war exodus of women from paid employment was not entirely compulsory. Many women left to start families when their husbands returned from the armed forces. The exodus was sufficient to cause concern in industries involved in reconstruction. A survey in 1947 (Thomas, 1948) investigated the problems of recruiting women into industry. One conclusion was: 'The principal factors which dissuaded women from work were, in order of importance, marriage, children, economic position and age. Marriage was several times more important than children.' Only 20 years later was it possible to say that the birth of the first child, rather than marriage, had become the most usual occasion for a woman to give up work, whether or not she resumed later (Hunt, 1968). In June 1947 just over six million women were occupied, a decrease of one and three quarter million since June 1943. Approximately 30 per cent of all women were in full-time employment and a further 9 per cent were in part-time employment (Thomas, 1948). By mid-1955 the female labour force had risen to over seven and a half million (35 per cent of the total labour force), this in spite of the raising of the school-leaving age to 15 in 1947. In that year unemployment stood at 1 per cent of the total labour force. By 1980 the number of women had risen to more than 9 million (42 per cent of the total labour force). This increase is almost entirely due to the increase in part-time working by married women. For example, among women born during the years 1921–4, the percentage in employment fell from 71 per cent in 1944 to 40 per cent (5 per cent part-time) in 1949, but rose to 66 per cent (32 per cent part-time) in 1974 (Martin and Roberts, 1984a). Owen and Joshi (1984) analyse female activity rates in successive post-war censuses in some detail. In 1980 unemployment exceeded the two million mark for the first time, since when it has risen to its present level of approximately three and half million (a figure which is widely held to underestimate the true figure because of the exclusion of those who do not register).

In the early post-war years the demand for workers for post-war reconstruction ensured that there were jobs for virtually all who wanted them. Nevertheless, the pre-war resentment against married women workers resurfaced. This attitude was officially condoned by the discriminatory treatment of married women in matters such as taxation and national insurance (Rimmer in Chapter 3 discusses taxation in detail). The 1946 National Insurance Act (operative in 1948) was based on Beveridge principles. It introduced the 'married women's option', under which a married woman could opt out of paying almost all her national insurance contribution (the employer had to pay in full in order to prevent discrimination against single women). A married woman who opted out lost her right to unemployment and sickness benefit and to a pension in her own right (she could receive a pension based on her husband's contribution). It has been estimated that about two-thirds exercised this option, influenced, no doubt, by their low wages and by the fact that a married woman who paid the full contribution (the same as a single woman's) received sickness and unemployment benefit at a lower rate than a single woman. As recently as 1965 the General Council of the Trades Union Congress (TUC), in reply to a resolution from its Women's Conference asking for equal treatment for married and single women, said that they could not accept the principle because:

> (i) Benefit rates were based on subsistence needs and normally in the case of the married woman the need for rent would not arise.
> (ii) The gainfully occupied married women's lower rate for sickness and unemployment was balanced by their entitlement to maternity benefits.
> (iii) The incidence of sickness was higher among married women than among single women.
> . . . the suggested increase would involve an increase in contributions and the question would then arise how such an increase should be divided between the contributions of men and single women. (Women's Advisory Committee of the TUC, 1965)

This Beveridge-based attitude of the predominantly male General Council has been modified over the years by pressure from women trade unionists, an increasing proportion of whom are married. Recent changes in national insurance have partially rectified this particular injustice. Another official example of the Beveridge influence was the Family Allowance Act of 1945, which introduced from 1946 a small weekly allowance for the second child and subsequent children in a family. This provision took no account of the fact that it is the *first* child which usually reduces or eliminates a wife's earning capacity, the assumption being that she would not be earning at all after her marriage. This anomaly was not rectified until 1977, when family allowances were replaced by child benefit, which applied to all children. It is worth noting that only after much controversy was the government persuaded to agree that family allowance should be paid to the mother as of right.

The attitudes of women themselves to the issue of whether or not married women, with or without children, should work were investigated by Hunt (1968) and Martin and Roberts (1984a). The latter give a comparison of these data, showing that attitudes were more favourable in 1980 than in 1965 in all cases, but that a substantial majority still thought that a woman with children under school age ought to stay at home (60 per cent in 1980, 78 per cent in 1965). Not surprisingly, a majority of working women with children under school age defended their right to work.

The right to work is meaningless unless conditions are such that it is possible to do so. Dex and Puttick in Chapter 7 show how the exercise of that right is subject to constraint. As already stated, the right of women with young children to help the war effort was recognised by the provision of nurseries. Riley (1983) describes how the rapid closure of these nurseries after 1945 was officially justified with a mixture of (often contradictory) social, medical and psychological arguments. Hunt (1968) estimated a demand for about half a million nursery places for the children of women workers or potential workers. On this the Ministry of Health commented:

> As far as day nurseries are concerned, they have been provided by local authorities since 1945 primarily to meet the needs of certain children for day care on health and welfare grounds. The service is not intended to meet a demand by working women generally for subsidised day care facilities. The number of places provided is therefore considerably less than the demand shown in this survey. (Hunt, 1968)

At that time there were 24 000 nursery places in Great Britain.

The increased participation of women in the labour force following the Second World War was common to all industrialised countries. International bodies as well as individual governments became concerned with the unequal treatment of women workers. The International Labour Office, on 29 June 1951, adopted Convention No. 100 (the Equal Remuneration Convention) which required member states to 'ensure the application to all workers of the principle of equal remuneration for men and women workers for work of equal value'. The Treaty of Rome of 25 March 1957 which established the European Economic Community contained Article 119: 'Each Member State shall . . . ensure and subsequently maintain the application of the principle of equal remuneration for equal work as between men and women workers.'

In the United States of America the Civil Rights Act (Title VII) was passed in 1964. Section 703(a) forbids employers:

(1) to fail or refuse to hire or to discharge any individual or otherwise to discriminate against any individual with respect to his compensation, terms, conditions, or privileges or employ-

ment, because of such individual's race, color, religion, sex, or national origin; or

(2) to limit, segregate, or classify his employees or applicants for employment in any way which would deprive or tend to deprive any individual or employment opportunities or otherwise adversely affect his status as an employee, because of such an individual's race, color, religion, sex or national origin.

This was followed in 1978 by the Pregnancy Discrimination Act of 1978, which required that women affected by pregnancy, childbirth or related medical conditions be treated on the same basis as other employees, including receipt of fringe benefits.

In 1972, Congress approved the passage of the Equal Rights Amendment (ERA) which states that 'equality of rights under the law shall not be denied or abridged by the United States or any State on account of sex'. The amendment requires ratification by thirty-eight state legislatures in order to become part of the Constitution. So far, this has not been achieved.

Many countries, such as the USSR, have equality for women embodied in their constitutions. This is particularly the case with countries which underwent revolutionary changes after the Second World War, such as the Eastern European States, Egypt and Israel. This does not necessarily guarantee women equality of opportunity, as the occupational distributions of women and men in these countries illustrate. The extent to which legislation can be effective depends both upon its terms of reference and statutory powers, and on how it is implemented and regarded in the society in question.

In the United Kingdom the Equal Pay Act was passed in 1970, to come fully into force in 1975. Prior to this, equal pay had been introduced into the non-industrial public service by stages between 1955 and 1962, mainly as a result of pressure by trade unions in this sector. Women's demands were strongly supported by their male colleagues. This support was not wholly disinterested, because men realised their own jobs might be at risk when women with identical qualifications and experience could be employed at a much lower rate of pay. Nevertheless, the support of more enlightened men has been an essential feature of the long struggle of women for equality at work.

The Equal Pay Act provided for equal pay as between men and women doing the same or broadly similar work, or doing work which, as the result of a job evaluation, had been equally evaluated. The extent to which women benefited as a result has been limited because of the extent to which the occupational structure is characterised by gender segregation (Hakim, 1981). Following pressure from the EEC, the Equal Opportunities Commission (EOC), the TUC and other organisations, the British government introduced an amendment to the Equal Pay Act to establish the principle of 'equal pay for work of equal value' in 1984, which has the major potential to undermine gender segregation but which has so far been implemented with extreme caution. A significant unresolved issue is whether working part-time is, of itself, a material difference from working full-time. In other words, a part-time worker may not be able to claim the same hourly rate as a full-time worker. In view of the importance of part-time work in women's lives, as shown by all the chapters in this book, it is essential that the principle be established, by legislation if necessary, that it is the nature of the work itself which is taken into account, not the number of hours worked. Many trade unions are now actively taking up the cause of part-time workers, but there is still hostility in some sections.

The Sex Discrimination Act 1975 made it illegal to discriminate on the grounds of sex in employment, education and the provision of services. The Act also provided for positive discrimination where one sex is manifestly at a disadvantage. Subject to the constraints imposed by its terms of reference, the Act has made some impact, but it has its limitations, notably in the specific exclusion of pensions and taxation.

Other UK legislation which has affected women's working lives includes the Employment Protection Act 1975 and the Employment Acts of 1980 and 1982. Various provisions of these Acts gave both women and men greater security in employment. The 1975 Act introduced the maternity pay fund and established the right to maternity leave. The UK provisions are, however, inferior to those in most EEC member states. For example, in France a mother is entitled to sixteen weeks' maternity leave at 90 per cent of salary plus post-natal allowances with the option of a further two years' unpaid leave. The UK entitlement is for six weeks at 90 per cent of average earnings, eighteen weeks at £22.50 per week plus maternity grant and an additional one year's unpaid leave (European Information Bulletin No. 1, 1985). Unlike virtually all other EEC countries, the UK imposes stringent conditions on entitlement to these provisions, related to length of service with the employer and hours worked, which discriminate heavily against part-time employees. At the present time a reduction, rather than an extension, of these rights is being considered by the UK government, as will be discussed in Chapter 9.

One theme common to all the chapters of this book is the increased participation of married women as well as single women in the workforce in Great Britain in the post-war years. This phenomenon is common to all industrialised countries, but its magnitude varies considerably even across a geographically compact group such as the EEC (see Davidson and Cooper, 1984). Exact comparisons are difficult because definitions vary, but it can be said that the participation rate of married women is higher in Great Britain than in any other EEC country except Denmark. Many British women, particularly those who return after childbirth and completion of their families, work part-time. This does not appear to be the case in other European countries, though comparisons are difficult because definitions vary: for example, in West Germany part-time work is defined as less than 40 hours a week in some circumstances. In their chapter Dex and Shaw use the British definition of 30 hours a week or less, and show that in the USA fewer women overall work part-time but that among younger women part-time work is more common in America than in Great Britain, while among older women the reverse is true. In Chapter 7 the author shows that some older British women who work part-time have caring responsibilities for the elderly and infirm.

Part-time working is shown, particularly by Elias in Chapter 4 and Main in Chapter 5, to be accompanied by a downgrading of jobs and hence loss of earning capacity. There seems no inherent reason why this should be so. When one considers, for example, the exceedingly complex system of shift-working devised for male workers in the chemical industry to accommodate the need for supervision, different skills, continuous and non-continuous processes and local customs, it is obvious that, given the will, higher level work could be made available on a part-time basis for most of those men and women who desire it. There may in fact be a financial advantage to the employer for some higher level posts to be shared between two part-timers with different expertise.

One reason for the popularity of part-time work is the limited amount of help with domestic tasks which most women receive from their husbands. Rimmer in Chapter 3 shows that even in households where wives are working full-time a majority do more than half the housework. This inequality exists in most industrialised countries (Davidson and Cooper, 1984). In many emergent countries, where women's rights to education and work are theoretically legally guaranteed, domestic responsibilities are seen as the major impediment to women's real equality. 'It is rare to find an Egyptian husband who will help out in the home on a regular basis'; 'My husband can't even fetch a glass of water for himself'; such statements by highly educated Egyptians (Lebo, 1984) illustrate both the power of established cultural relations between the sexes to impede progress towards greater equality of opportunity between women and men and the extent of men's socialised roles and women's reluctance to challenge such 'incapacities'.

The proportion of part-timers is above average among women who have the responsibility for elderly or infirm people, described in Chapter 7. It is only comparatively recently that the problems of carers have been recognised. Neither the 1943 survey nor the 1947 survey (Thomas, 1944 and 1948) touched on them. There was some recognition during the Second World War of the demands of caring in that women with such responsibilities could be exempted from direction to work away from home. Very rarely men could obtain similar exemption. The increase in interest in recent years can be ascribed to two main causes: the change in the sex ratio which means there are fewer unmarried daughters to undertake these responsibilities, and the growth in the proportion of very old people in the population. Present government policies directed towards caring for the elderly and infirm in the community make little financial provision for carers within the family and, until fairly recently, specifically excluded married women carers. The official leaflet (N1 12/Sep 84) stated categorically: 'You can't get Invalid Care Allowance if you're married and living with your husband . . . This rule applies whoever gets your help.' This rule was challenged by Mrs Jacqueline Drake, who won a test case to a Social Security Appeals Tribunal on the grounds that the regulations were contrary to an EEC directive which states that there should be no discrimination against women. Mrs Drake also took her case to the European Court which, in June 1986, pronounced in her favour. In June 1986, the government finally came into line with EEC policy, granting invalid care allowance to married women carers and backdating its award to December 1984. This was a major step forward in the legitimisation of women's right to employment.

Another aspect of caring which has received no attention is that of married women who feel compelled to work beyond retirement age because their husbands are invalids and their own occupational pension scheme contains no provision for widowers' and dependants' benefits. The EOC has produced a report which shows that introducing widowers' benefits might cost very little (EOC, 1985b).

The European Community has prepared a draft directive which would require member states to introduce leave for pressing family reasons, which would provide a minimum number of days' leave, maintain social security cover, and guarantee a return to the same job, (House of Lords, 1985. Appendices 1 and 2).

WHAT OF THE FUTURE?

Policy issues as a whole are discussed in detail in Chapter 9. Here there is room only to raise the question of how the policy objectives are to be achieved.

Dex and Shaw in Chapter 8 show that in some ways working women in the United States are in advance of those in Britain, and they ascribe this in part to the earlier dates and more forceful provisions of legislation in the USA. However, we have seen in Britain that the effect of laws designed to promote equality has been less than was hoped. After an early improvement in women's rates of pay and some movement towards occupational desegregation, the situation has become static. Women's employment in many industrialised countries appears to have responded in similar ways to international and national legislation (Davidson and Cooper, 1984).

There are, however, some ways in which legislation can effect equality. The discriminatory social security provisions and taxation laws described by Rimmer in Chapter 3 can only be rectified by legal action. Such action is long overdue.

Legislation which is enacted with the positive support of a minority and the apathetic indifference of a majority can have some influence on public opinion. The sex and race equality laws in this country have at least made many people examine their own attitudes to these questions. This can be a first step towards changing attitudes. It is only by pressure of public opinion that, in a democracy, conditions will be changed. Progress towards equality at work has been slow: it takes overwhelming necessity such as that produced by two world wars to achieve even modest gains, of which a large part have subsequently been lost.

Over a hundred years ago J. S. Mill wrote:

> I believe that women's disabilities elsewhere are only clung to in

> order to maintain their subjection in domestic life; because the generality of the male sex cannot yet tolerate the idea of living with an equal. Were it not for that I think that almost everyone ... would admit the injustice of excluding half the human race from the greater number of lucrative occupations. (Mill 1869)

It seems to many of us that these words are almost as true today as when they were written. However, a century is a short time in history, and one cannot hope in that time to rectify all the injustices of many thousands of years. All the great civilisations and all the great religions have effectively relegated women to a subordinate role. Women's inferior position in paid work is only one aspect of inequality, but a very important one. We hope that the contributions to this book, by highlighting some of the factors which at present prevent women from achieving equality in paid work, will provide a basis for action to secure more equitable treatment in future.

2 The Lifetime Attachment of Women to the Labour Market

Brian G. M. Main

INTRODUCTION

This chapter examines the attachment of women to the labour market, as defined by the extent to which they are engaged in paid full-time or part-time employment over the life-cycle. This is, of course, but one aspect of the phenomenon of women's work. In Chapter 5 the author examines the relationship between work experience and women's earnings. Other authors of this book have explored issues concerning occupational mobility, and the role of women in the family as wife, mother and carer.[1]

The empirical findings presented here come almost entirely from analysis of the 1980 Women and Employment Survey. The next section of the chapter discusses this survey and the data, its validity, and the method of analysis. The third section offers an overview of women's working lives by discussing a series of figures which describe, for various groups of women, the most common patterns of work histories followed. Some attention is paid to the extent to which these work histories have changed during the last few decades. The fourth section extends this analysis by devising several summary measures of work histories and examining these at a given stage in the life-cycle for women in different age groups. This approach attempts to highlight intergenerational changes in behaviour by controlling for life-cycle effects.

Following this analysis are two sections which concentrate on the division of periods of paid employment within women's work histories into full-time or part-time employment. The second of these two sections pays particular attention to movements *between* the two modes of employment. Finally, the concluding section offers an overview and a commentary on the policy implications of the findings discussed in this chapter.

THE WOMEN AND EMPLOYMENT SURVEY

The Women and Employment Survey, conducted in May and June of 1980, yielded a nationally representative sample of 5588 women. The original report on the survey and a description of its technical background can be found in Martin and Roberts (1984a, 1984b). The survey was conducted by the Office of Population Censuses and Surveys.

The essential feature of the Women and Employment Survey used here is the extensive information relating to women's working lives. Not only were the start and finish dates for each period of employment and non-employment collected, but so too were the dates of life-cycle events such as marriage and the birth of children. For any birth cohort[2] of women in the survey it was therefore possible to construct a set of variables giving such information as the percentage of the cohort in employment at any time in a given year, the percentage of women working part-time, or the percentage of women married, etc. Such variables, describing the typical work experience, or fertility, of a birth cohort can be calculated for each year, from the year that women in each birth cohort were aged 16 years until 1980, the year of the survey.

The variables that describe the 'evolution' of each cohort have the triangular structure illustrated in Figure 2.1. In this diagram the current age of each cohort is listed for each year in the life of the cohort. The variables of interest, such as the percentage of the cohort in full-time or part-time employment in each year, can also be portrayed in this fashion. It was not possible, however, to distinguish periods of unemployment in the work history of each cohort.

In the design stages of the survey it was felt that, in the case of women, the definition of the unemployed state presented too many ambiguities to allow a single definition suitable for the collection of work history information. In their main report, Martin and Roberts (1984a) spend some time analysing this labour market status and attitudes of women in the survey. They conclude, as do Cragg and

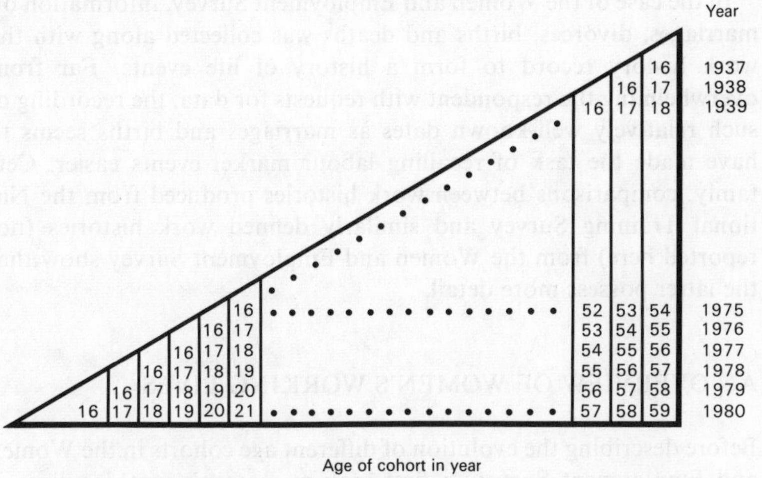

* The variable recorded is the cohort's contemporaneous age, but it could equally be the cohort's employment rate or any other such variable.

FIGURE 2.1 *A representation of the cohort data structure*

Dawson (1984) in their follow-up survey of a group of women who were unemployed at the time of the main survey, that female unemployment is best viewed as a continuum of states rather than in terms of a single definition.

Concern is often expressed about the quality of any work history information collected by such recall methods, given the fallibility of memory. A test on the reliability of recall work history data was conducted by Elias and Main (1982) on the National Training Survey. This survey collected work history information in 1975 for approximately 25 000 women. Elias and Main used these data to compute age-specific activity rates for particular years. For example, those women who were aged 49–53 years in 1975 would have indicated through their work histories an activity rate for 25–29 year olds in 1951, which could then be compared with the findings of the 1951 census. This procedure yielded a high correlation between the two data sources and, therefore, added confidence to the veracity of recalled work histories. Martin and Roberts (1984b) conducted a similar test on the Women and Employment Survey data, reaching the same conclusion. Comparison with four common cohorts from Hunt (1968) also shows a high correlation.

In the case of the Women and Employment Survey, information on marriages, divorces, births and deaths was collected along with the work history record to form a history of life events. Far from overwhelming the respondent with requests for data, the recording of such relatively well-known dates as marriages and births seems to have made the task of recalling labour market events easier. Certainly, comparisons between work histories produced from the National Training Survey and similarly defined work histories (not reported here) from the Women and Employment Survey show that the latter possess more detail.

AN OVERVIEW OF WOMEN'S WORKING LIVES

Before describing the evolution of different age cohorts in the Women and Employment Survey, a first look at women's working lives is taken in Figure 2.2, using a technique borrowed from Elias and Main (1982). This represents the patterns of working life experienced by women in the form of a bar-chart or histogram, where the width of each column represents the relative frequency of that particular pattern of working life among all women in the group. The actual type of pattern experienced is represented in the vertical direction, where the height of each component of the bar chart represents the average years spent in either paid employment or non-paid employment. Paid employment phases are denoted by shaded areas in contrast with blank areas, which represent non-employment phases. For ease of comparison between such histograms, the first eight columns are always presented from left to right in the same order. These start with a continuous employment phase and then increase the number of phases by adding alternate non-employment and employment phases. After the pattern with four employment and four non-employment phases has been presented, the successive order is determined by ranking the frequency of the observed work history patterns. For clarity of presentation a few complex and rare work history patterns have been omitted, and therefore the charts do not display 100 per cent of the recorded work histories.

In Figure 2.2 the working lives of all women in the Women and Employment Survey who had identifiable work histories are shown as they were recorded in 1980. Two impressions are gained immediately. First, this is a picture of working lives punctuated by periods of non-labour-market activity. It differs sharply from the equivalent picture

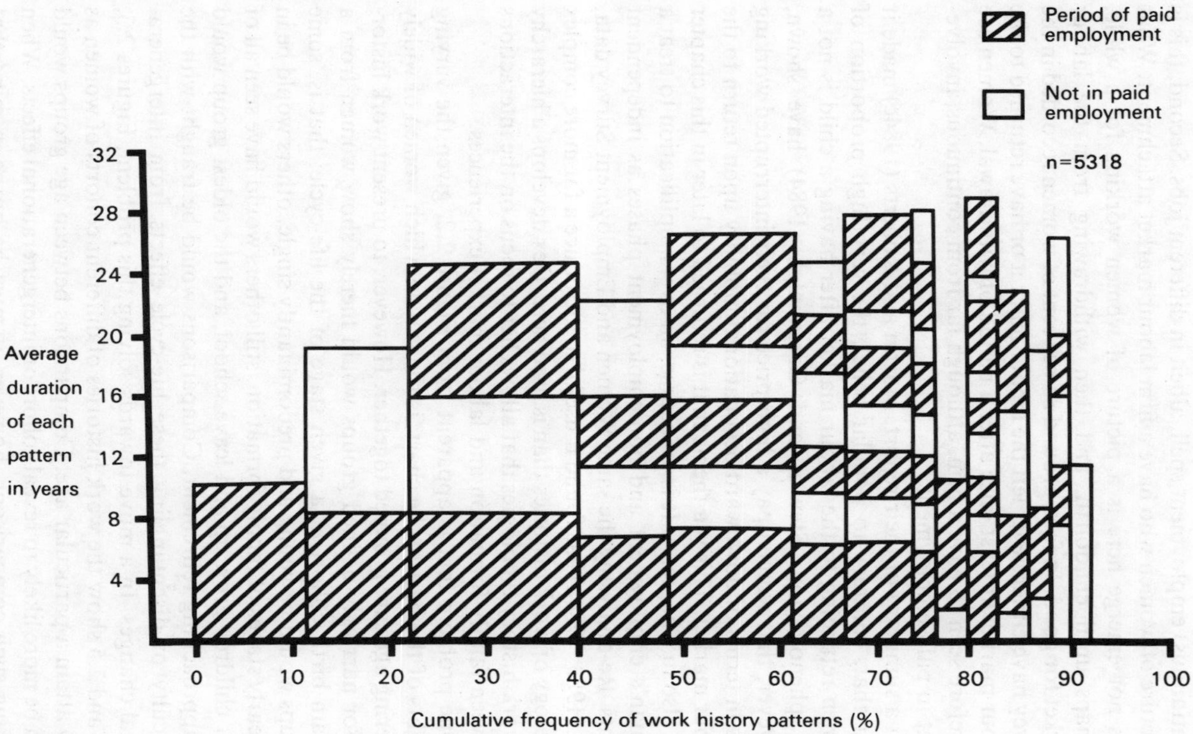

FIGURE 2.2 *Distribution of work history patterns, all women, 1980*

for males produced in Elias and Main (1982) from the National Training Survey. There, over 80 per cent of men had only one (continuous) employment spell, albeit in different jobs. Second, this is a picture of women who have a firm labour market attachment. What does not emerge here is a picture of women working for a while, perhaps until childbirth, and then withdrawing from the labour market for good. In fact, around 85 per cent of women recorded in the survey have either never left the labour market or have returned to the labour market at least once after a period of withdrawal. Women are therefore seen to have a firm, although far from continuous, involvement in paid employment.

In a summary of their report, Martin and Roberts (1984c) made it clear that, contrary to popular belief, the very high proportion of women returning to the labour market after having a child is not a new phenomenon. Stewart and Greenhalgh (1984) have shown, however, that women pay a high price for their interrupted working lives in terms of downward occupational mobility upon return to the labour market. This is a theme that is returned to later in this chapter and also in Chapter 4. It is, of course, an oversimplification to treat a woman's employment and non-employment phases as independent events. Re-analysing the same Women and Employment Survey data, Dex (1983, 1984a) has found it useful to introduce a far more complex typology of work histories than is used here. Dex develops a hierarchy of work history typologies that allows her to focus on the interactions between family formation and labour market experiences.

One problem that is apparent from Figure 2.2, given the varying heights of the bars in the chart, is the way in which women of widely differing ages are grouped together. However, to present work histories for narrowly defined groups would merely show women from a certain birth cohort at a given stage of the life-cycle: that is, some groups would be young and predominantly single, others would be in the early stages of family formation, still others would have seen all of their children grow up and leave school, and the oldest group would be approaching retirement. Comparisons would be fraught with the difficulty of disentangling these life-cycle effects from intergenerational changes. In a move towards solving this problem, Figures 2.3, 2.4, and 2.5 show the work histories of different cohorts of women as they attain a particular age. Comparisons between age groups would then be more likely to reveal cohort or intergenerational effects. When making such comparisons, however, it must be borne in mind that women born in 1930 reached the age of 30 after a very different

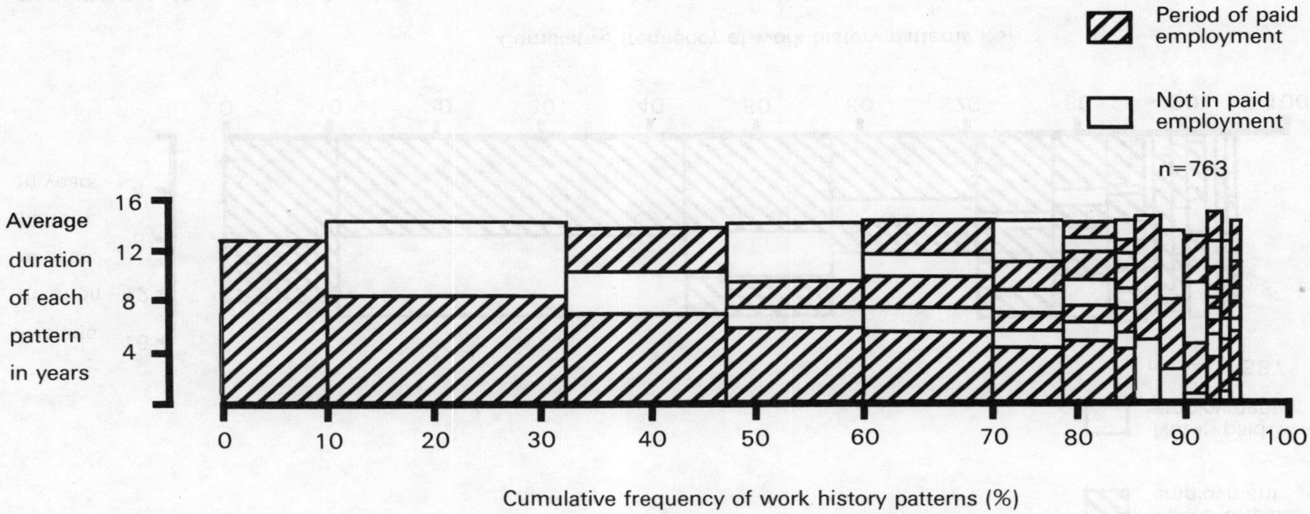

FIGURE 2.3 *Distribution of work history patterns at age 30, women aged 30–34 years in 1980*

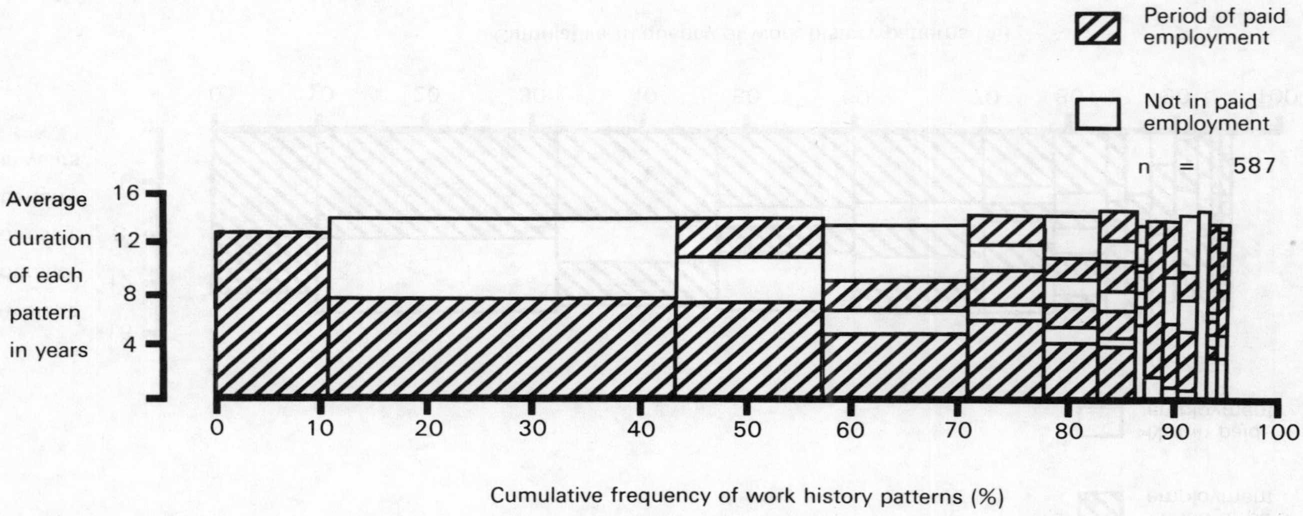

FIGURE 2.4 *Distribution of work history patterns at age 30, women aged 40–44 years in 1980*

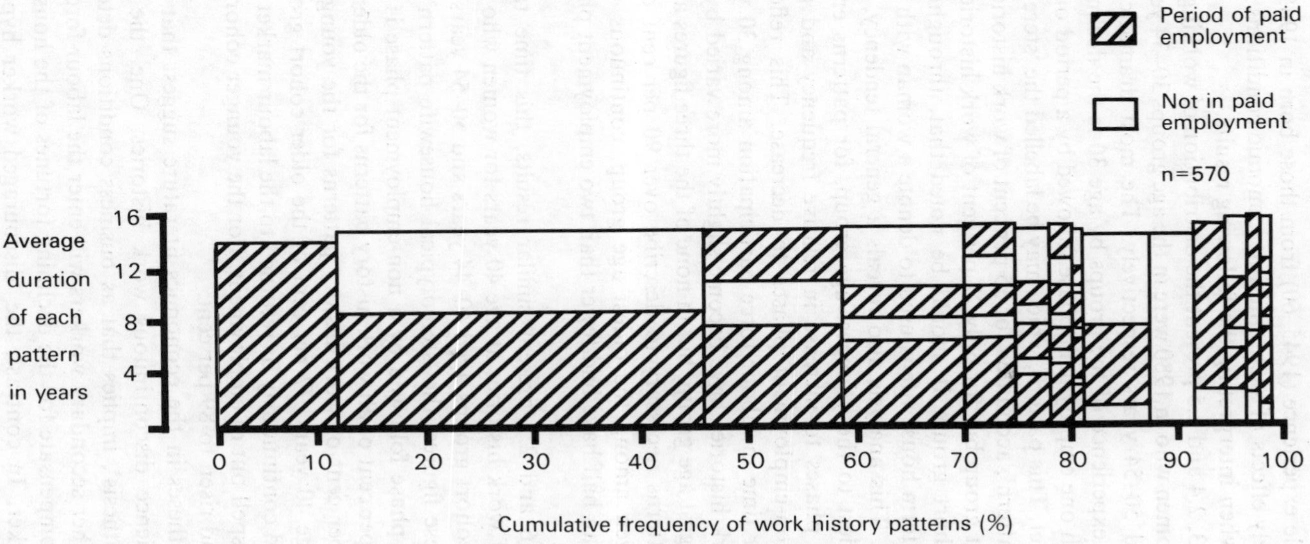

FIGURE 2.5 *Distribution of work history patterns at age 30, women aged 50–54 years in 1980*

business cycle experience (1945–60) from those born in 1945 (1960–75). The likely effects of such differing economic conditions must be considered when interpreting the following results.

Figures 2.3, 2.4 and 2.5 present the distribution of working lives at age 30 for women who in 1980 were in the age groups 30–34 years, 40–44 years and 50–54 years respectively. The most dramatic change between the experience of the groups by age 30 is the decline in the category with one employment phase followed by a period out of the labour market. This pattern, which may be labelled the 'stereotypical housewife pattern', accounted for 35 per cent of work histories in the oldest cohort group but for only 22 per cent of work histories in the youngest cohort group. It should be noted that, throughout this chapter, the term housewife is used to denote a woman with no paid employment. This analysis also reveals a general tendency, moving from the oldest to the youngest age group, for patterns ending in employment phases to increase in relative frequency and patterns ending in non-employment phases to decrease. This reflects the increase over time in labour force participation among 30 year-old women. Work histories have become slightly more varied by age 30 for the youngest age group, but in none of the three figures are more than ten patterns necessary to describe over 90 per cent of work histories. Even among the oldest age group, continuous workers aside, less than half have had fewer than two employment phases by age 30 years.

Figures 2.6 and 2.7 present similar results, this time taking a 'snapshot' of work histories at age 40 years for women who in 1980 were in the cohort groups aged 40–44 years and 50–54 years respectively. In these figures, the 'stereotypical housewife pattern' of one employment phase followed by a non-employment phase is seen to fall from 17 per cent of all work history patterns for the older cohort group to 9 per cent of work history patterns for the young cohort group. By age 40 years, 77 per cent of the older cohort group had either worked continuously or returned to the labour market at least once after a spell out of employment. For the younger cohort group this figure had risen to 89 per cent.

Two hypotheses in the economics literature suggest that women might experience discontinuous work histories. One, the 'added worker hypothesis', implies that as business conditions deteriorate women or other secondary workers will enter the labour force in an attempt to compensate for the declining fortunes of the household's primary worker. In contrast, the 'discouraged worker hypothesis'

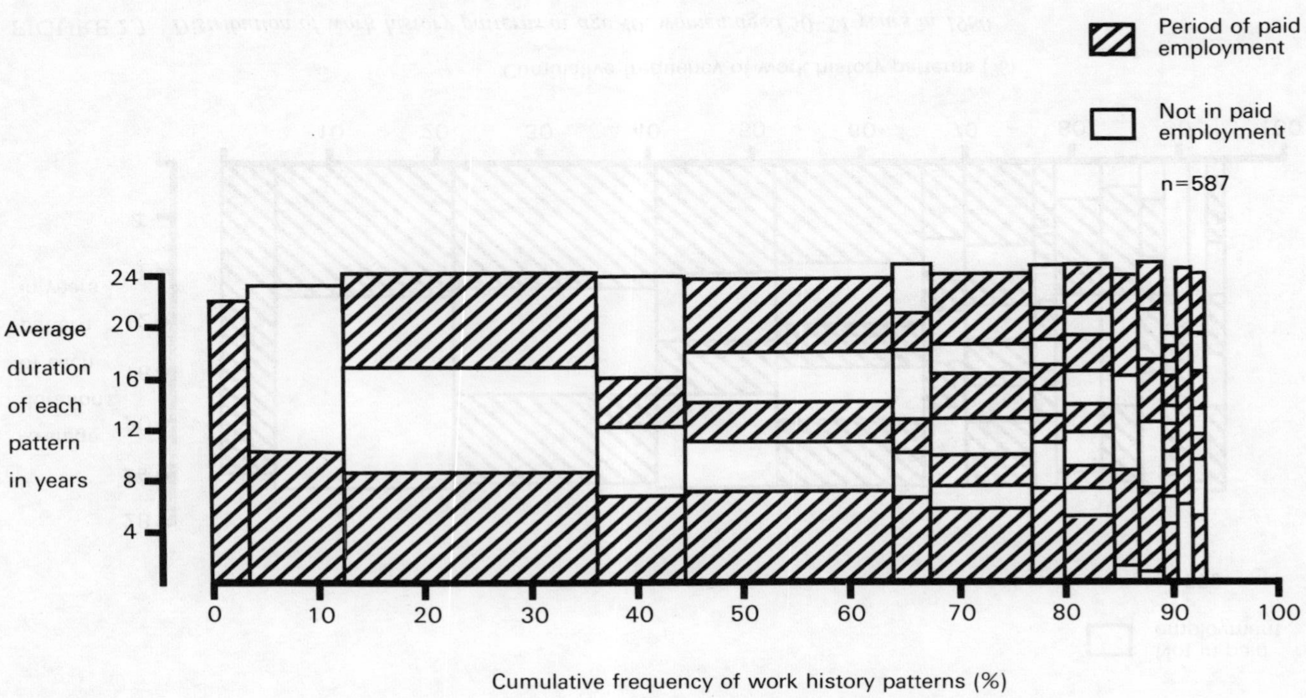

FIGURE 2.6 *Distribution of work history patterns at age 40, women aged 40–44 years in 1980*

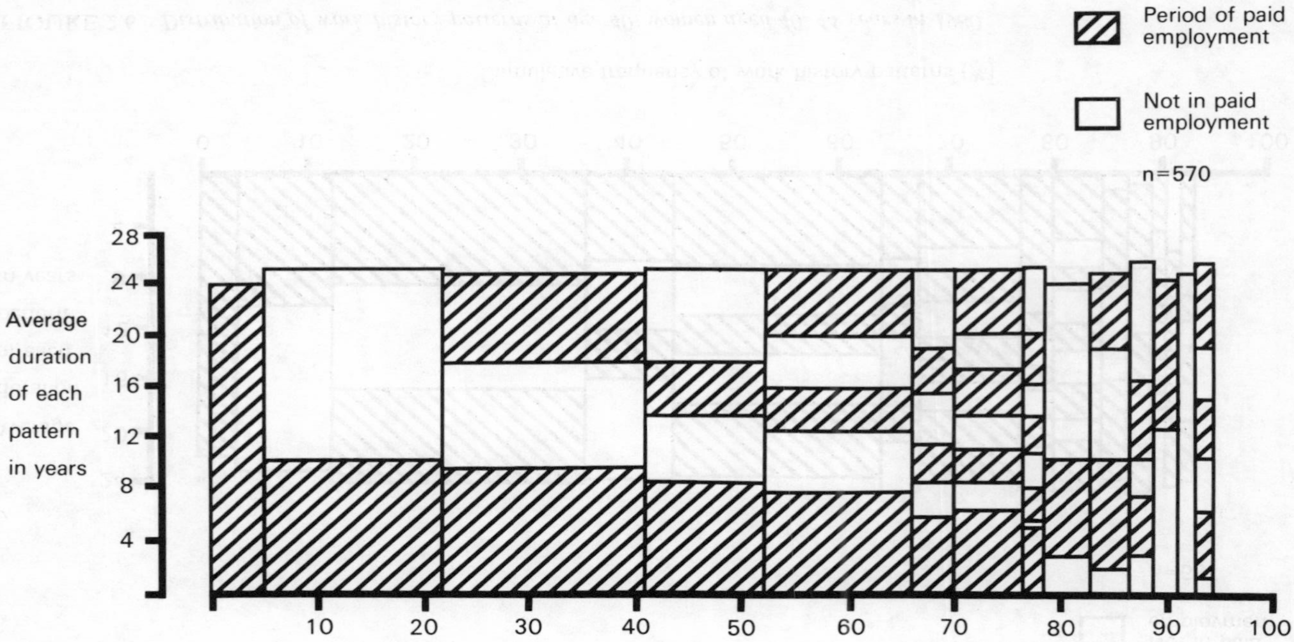

FIGURE 2.7 *Distribution of work history patterns at age 40, women aged 50–54 years in 1980*

suggests that, as secondary workers, women will be quick to refrain from employment search when business conditions, and hence the prospects of finding a job, deteriorate. These hypotheses are not well supported by the detailed analyses of women's work histories given in Figures 2.6 and 2.7. The fact is that over 90 per cent of women's work histories as portrayed at age 40 years can be summarised in one of twelve patterns. Well over 70 per cent of these work histories fall into one of six patterns.

These pictorial representations of women's work histories show that the vast majority of women return to the labour market after one, two or three breaks from employment. The dichotomy suggested by Applebaum (1981) for the USA, of women following either 'chaotic career lines' or 'orderly career lines' (p. 67), does not seem to fit the British experience. Indeed, Dex and Shaw in their comparison of women's working lives in the USA and Great Britain (Chapter 8) emphasise this very difference. They point out that while American women have been moving towards taking very little time off work for childbirth, the British, while experiencing a trend to shorter non-employment durations, still take much more time out of paid employment. Part of the difference is credited to tax concessions for child-care expenses available in the USA. One of the consequences that will be expanded on below and pursued further in Chapter 4 is that British women very often return to employment via part-time jobs and experience substantial downward occupational mobility.

The underlying trend in these figures is towards higher labour force participation among women. This has been documented by Joshi, Layard and Owen (1985) and by Martin and Roberts (1984a). What the above figures bring out is that most women born since the end of the First World War have always had an involvement in paid work throughout their working lives, and this involvement is becoming more extensive with the passing of time. Of course, in earlier years women were often constrained in their choices by the operation of the 'marriage bar'. Hunt (1968, Tables D4 and D5) shows that 21 per cent of women aged 40 years and above in 1965 had either never had paid employment or had given up paid employment permanently upon marriage or birth of first child. In addition, Thomas (1944) shows that only 20 per cent of women who came into employment from the home during the war had had any intention of returning to paid employment were it not for the war. The results discussed in this chapter therefore represent what is very much a post-Second World War phenomenon, although as was pointed out in the preceding chapter, married women's employment is by no means a new thing.

COHORT WORK HISTORY SUMMARY MEASURES

The analysis of work histories is made difficult by the need to represent what is often a complex series of events in some summary form. In an attempt to simplify matters somewhat, this section presents a few summary measures of each cohort's behaviour. To control for life-cycle events such as family formation, these measures are taken at certain ages. To reduce the loss of information through aggregation, the results are presented for single-year birth cohorts.

Four measures are used: participation in paid employment or 'labour force participation'; the fraction who are 'returners'; the average number of spells spent in non-employment; and the fraction of working life spent in non-employment. Each is reported as the cohort passes through four ages – 30, 35, 40, and 45 years – for all cohorts who have reached that age by 1980. Because single-year cohorts are chosen, the results display a degree of variability. This is due, among other things, to each cohort reaching a given age in a different calendar year and thus having experienced different economic conditions. Thus, women born in 1939 reached age 40 in 1979, and as they moved towards their fortieth birthday experienced the labour market conditions of 1954 to 1979. By contrast, women born in 1922 moved towards their fortieth birthday experiencing the different labour market conditions of 1936 to 1962. In spite of these different labour market experiences, it is hoped that any underlying trends will emerge clearly.

Figure 2.8 presents the fraction of each cohort in employment at each of the four ages, 30, 35, 40 and 45 years. This is, of course, not strictly equivalent to labour force participation rates, but, due to the difficulty of defining female unemployment in an unambiguous way here, it is used as a proxy. The results are similar to those in Table 9.1 in Martin and Roberts (1984a), where aggregated five-year groups are used. The marked upward trend in labour market activity among younger (later born) cohorts is clearly visible at all ages. If anything, the trend is stronger at ages 35 years and above where the underlying trends represent a gain of around 2 per cent as opposed to the 1 per cent per year growth in 'labour force participation' at age 30. Only in very recent cohorts, those born after 1943, does the trend at age 30 increase sharply. The extent to which the various lines in Figure 2.8 move in a synchronous manner around the trend represents influences particular to each year's birth cohort. Thus, the fact that those born in 1924 are observed above the trend line at ages 30, 35, 40 and 45 years

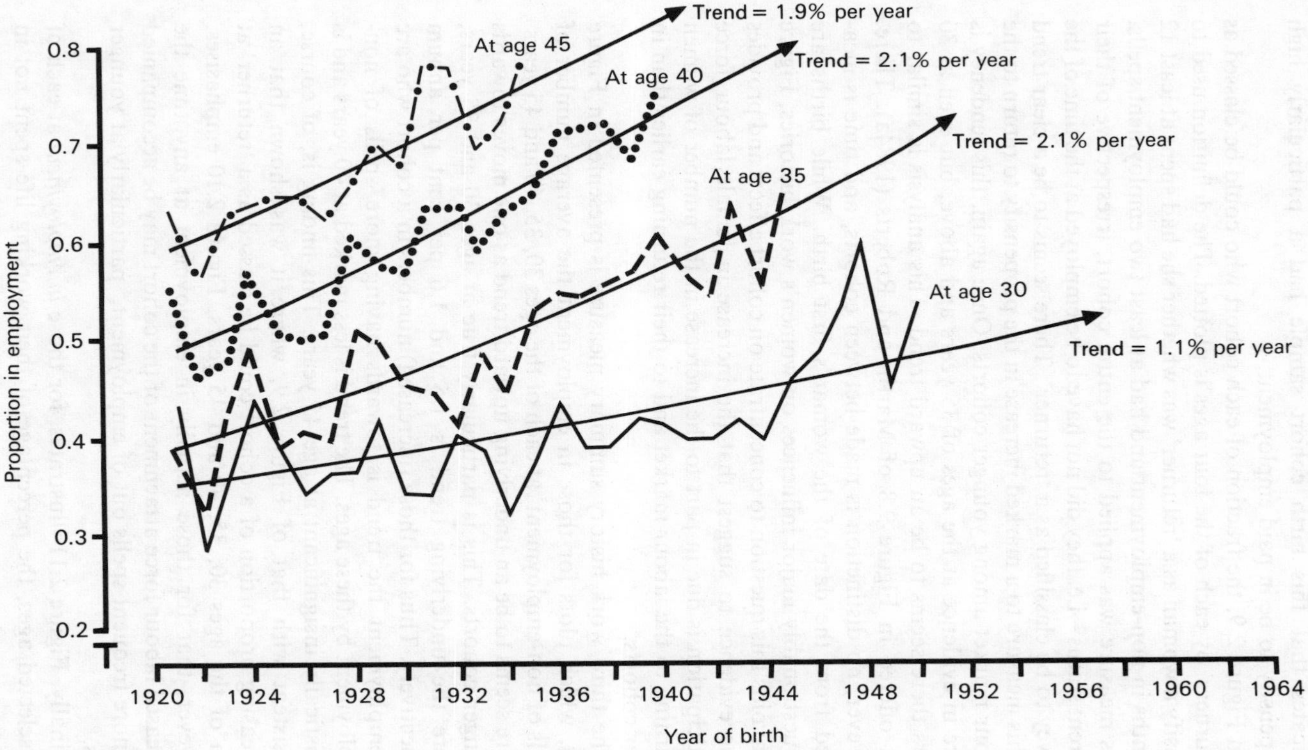

FIGURE 2.8 *Proportion of respondents who are in employment at a given age, by year of birth*

indicates that this birth cohort sample had a particularly high propensity to be in paid employment.

In Figure 2.9, the fraction of each cohort who could be classed as 'returners' by each of the four ages is plotted. The definition used to classify a woman as a 'returner' was whether she had spent at least 12 months in non-employment and had at least two employment spells. This measure was applied to the entire cohort, irrespective of their current status – i.e. they did not have to be employed at the time of the survey to be classified as a 'returner'. There seems to be a clear trend in this measure to a marked increase in the propensity to return to the labour market among younger cohorts. Once again, this tendency is more in evidence at the ages of 35 years and above, but even at 30 years there seems to be an upward trend. This analysis is similar to that offered in Figure 9.8 of Martin and Roberts (1984a). There, however, no distinction is made between cohorts, and time is measured from the date of the woman's first birth. While births are unquestionably major influences on women's work histories, Figure 2.9 avoids this question to concentrate on cohort effects and provides some evidence to suggest that the increase in female labour force participation is due in part to the increase in the number of women returning to the labour market and to their returning earlier than in older cohorts.

The third work history summary measure is presented in Figure 2.10, which plots for those in employment the average number of spells of non-employment[3] at each of the ages 30, 35, 40 and 45 years. There seems to be an underlying upward trend as one moves towards younger cohorts. This is particularly true at ages 30 and 35 years, where the underlying trend is 1.5 and 1.6 per cent per annum respectively. Thus for those (increased) numbers in a cohort who are in employment the trend is towards having more spells of non-employment by these ages. The trend is less marked at 40 years and is statistically insignificant at age 45 years. This finding is, of course, consistent with that of Figure 2.9, where it was shown that an increasing proportion of a cohort could be classed as a 'returner' at each of the ages 30, 35, 40 and 45 years. Figure 2.10 emphasises, however, that for those actually in employment at any time the increased labour force attachment of the cohort may be accompanied by more frequent spells out of employment,[4] particularly at younger ages.

Finally, Figure 2.11 illustrates, for those *in employment* at each of the selected ages, the percentage of their working life spent not in

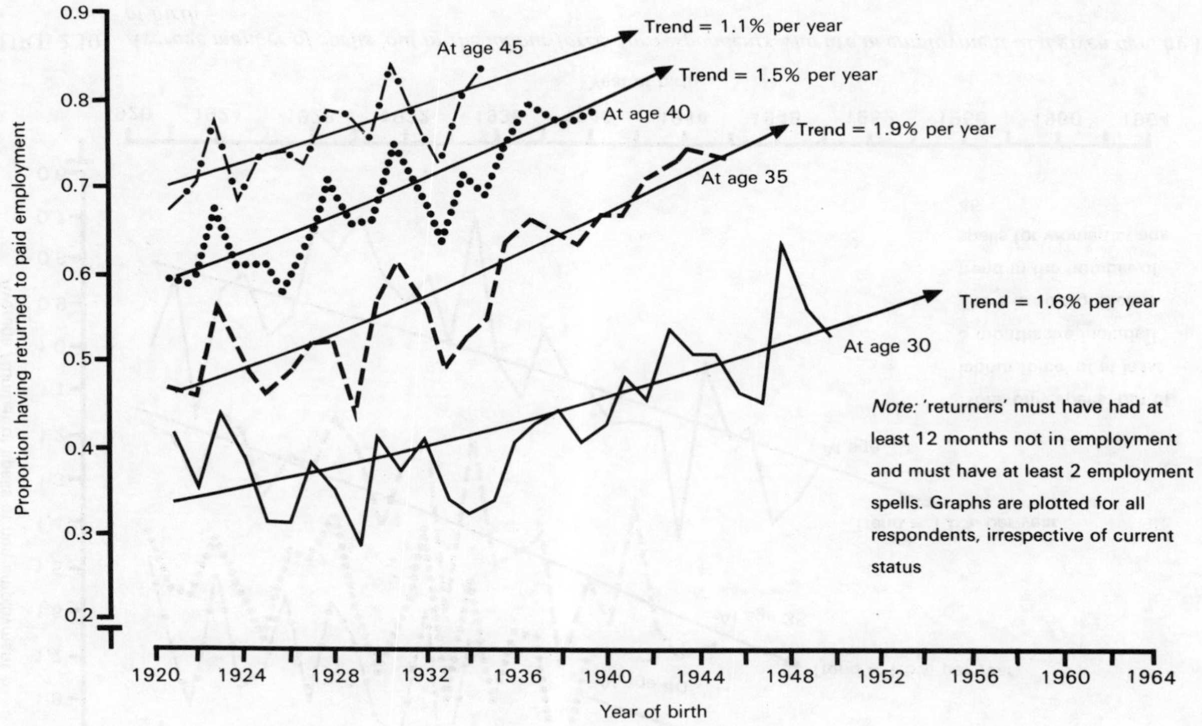

FIGURE 2.9 *Proportion of respondents who are returners at a given age, by year of birth*

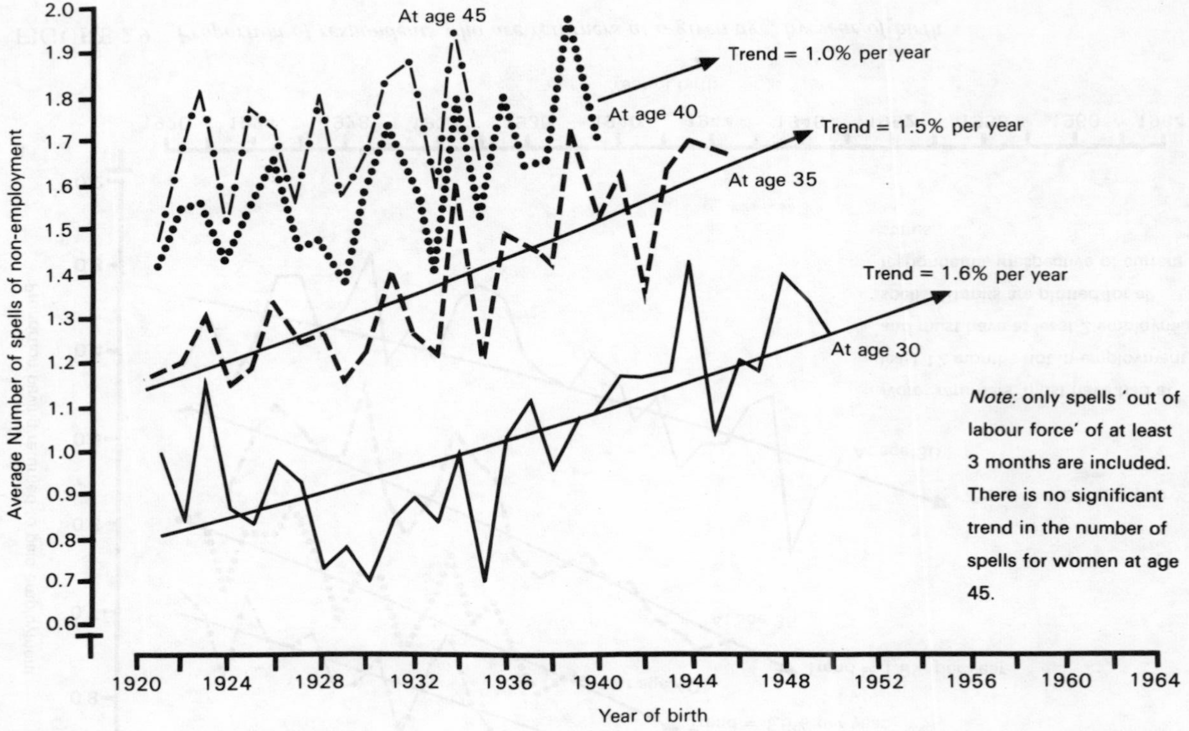

FIGURE 2.10 *Average number of spells 'out of the labour force' for respondents who are in employment at a given age, by year of birth*

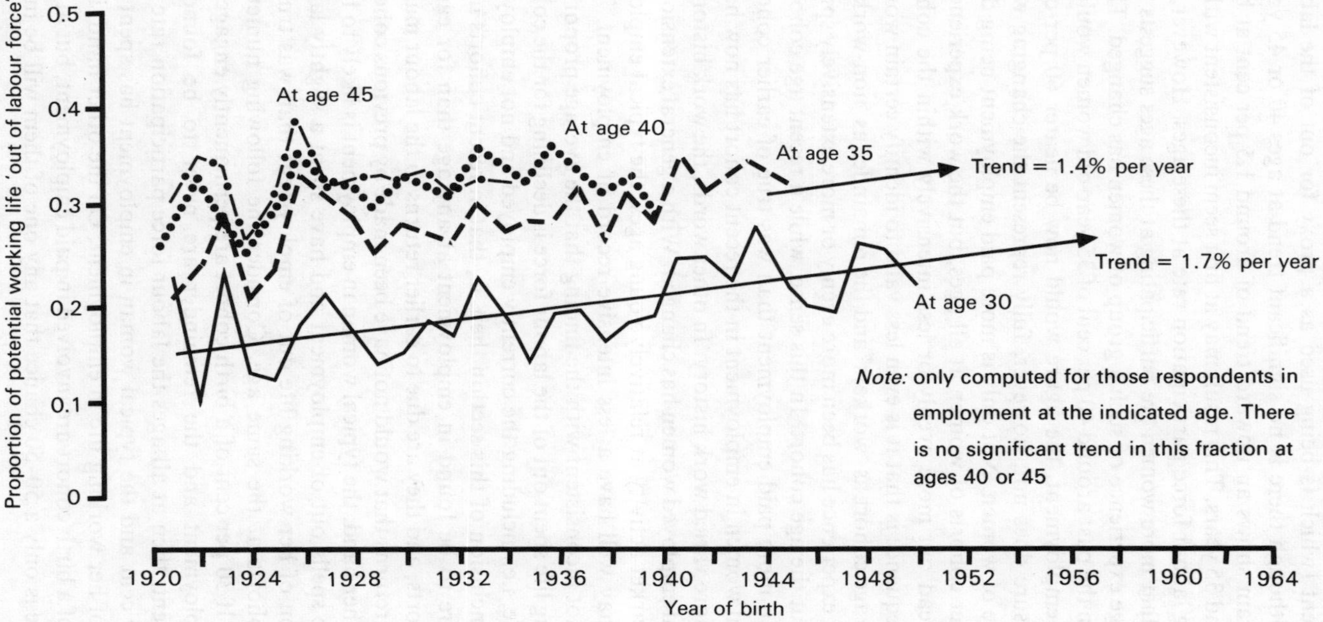

FIGURE 2.11 *Proportion of potential working life spent 'out of the labour force' at a given age, by year of birth*

employment (which is being used as a proxy for out of the labour force). Although there is no significant trend at ages 40 or 45 years, this diagram shows an upward trend of around 1.5 per cent at both ages 30 and 35 years. This result may at first seem inconsistent with an increasing labour force participation rate at these ages. However, the very fact that more women are participating at these ages suggests that the average experience of such a group of women has changed. Thus, whereas in the past around 40 per cent of 35 year-old women would be found in employment, the figure would now be nearer 60 per cent. This measure does not, however, fully represent the changing work experience of women. Not only is more paid employment being done by younger cohorts of women at all ages, but the work experience is being spread out more evenly or less intensively within the cohort. The consequence is that it is even less valid to identify certain women within an age cohort as 'workers' and the remainder as 'non-workers. The work experience has been more evenly or more extensively spread throughout the age cohort. In this sense, while a recent age cohort is engaged in more paid employment than was true of earlier cohorts, the typical women in employment in the recent cohort has now had a slightly more varied work history. In other words, the work history of the typical employed women has changed. With a general extension of labour market activity at relatively young ages, the typical employed woman may well have a less intensive record of employment. This result is not inconsistent with the finding that the average proportion of working life spent out of the labour force is declining for the cohort as a whole, i.e. including the currently employed and not employed.[5]

The conclusion of this section then, is, that in recent cohorts more women are to be found in employment at any age than for earlier birth cohorts, and they are due to earlier returns to the labour market or due to returns that would not have been made by previous cohorts. On the other hand, the typical woman in employment is likely to have had more spells out of employment and have spent a slightly larger proportion of her working life out of employment than was true of earlier cohorts at the same age. Consider the following numerical example. If 30 per cent of a birth cohort are permanently engaged in paid employment and the remainder are never to be found in employment, then at all ages the labour force participation rate will be 30 per cent and the typical woman in employment has spent 100 per cent of her working life in employment. On the other hand, if 80 per cent of a birth cohort are involved in paid employment, but at any time there is only a 50–50 chance that any one of them will be in the labour force, then at all ages the labour force participation route of such a cohort will be 40 per cent, and yet the typical woman in employment has spent only 50 per cent of her working life in employment. This is a simplistic example, but it serves to make the point that the employment experience of a cohort can rise by employment becoming more extensive within the cohort. It is therefore important not to lose sight of the fact that the increase in labour market activity among women has been an extensive as well as an intensive phenomenon.

THE FULL-TIME/PART-TIME BREAKDOWN OF LIFETIME EMPLOYMENT

The rise in the importance of part-time employment in Britain over the past few decades has attracted considerable research interest.[6] Work by Elias and Main (1982) emphasised the fact that part-time employment is essentially the domain of women returning to the labour market after a period of withdrawal, usually for family formation reasons. In a series of case studies, Robinson and Wallace (1984) illustrate how demand-side considerations result in much part-time employment being in low-paid jobs. In Chapter 4, Elias pursues the interaction of the supply of women returners and the demand structure of part-time jobs. What is attempted below is an illustration of the growing importance of part-time employment over the lifetime labour market experience of women.

Figure 2.12 plots the percentage of women in employment (full-time and part-time) over the life-cycle for a range of five-year cohorts in the Women and Employment Survey. The profiles that emerge are consistent with what Gustaffson (1980) has labelled the 'M-shaped pattern'. In the early years there is a rise in employment as women leave full-time education. The following dip is attributable to family formation activity, and the subsequent rise is due to women then returning to the labour market. Towards the end of the life-cycle, early withdrawal and retirement cause the final fall in the employment rate. This picture is essentially that produced as Figure 9.3 in Martin and Roberts (1984a). There, however, the effects of full-time education and its increasing importance to younger cohorts is not seen to emerge so clearly.

If the fraction of each cohort in full-time employment only is plotted, a very different picture emerges. Figure 2.13 illustrates that,

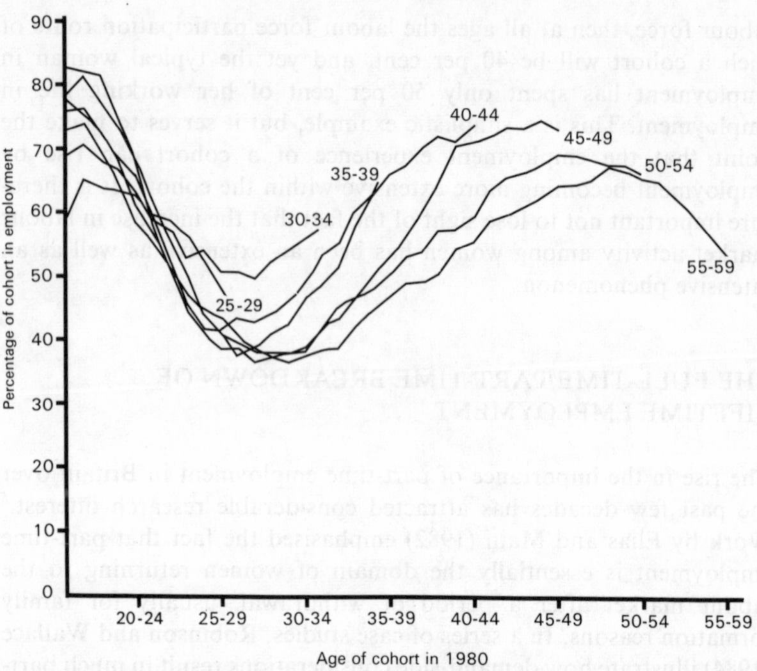

FIGURE 2.12 *Percentage of cohort in employment, for seven five-year age group cohorts*

apart from the effects of more extensive full-time education and earlier child birth among younger cohorts, subsequent profiles are very similar. The difference between the two sets of profiles in Figures 2.12 and 2.13 is due to the increasing importance of part-time employment. This is, indeed, confirmed in Figure 2.14, where the proportion of each cohort engaged in part-time employment is plotted by age. While part-time employment was not unknown to the older cohorts, there has been a marked increase at every age in the proportion of younger cohorts engaged in such employment. Taking these figures together, it is clear just how important a role part-time employment has played in the increased labour force participation of women over time.

Dex and Shaw (Chapter 8), in their comparison of the experience of women in the USA and in Great Britain, emphasise the importance of child-care consideration. In Britain this is much more likely to be an informal arrangement among family and friends, placing greater

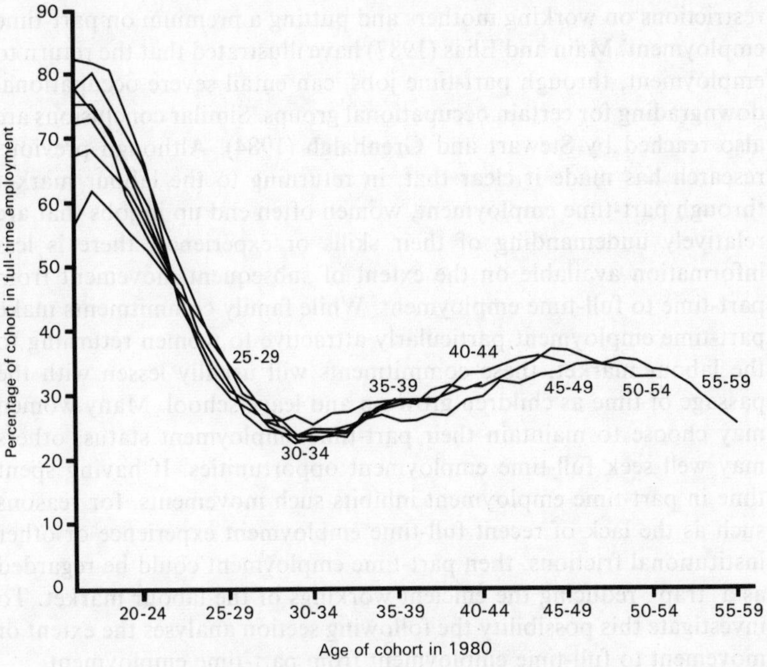

FIGURE 2.13 *Percentage of cohort in full-time employment, for seven five-year age group cohorts*

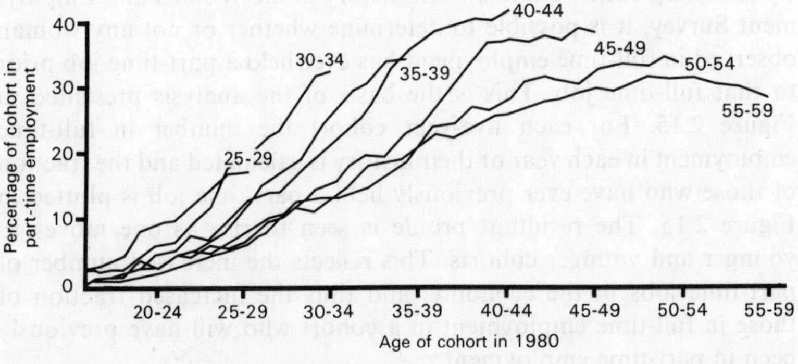

FIGURE 2.14 *Percentage of cohort in part-time employment, for seven five-year age group cohorts*

restrictions on working mothers and putting a premium on part-time employment. Main and Elias (1987) have illustrated that the return to employment, through part-time jobs, can entail severe occupational downgrading for certain occupational groups. Similar conclusions are also reached by Stewart and Grenhalgh (1984). Although previous research has made it clear that, in returning to the labour market through part-time employment, women often end up in jobs that are relatively undemanding of their skills or experience, there is less information available on the extent of subsequent movement from part-time to full-time employment. While family commitments make part-time employment particularly attractive to women returning to the labour market, these commitments will usually lessen with the passage of time as children grow up and leave school. Many women may choose to maintain their part-time employment status, others may well seek full-time employment opportunities. If having spent time in part-time employment inhibits such movements, for reasons such as the lack of recent full-time employment experience or other institutional frictions, then part-time employment could be regarded as a 'trap', reducing the efficient workings of the labour market. To investigate this possibility the following section analyses the extent of movement to full-time employment from part-time employment.

THE TRANSITION TO FULL-TIME FROM PART-TIME EMPLOYMENT

By analysing each woman's work history in the Women and Employment Survey, it is possible to determine whether or not any woman observed in full-time employment has ever held a part-time job prior to that full-time job. This is the basis of the analysis presented in Figure 2.15. For each five-year cohort the number in full-time employment in each year of their history is calculated and the fraction of those who have ever previously held a part-time job is plotted in Figure 2.15. The resultant profile is seen to rise as one moves to younger and younger cohorts. This reflects the increased number of part-time jobs in the economy, and thus the increased fraction of those in full-time employment in a cohort who will have previously been in part-time employment.

Figure 2.15 does suggest that part-time employment does not, in itself, represent a complete barrier to movement into full-time work.

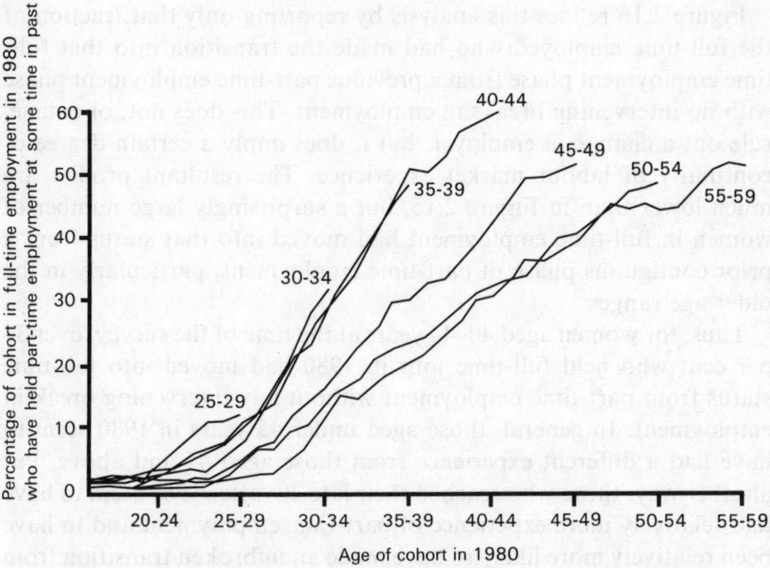

FIGURE 2.15 *Percentage of cohort in full-time employment in 1980 who have held part-time employment some time in the past, for seven five-year age group cohorts*

For the 40–44 year-old age group almost 60 per cent of those in full-time employment in 1980 had held a part-time job at some time in the past. By contrast, for those aged 55–59 years in 1980, when they were aged 40–44 years just over 30 per cent of those in full-time employment had experienced part-time employment. There is, of course, a gap of fifteen years between these two observations, and part-time employment in the economy had grown dramatically in that time, as Figure 2.14 illustrates. The fact remains, however, that a large proportion of those in full-time employment had made the transition from a part-time job. Combining the findings of Figure 2.14 and Figure 2.15 allows the importance of part-time work in women's work histories to be highlighted. At any time a large proportion of women are actually in part-time employment. And of those who are in full-time employment an equally large proportion will have had experience of part-time employment. It would clearly be misleading when discussing women's employment to regard full-time employment as the dominant 'norm'.

Figure 2.16 refines this analysis by reporting only that fraction of the full-time employed who had made the transition into that full-time employment phase from a previous part-time employment phase with no intervening breaks in employment. This does not, of course, rule out a change in employer, but it does imply a certain degree of continuity of labour market experience. The resultant profiles are much lower than in Figure 2.15, but a surprisingly large number of women in full-time employment had moved into that status from a prior contiguous phase of part-time employment, particularly in the older age ranges.

Thus, for women aged 40–44 years at the time of the survey, over 35 per cent who held full-time jobs in 1980 had moved into full-time status from part-time employment without any intervening break in employment. In general, those aged under 45 years in 1980 seem to have had a different experience from those aged 45 and above. Put another way, those who reached their late 20s after 1965 seem to have had relatively more experience of part-time employment and to have been relatively more likely to have made an unbroken transition from part-time to full-time employment. This may well be due to these

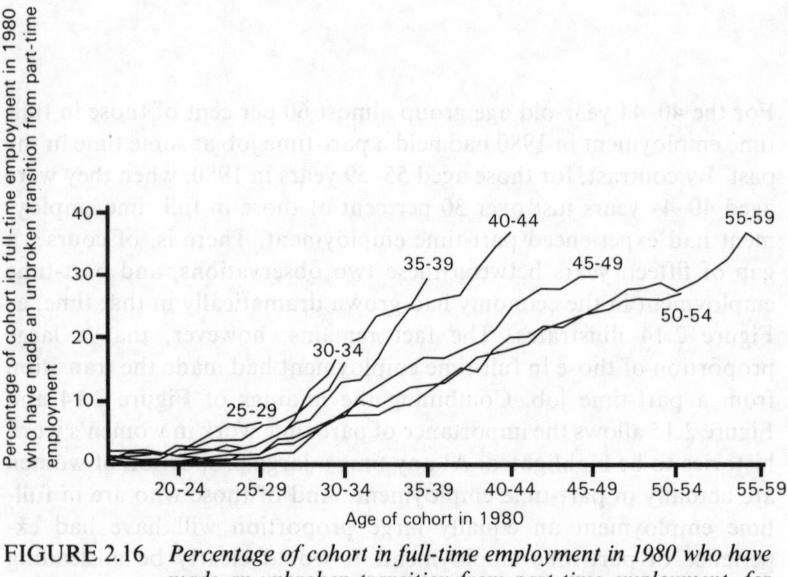

FIGURE 2.16 *Percentage of cohort in full-time employment in 1980 who have made an unbroken transition from part-time employment, for seven five-year age group cohorts*

cohorts living through different time periods. The growth of part-time jobs in the economy was particularly notable in the period after 1965.

Of course, the finding that the majority of women were able to make the transition from part-time employment to full-time employment does not remove the possibility of lasting downward occupational mobility suffered by women returning to the labour market. It does seem clear, however, that part-time employment itself is not acting as a trap by preventing women from moving into full-time employment status. This concern of a part-time 'trap' seems to be discounted by the finding here that the majority of women from the older cohorts who are in full-time employment have held part-time employment some time in their past. There are other ways in which the experience of part-time work can have an influence on women's subsequent labour market status. None of the evidence presented above rules out the possibility that the transition to full-time employment was delayed or hindered by the experience of part-time working. Nor can it be ruled out that the occupational status in any subsequent full-time job is lower than it would have been if the woman had remained in full-time employment. Evidence from the reported hourly earnings in the Women and Employment Survey does suggest that the effect of experience of part-time employment is to lower wage rates even after the woman has moved to full-time employment.[7]

CONCLUSIONS AND POLICY IMPLICATIONS

This chapter has examined the nature of women's working lives by using the work history data from the Women and Employment Survey. Women today emerge as having a firm and indeed lifetime attachment to the labour market. Although their work histories are interrupted by periods out of the labour market, the typical woman returns to paid employment after such breaks. This is not a finding that applies only to younger cohorts. The 'stereotypical housewife' who works and then withdraws permanently from the labour market upon marriage or childbirth has always been in a minority class since the Second World War. The vast majority of women continue their attachment to the labour market through one, two or three interruptions.

The increased labour market activity displayed by younger cohorts is in part due to an extension of the phenomenon of returning to the labour market. This can occur through shorter spells out of the labour market and/or through more frequent returns to the labour market. If anything, the typical woman in employment will have spent a shorter proportion of her working life in employment at a given age than was true of a typical employed woman from an older cohort at that same age. If, in the inter-war years, the dichotomy of women into workers and housewives was fairly generally applicable, it is certainly not the case in the 1980s, as women's labour market behaviour moves to a more varied pattern.

Part-time employment has come to be of greater importance in the economy and in the labour market experience of younger cohorts. What sets the experience of younger cohorts apart from their predecessors is to a large extent their involvement in part-time employment. For many women who have young children and who want to work, part-time working reflects the greater time that they spend on domestic work and child-rearing. However, as children grow older, a preference for full-time work may be re-established. Evidence presented in this chapter suggests that part-time employment does not present an insuperable barrier to securing full-time employment. This said, however, the possibility remains that the transition to full-time employment is difficult. Indeed, such a fact would go part way to explaining why so many women remain in part-time employment throughout the later stages of their working lives, as Figure 2.14 illustrates. Nevertheless, Figure 2.15 indicates that an ever increasing proportion of women in full-time employment have held part-time employment some time in their past. In addition, Figure 2.16 illustrates that in a large proportion of these cases the move from part-time to full-time employment had been made continuously, in the sense that there was no intervening period of non-employment.

The policy implications of this work rest on three interrelated findings: namely, women are involved in the labour market throughout their working lives, their employment experience is interrupted, and after their first employment spell part-time employment plays an important part. Thus women do two things in the labour market that are quite foreign to men: they experience a return to paid work and at some time they work part-time. In future years it is increasingly likely that this will be true of almost all women. The dynamics of the return and the concomitant experience of part-time work have received relatively little attention when measured against the quantitative importance of these phenomena.

Work by Dex (1984a), Elias (Chapter 4), Main and Elias (1987), and Stewart and Greenhalgh (1984) has called into question the efficiency of the labour market in this area. Constraints on the provision of child-care facilities, barriers imposed by the segmented nature of labour markets, and disincentives introduced by the tax/benefit system all combine to prevent qualified and experienced women finding labour market employment consistent with their attributes. This chapter does not address these issues directly, but by illustrating the nature of women's working lives and by exposing some of the underlying trends it can be argued that such issues are of potential quantitative significance.

None of this argues against part-time jobs. It does, however, suggest that perhaps some of the imaginative divisions of jobs into varying hours as outlined by Olmsted (1983) could reward both employers and employees. At any time there is a large number of women moving in and out of the labour market. In general these women are individually engaged in what is one of very few such moves in a lifetime. Part-time employment clearly appeals to such women at certain stages of their work history. It seems unfortunate, then that the majority of part-time jobs are found in a narrow range of low-paying activities.

NOTES

1. A broad and thorough introduction to the topic of women and work can be obtained from Joseph (1983). For references on the specific authors mentioned see Main (Chapter 5), Elias (Chapter 4), Rimmer (Chapter 3) and Hunt (Chapter 7) respectively.
2. Birth cohort is defined as that group of women who were born in a given year or in a given set of contiguous years.
3. Only spells of non-employment of at least three months' duration are counted.
4. Table 9.6 in Martin and Roberts (1984a) shows a trend towards fewer spells out of employment, but this table confounds cohort effects and life-cycle effects.
5. Table 9.6 in Martin and Roberts (1984a) represents the proportion of working life worked for the entire cohort, not just for those currently in employment. It also fails to separate out life-cycle and cohort effects.
6. Examples of recent work are Clark (1982) and Dex and Perry (1984).
7. This is a finding consistent with Stewart and Greenhalgh (1984).

3 The Intra-family Distribution of Paid Work, 1968–81

Lesley Rimmer

INTRODUCTION

The changes that have taken place in women's employment patterns, and the family changes with which they are associated, are at the heart of a number of contemporary issues of public policy. Public expenditure constraints and concern about the growing complexity of the social security systems have prompted a review of the social security system and have increased pressure for the integration of the tax and social security structures. The existing system derives from the Beveridge Report of 1942. Beveridge clearly related his social security system to *interruptions* from paid employment – both short-term interruptions in a person's working life (sickness, unemployment) and longer-term withdrawal from the labour market (family formation, retirement). If calls for a new Beveridge Report are to be taken seriously, then the issues raised by the changes in women's employment profiles should be at the very centre of the current political debate. Indeed, Beveridge's assumptions about women's employment and the economic dependence of married women have been under scrutiny over the last few years.

Beveridge's view of the status of married women can be summed up as follows:

> all women by marriage acquire a new economic and social status, with risks and rights different from those of the unmarried. On marriage a woman gains a legal right to maintenance by her

> husband as a first line of defence against risks which fall directly on the solitary woman; she undertakes at the same time to perform vital unpaid services and becomes exposed to new risks, including the risk that her married life may be ended prematurely by widowhood or separation. (Beveridge, 1942)

Critics of Beveridge's approach in today's world have pointed to the increased participation of married women in paid work, to the reduced differential in participation between mothers and other women, and the consequent increase in dual-earner families. This chapter describes some of the changing array of risks to which women are exposed: the risk of being a working wife and mother in a two-parent family, the risk of being the sole breadwinner in a one-parent family, and the risk of being an actual or potential earner in a family where the husband is unemployed. It is based on an analysis of Family Expenditure Survey (FES) data covering the period 1968 to 1981. This period was chosen for two reasons. First, a major increase in married women's participation in paid work took place through these years, followed by the onset of a recession. Second, Audrey Hunt's influential report *A Survey of Women's Employment* was published in 1968, and the report of the 1980 Women and Employment Survey was published in 1984. The analysis of FES data covering the years 1968 to 1981 sheds more light on the changes in the situation of women described in these reports.

In this chapter we document the increase in women's participation between 1968 and 1981, highlighting the substantial increase in two–earner families, and explore the impact on participation and working patterns of family size and family composition. It is clear that within similar levels of participation, groups of women can have significantly different working patterns, reflecting their varying family circumstances and their previous work history. These working patterns are examined in cross-sectional terms, and the significance of part-time working and self-employment are investigated.

The FES shows in effect a 'snapshot' of families and individuals at different stages in the family cycle. This cross-sectional approach to data analysis has a number of limitations. For example, it is clear that women's participation rates over a longer period of time are higher than the instantaneous or 'point in time' rate suggests. Cross-sectional data cannot, then, give the full perspective which we would derive from longitudinal or retrospective surveys such as the Women and Employment Survey (Martin and Roberts, 1984a). However, comparison between cross-sectional information at different dates can give a valuable picture of changes over time for different groups, and can be used as a basis for exploring differences between those in different family settings.

Linked to women's increasing participation in paid work is the increase in their contribution to family incomes. We examine the scale of this contribution and how it has changed, and the relative earnings of husbands and wives in married couple families.

While the major focus is on the distribution of paid work in married couple families, it is clear that changes in marriage patterns cannot be ignored. More and more women can expect to experience a period of time as a lone parent, and there have been some recent changes in the law governing financial arrangements after divorce which may influence the way in which women regard their own employment. By giving greater weight to the objective of self-sufficiency after divorce the new provisions emphasise the income women might generate from their paid employment. Even prior to the new legal framework, it has been increasingly recognised that few lone mothers can rely on maintenance payments from their former spouse as a major means of support. Hence the level of pay they can command, and the hours they are able to work, may well prevent them from living in, or on the margins of, poverty. In this chapter we consider the employment patterns of lone parents – both men and women – and relate this to policies for their financial support. In particular we consider the appropriate balance between income support through transfer payments and through employment measures.

Towards the end of the period under consideration the first indications of the high levels of unemployment which afflict the 1980s begin to emerge. It is important to recognise that unemployment is a family affair. Far too often the focus is on the unemployed person in isolation, whereas in reality the unemployment of one member of the family clearly affects other family members – their standard of living, roles and relationships, and even their health. How is unemployment distributed between various family types, and how far does the employment of a husband or wife act as a safety net when the other is unemployed? Is there a growing tendency for unemployment to be concentrated within certain families, making income distribution between working and unemployed households even more unequal? Answers to these questions become imperative as high levels of unemployment persist, and long-term unemployment emerges as a significant aspect of family life.

Changes in women's employment patterns, in the participation of single parents, and in the incidence of unemployment affect the social security system and also the tax system. Substantial pressure has been building up for a move to an individual unit of taxation, as opposed to the married couple as at present. This will remain an important issue even if more radical solutions to the overlap of the tax and benefit systems, such as negative income tax are adopted. The final section below discusses these policy-related issues in the light of the trends documented in this chapter.

CHANGES IN HOUSEHOLD COMPOSITION

In the analysis which follows, employment and income have been studied within a household context. To a large extent this centres upon those households in which there are married couples only, or married couples with dependent 'children' (defined broadly to cover all young people aged 0–17 years). The analysis categorises the FES households into eight, mutually exclusive groups. These are:

1. Single adult households, no children
2. Single adult, with children
3. Married couple, no children, no other adults in household
4. Married couple with children
5. Married couple, plus other adults, no children
6. Married couple, plus other adults, with children
7. Other households without children
8. Other households with children

Four years were selected for analysis: 1968, 1974, 1979 and 1981. Where the trends in household composition between 1968 and 1981 were reflected in 1974 and 1979, the information for these intervening years is not shown.

Figures 3.1 and 3.2 show the distribution of the population between these household types for the years 1968 and 1981. The height of the histograms shows the distribution by household types, and within this the proportion of children in various age groups is shown.

The most dramatic change is the increase in the proportion of single-person and single-parent households. While the former increased from 16 per cent to over 20 per cent of all households, the latter rose as a proportion of all households from 1.9 per cent in 1968 to 3.5 per cent by 1981. These changes in household composition

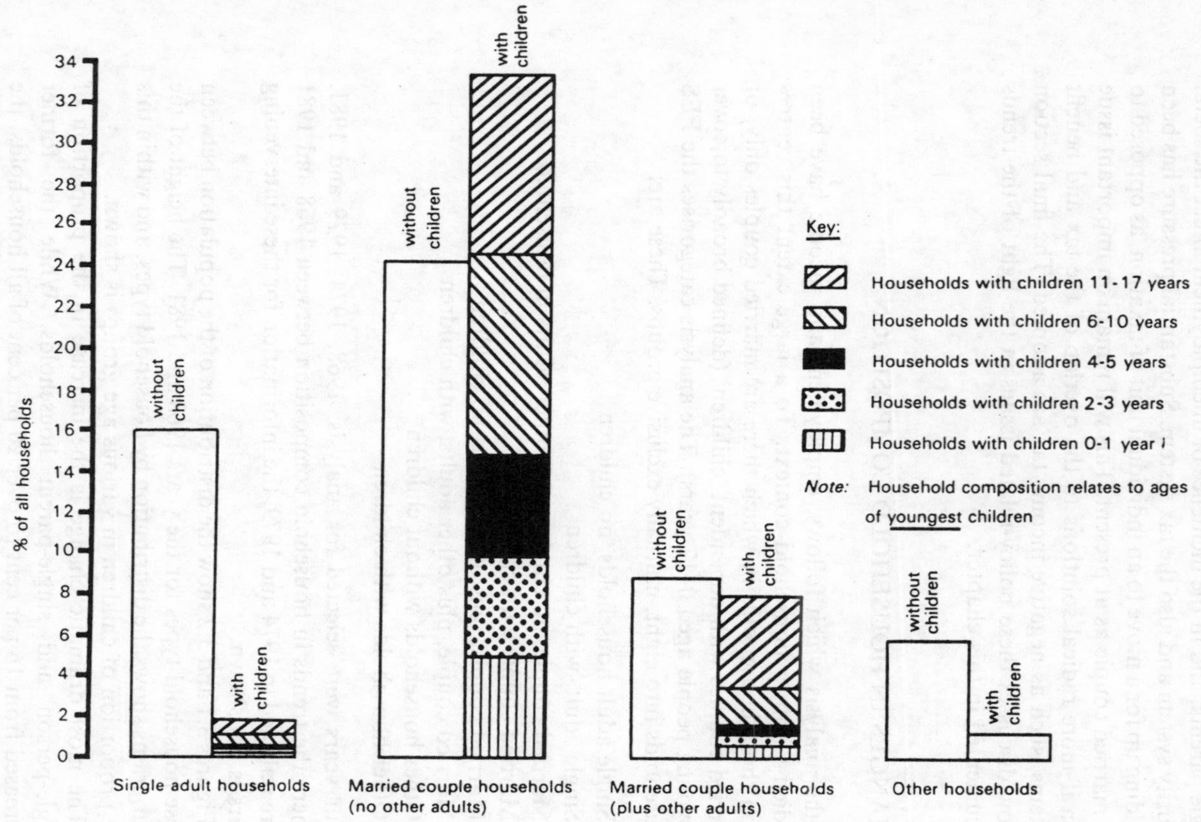

FIGURE 3.1 *Household composition: Family Expenditure Survey households, 1968*

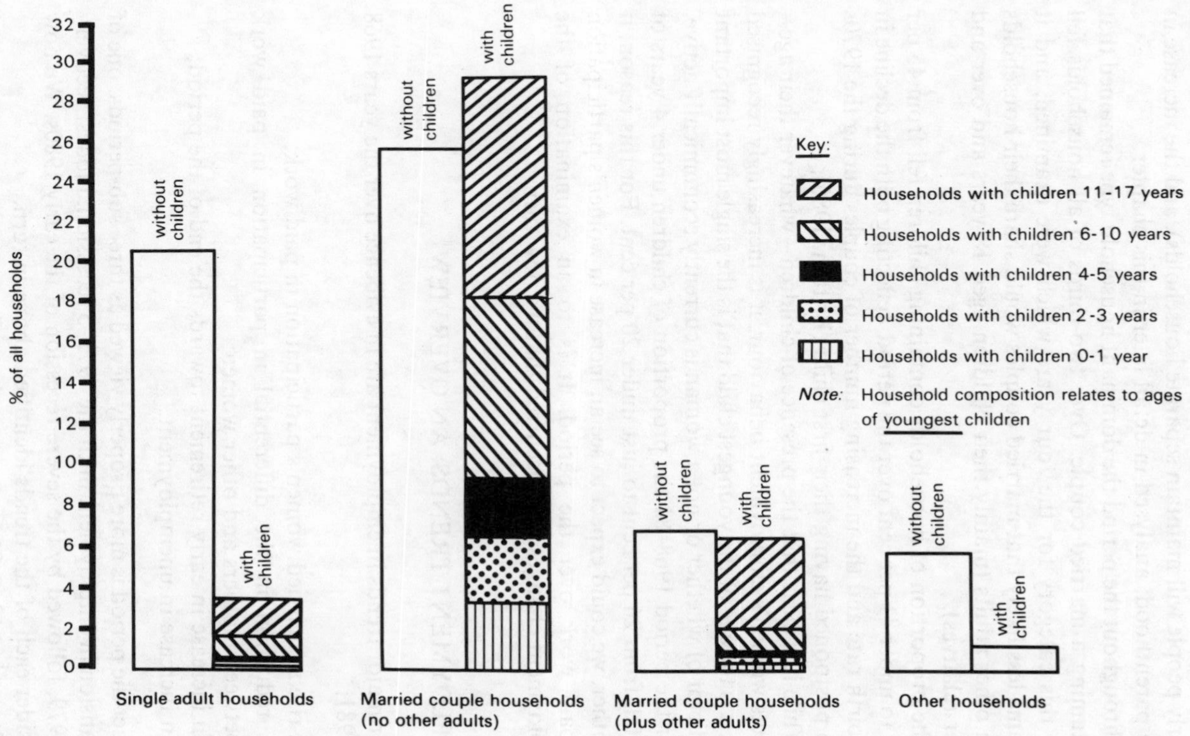

FIGURE 3.2 *Household composition: Family Expenditure Survey households, 1981*

reflect two major social changes which characterized the period: the growth in the elderly population (and the increasing likelihood that elderly people will maintain separate households), and the increase in lone parenthood, analysed in detail later in this chapter.

Throughout the period the dominant household type remained that containing a married couple. Over two-thirds of all households fell into this category for the four years which were examined, and it became less likely that married couples would share their households with other adults (mainly their children aged 18 years and over and other relatives).

The proportion of households containing children fell from 45 per cent to under 41 per cent over the period, reflecting both the decline in the birth rate and the increasing number of couples during the 1970s who postponed having their first child (Britton, 1980).

While it is clear that the presence of children – whatever their age – affects women's employment behaviour, it is increasingly recognised that it is the age of the youngest child that is the single most important predictor of whether or not a woman is currently economically active. Over the period 1968–81 the proportion of children under 4 years of age fell from 26 per cent to just under 20 per cent. For this reason, if no other, we could expect to see an increase in women's participation in paid work over the period. It is to an examination of the employment changes that occurred that we now turn.

EMPLOYMENT TRENDS: AN OVERVIEW

Four major trends in employment are in evidence over the years 1968 to 1981:

1. a rise in married women's participation in paid work;
2. a reduction in the differential in participation in paid work between mothers and other women;
3. an increase in early retirement towards the end of the period;
4. an increase in unemployment.

In fact the period is more properly viewed as three sub-periods: one of expansion in employment until the 1973–5 recession, modest recovery to 1979, followed by the severe recession of the early 1980s. We now consider each of the trends identified above in turn.

The period 1968–81 saw a continuous rise in women's participation in the labour market. Within this, however, there is the complex picture of continuity and change in women's position in the paid labour market, documented in Chapters 2 and 4. Change is mostly evident in the increased levels of participation particularly for married women, and the proportion of married life devoted to paid work. Continuity arises through high levels of part-time work among women workers and mothers of young children in particular, and in the concentration of women within low-paid occupations characterised as 'women's jobs'.

Over the period the proportion of married women in paid employment rose from 45 per cent in 1968 to 64 per cent in 1981. This significant increase is reflected in the FES households under analysis. For households with a married couple only, the proportion of married women economically active rose from 42 per cent to 48 per cent in the households without children, and from 45 per cent to 63 per cent in households with children. In households with married couples and other adults, the rise in the labour force participation of married women was from 45 per cent to 59 per cent for households without children, and from 52 per cent to 71 per cent for households with children. Looking at it the other way round, the proportion of married women in these households who described themselves in the FES as 'unoccupied' fell from around a half in 1968 to around one-third in 1981.

These figures for economic activity derived from the FES include the self-employed. It is probable that, in some cases, this employment involves few hours and limited earning. If we limit the analysis to married women who are employees, the underlying rise in their participation in paid work is easier to discern. In those households which consist of a married couple with children (and no other adults) 40 per cent of wives were employees in 1968. For comparable households with children the figure was 34 per cent. By 1981 the situation had reversed: 47 per cent of wives in the households with children were employees compared to 43 per cent in households without children. There are significant differences between the proportions of couples in the different household types in different age groups. Both husbands and wives in households without children are older on average than in households with children. Over half of the husbands in 'married couple only' households without children were over 60 years of age in 1968, compared with just 2 per cent for comparable households with children. For wives in these households the figures are 45 per cent and 0.5 per cent respectively. This age distribution affects the proportions who are retired, and distorts somewhat the picture of the changes in economic activity. In later sections, therefore, we focus on couples in which both are employees.

Referring to Figures 3.3 and 3.4, it can be seen that, in the 'married couple only' households without children, about six out of ten of the wives under 60 were employed or unemployed in 1968, compared with about one in three of the wives in households with children. By 1981 this differential was much reduced. While nearly eight out of ten women without children in the household were employed or unemployed, this was true of half of the women with children. And whereas in 1968 a woman without children in the household was nearly twice as likely to be an employee as her counterpart with children, by 1981 the differential had fallen to one and a half times. Overall, then, women in these households were significantly more likely to be economically active in 1981 than in 1968, and the differential between women with and without children in the household was substantially reduced.

Increasingly, therefore, households were reliant on two earners, and the proportion of households reliant on two employees rose from 30 per cent for 'married couple only' households including children to 39 per cent, but remained fairly constant for such households without children – 35 per cent and 33 per cent in 1968 and 1981 respectively.

In contrast to the experience of women, the proportion of men who were economically active fell between 1968 and 1981, with a particularly sharp decline in the latter part of the period and for men over 60 years of age. This decline was accompanied by a significant rise in unemployment.

In households containing only a married couple, which includes a high proportion of men nearing retirement age, some 27 per cent were retired in 1968. By 1981 this had risen to 34 per cent. For women the increase in retirement is greater, although rising from a smaller base. Six per cent of married women in households without children were retired in 1968, compared with nearly 16 per cent in 1981.

Early retirement is an alternative to unemployment for those nearing retirement age, and in some ways those who retire early should be regarded as much casualties of the recession as those who are unemployed. Over the period with which we are concerned, the level of unemployment in the UK rose from 300 000 to 2.5 million, or from about 1.5 per cent to over 10 per cent of the labour force. Again, we find this reflected in the levels of unemployment found in the FES households.

In 'married couple only' households without children just over 1 per cent of men under 60 and less than 1 per cent of women were unemployed in 1968. By 1981 the figures were 6 per cent and 4.5 per cent respectively. In households of this type with children the rises were even more substantial, from under 2 per cent to 9 per cent for men, and from less than half a per cent to about 4 per cent for women. Again the FES cannot tell us a great deal about the nature of the unemployment it identifies: how far it is a period of short-term dislocation between jobs, or a long-term situation; or whether it is one period in a lifetime of otherwise secure employment or part of a pattern of job insecurity and disadvantage.

These overall trends in employment are associated with different working patterns for men and women in a variety of household settings. In the next section we consider how working patterns are affected by household composition, and how men and women divide paid and unpaid work between them.

WORKING PATTERNS

Women's employment is integrally related to the care they provide for others – for children, for elderly or handicapped relatives, and for spouses. Central to the analysis which follows is the distinction between families with and without children. This is partly because the issue of income support for families with children is likely to remain high on the political agenda and partly because of the impact of their responsibility for child care on women's paid employment. In Chapter 7 Audrey Hunt complements this analysis by looking at the implications of caring for elderly or disabled relatives on the employment of women.

Husbands and wives

We have shown that the period 1968–81 saw a rapid rise in the participation of married women in paid work. The differential in economic activity between husbands and wives declined significantly, and in consequence an increasing proportion of families relied on the earnings of both husband and wife. However, the broad nature of the concept of 'economic activity', based upon any participation in paid employment during a particular period, masks the implications of these changes in terms of the distribution of weekly hours in paid

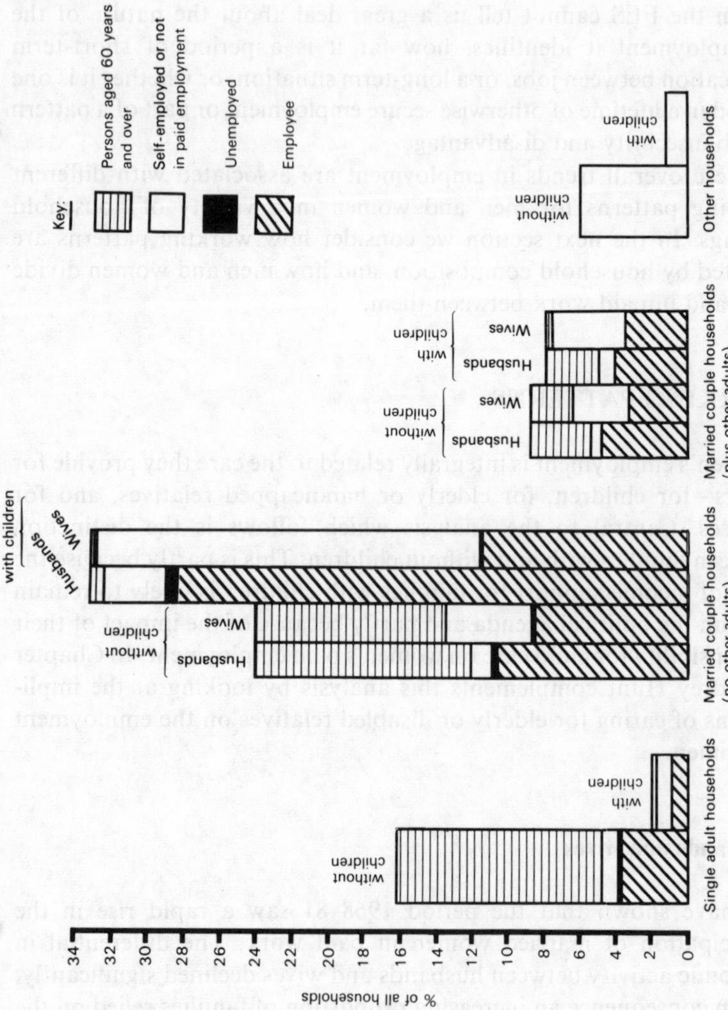

FIGURE 3.3 *Household composition and economic status of adults within households, 1968*

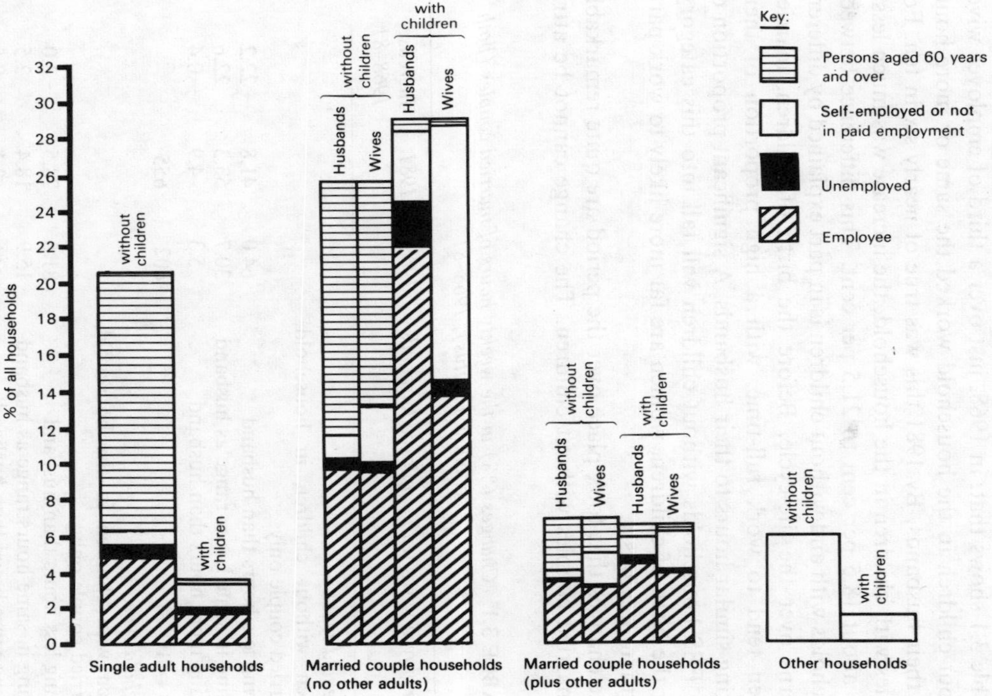

FIGURE 3.4 *Household composition and economic status of adults within households, 1981*

employment between husbands and wives. Women remain less likely to work the same number of hours in paid employment as their husbands, but the analysis below, confined to married couples where both are employees, will show how the pattern has changed over the years.

Table 3.1 shows that, in 1968, just over a third of employee wives without children in the household worked the same or more hours than their husbands. By 1981 this was true of nearly six in ten. For couples with children in the household, the increase was much less – from about 18.5 per cent to 21.5 per cent. This difference between households with and without children is in part explained by different patterns over the life-cycle. Before the birth of children, married women tend to work full-time, with a high proportion of them working similar hours to their husbands. A significant proportion of these FES households without children will fall into this category. After the birth of children, women are far more likely to work part-time than previously.

The changes that took place over the period are quite remarkable for married couples without children. The change cannot be attri-

TABLE 3.1 *Changes (%) in the weekly hours of married couples (both employee status), 1968–81*

All employee wives with employee husbands	*1968*	*1981*	*Increase 1968–81*
Household type:			
Women without children in household, married couple only:			
Working less hours than husband	64.0	41.8	−22.2
Working in same hours range as husband	30.7	53.3	22.6
Working more hours than husband	5.3	4.9	−0.4
Base (=100%)	602	655	
Household type:			
Women with children in the household, married couple only:			
Working less hours than husband	81.5	78.5	−3.0
Working in same hours range as husband	15.9	18.4	2.5
Working more hours than husband	2.6	3.1	0.5
Base (=100%)	723	848	

Note: information on normal weekly hours worked has been grouped. The class intervals are: 1–8, 9–16, 17–24, 25–32, 33–40, 41–48 and 49+ hours.
Source: FES base tapes, 1968, 1981.

buted to the reduction in normal weekly hours in the manufacturing sector, bringing the average weekly hours of male employees closer to that of women who predominate in the service sector, for if this were the case the differential rate of change between married couples with children and married couples without children would not be so great. Rather, it seems likely that there is less part-time employment among young women without children in the early 1980s, than was the case in the late 1960s.

Thus, although the period in question can be seen as the beginning of a fundamental shift in the relationship between men and women in work and family roles, it is important to recognise that a major part of the expansion in labour force participation for women with children has been in part-time work. Such work has traditionally been the way in which mothers have combined the often conflicting demands of work and family. Such advantage, however, is bought at the cost of low pay in the short term and restricted opportunities and de-skilling in the longer term. These issues are dealt with in Chapters 4 and 5, but it is important to stress here that part-time work is an option particularly linked to the stages in the family building cycle when mothers are responsible for intensive periods of child care and when they are returning to work after the birth of children. Conversely, we have shown the remarkable increase in weekly hours, relative to their husbands, for married women without children. A later section will examine the implications of these changes in terms of the earnings of married couples.

Fathers and domestic work

Figures 3.3 and 3.4 indicate that the working patterns of mothers are quite dissimilar to those of fathers. While it is difficult to discern trends from these cross-sectional data, Moss (1980) has shown that fathers of young children work more hours than their childless counterparts, leaving them less time to spend with their children. Part of the explanation of these dissimilarities may lie in the extra financial demands which families entail, and we discuss these issues in the next section, but they are most closely related to the division of paid and unpaid work between husbands and wives.

Does greater sharing of paid work lead to greater sharing of domestic work, or do women continue to bear the double burden of paid and domestic work? Such questions are not easily answered.

Although a number of surveys have addressed this issue, there is little reliable trend data. Changes between cohorts, the more general changes in social attitudes and values affecting all cohorts, and the changing nature of the tasks involved need to be considered.

Gershuny's (1982) time budget data suggest that there are different degrees of specialisation among various sorts of households. His survey of 225 couples in South London compared young childless couples (wife under 35), couples with children, and older couples (wife aged over 35). He analysed three clusters of activity: cooking, cleaning and washing; leisure and recreational activities; and household repair and maintenance tasks. Within all these three clusters the older couples adopted more specialised roles in line with commonly held assumptions of male and female tasks. This division of domestic tasks, particularly into routine and non-routine tasks, is clearly important. While data from the mid-1970s show that husbands on average do less than one-quarter of all domestic work, their share declines to around 10 per cent of routine tasks. Conversely, they were found to do on average approximately half of the non-routine tasks (Gershuny and Thomas, 1982).

More recently the Women and Employment Survey shows greater sharing of non-paid employment than one might expect. Just over a quarter of wives said they shared the housework equally with their husband or that he did more than they, with 73 per cent saying that they did all or most of the housework. Some accommodation to the women's role in paid employment can be seen in the fact that a far higher proportion of women who worked full-time – 44 per cent – said they shared the housework equally, as opposed to only 23 per cent of women who worked part-time. Even so, 54 per cent of women working full-time were combining paid work with the major share of the housework at home.

As far as child care is concerned, a higher proportion of husbands were seen to share the work equally than for 'housework' tasks. But even here there is evidence to suggest that the routine basic tasks were the lot of women, while playing with children and taking them out were ways in which men contributed to their children's care.

Nonetheless, it is clear that the main burden of domestic responsibility still falls on women in the majority of households, and that this division of domestic labour sets limits to the effectiveness of labour market-based policies to promote equality of opportunity.

Self-employment

The FES identifies higher levels of self-employment than is obtained from other sources of information on labour market status. In the 1968 survey, about 10 per cent of men and 10 per cent of women under 60 with children in the household in 1968 defined themselves as self-employed. By 1981, one in eight men and women under 60 with children in the household claimed to be self-employed.

The nature of this self-employment is likely to vary, however, and it is doubtful whether it would be defined as 'employment' in other surveys. Of particular note is the level of self-employment among women with children in the household. They are some four or five times more likely to report themselves as self-employed as women without children in the household. Many of these mothers will, however, be engaged in mail order, child-minding and other types of activity which, although financially important to the household, often yield low incomes and occupy them for relatively few hours per week.

Some light on these issues comes from the Women and Employment Survey, where those women not currently in a paid job were asked whether they had regular or occasional paid work. Overall some 13 per cent of non-working women said they did this sort of work, but the vast majority of them did not think of themselves as 'working'. Most of them earned less than £6 per week in 1980 (compared to average earnings of full-time women workers in the survey of £71) and worked less than five hours per week.

In the FES, however, such work has been defined as self-employment, indistinguishable from the work of a small businessman or highly paid freelance computer programmer. But such work, despite sometimes being of limited financial value, is clearly important at particular stages in the life-cycle. Moss (1980), in an earlier analysis of the FES, found high levels of regular or occasional working by mothers of young children. Audrey Hunt's survey found that one working woman in sixteen was self-employed, of which one in twelve was working in her own home or in premises attached to them. The majority of this latter group could not be induced to work outside the home even if suitable work were readily available, because of domestic responsibilities. As Martin and Roberts conclude, 'looking at the description of the work done by these women, it was apparent that almost all the work could be carried out at home, or done from home, and most of these women were limited to this sort of work by the presence of young children' (Martin and Roberts, 1984a, p. 32).

The limitation of this type of work, however, was that despite likely psychological benefits, it would not necessarily help the woman's re-entry to the labour market. Martin and Roberts comment, for example, that 'among these non-working women who were not engaged on mail order work, there was no evidence that the paid work they were doing would help provide a way back into the labour market in terms of their being able to get a job doing similar types of work' (Martin and Roberts, 1984a, p. 32).

Earnings

There are perhaps three major questions surrounding the contribution of women's earnings to family incomes: how significant are they in relation to the contribution of their husband, and how is this changing; for what part of married life will women be contributing to family incomes; and, conversely, at what stages in the life-cycle will their earnings be absent or very low? Given the measurement problems associated with the information on earnings from self-employment, we consider here only those couples where both are employees.

Table 3.2 shows the proportion of wives in households containing a married couple (with and without children) whose weekly earnings were below, in the same range, or greater than those of their husband. The differential between those with and those without children reflects the pattern of hours worked described in Table 3.1. Only 2.5 per cent, or one in forty, of employee mothers were earning as much as or more than their husbands in 1968, compared to 5.8 per cent, more than one in twenty, of women without children in the household.

In both types of household the proportion of wives earning as much as or more than their husbands increased over the period, but again the convergence is far greater for the households without children. In such households the proportion of wives whose gross earnings were equal to or greater than those of their spouse rose from under 6 per cent to over 16 per cent, or from around one in twenty to one in six.

This increase in earnings is particularly marked in the case of those women without children in the household earning *more than* their husband – a possible difference in gross earnings per week of between £2 and £20 for a couple at either end of their respective earnings ranges in 1981. Since the major change in hours worked was to bring

TABLE 3.2 *Changes (%) in the weekly earnings of married couples (both employee status), 1968–81*

All employee wives with employee husband	*1968*	*1981*	*Increase 1968–81*
Household type:			
Married couple only, no children			
Earning less than husband	94.2	83.5	−10.7
Earning same as husband	2.3	5.0	2.7
Earning more than husband	3.5	11.5	8.0
Base (= 100%)	602	655	
Household type:			
Married couple only with children:			
Earning less than husband	97.5	94.6	−2.9
Earning same as husband	1.1	1.8	0.7
Earning more than husband	1.4	3.7	2.3
Base (= 100%)	723	848	

Note: Earnings information is grouped. For 1968 the class interval is £2 per week up to gross earnings of £38 per week, the open-ended class interval. For 1981 the class interval is £10 per week up to £200 per week, the open-ended class interval. These differences compensate for earnings inflation over this period. Earning 'less than' means that the wife's gross weekly earnings are in a lower class interval than her husband's; 'as much as' refers to husband and wife with earnings in the same class interval; 'more than' refers to a higher class interval.

Source: FES base tapes, 1968 and 1981.

more women into the *same* hours range as their husband, there must also be an increase in earnings levels being reflected here.

In an earlier analysis of FES data, Elias (1984) noted that the median earnings of married women in the FES sample who held employee jobs grew more rapidly over the period 1968 to 1977 than the seasonally adjusted increase in earnings in Great Britain. For women holding full-time employee jobs, with husbands working as full-time employees, the increase was even greater. From 1977 to 1980 the intra-household distribution of spouses' earnings was constant, indicating that the increase in women's earnings relative to men's, associated with the implementation of the Equal Pay Act in the early 1970s, was one of the principal reasons for the rise in a married woman's earning potential relative to her husband's. This analysis shows that the rise is concentrated in households without children, that is among the younger women covered in the Family Expenditure Survey.

While the FES can show the situation over time for different households, we need to draw on other sources to gain a fuller picture of women's contributions to family incomes *over the life-cycle* and the extent to which they are affected by childbearing. The re-analysis of the Women and Employment Survey by Joshi (1985a) is particularly important here. From multiple regression analyses of women's employment patterns and earnings, she compares an 'illustrative' mother of two children born three years apart with her childless counterpart. The mother spends some six fewer years at work – a combination of a loss of nine years of full-time employment, offset by a gain of three years' part-time work. Overall, Joshi suggests that this mother's lifetime earnings are reduced by as much as £49,000 at 1985 prices, if she has average earnings potential. While part of this loss of potential earnings is explained by reduced hours and by lost earnings while not in employment, a significant part of the reduction derives from rates of pay which are below those of women who have been continuously employed. She found that the average hourly pay after age 25 was reduced by nine, twelve and thirteen per cent for the mothers of one, two and three children respectively.

A further issue is whether women's earnings lead to more or less equality in the overall distribution of family incomes. Fry (1984) has shown that there has been a proportionately faster growth of paid employment among wives of non-manual as opposed to manual worker husbands. This she suggests, has tended to increase the inequality in family earnings across social classes. It is certainly the case that in the FES two-earner households investigated in this chapter, a higher proportion were in professional jobs in 1981 than in 1968. At the beginning of the period, one in five employed men in two-earner couples without children in the household were in professional occupations, compared to one in three in 1981. There was a larger increase for wives in these couples – from one in ten to one in five over the period. For couples with children in the household the improvement for men is greater than for women. One in three men were in professional occupations in 1981, compared to only one in six in 1968, whereas the increase for women was from one in eight to just under one in five. Fry's analysis was concerned with the inequality in family incomes *per se*, whereas our focus is primarily on the resources available to families with and without children, the most significant features being the increasing proportion of fathers in two-earner couples who were in professional occupations, and the doubling of the proportion of women without children in their household in these occupations. These findings would be consistent with Fry's hypothesis, and also with the higher participation rates commonly observed for professional women both before, during and after childbearing (Martin and Roberts, 1984b).

The rise in women's employment over the period has, as noted previously, largely been accounted for by part-time work. This in itself limits their contributions to family incomes. In the longer run it is arguable that the deskilling accompanying these occupational transitions around childbirth also limits a woman's potential contribution to the household income. Thus, it is becoming an increasingly urgent question to ask whether the division of paid and unpaid work within the family is efficient. The consequences for women of their greater share of domestic, especially childcare, tasks represents a considerable underutilisation of scarce skills. Would society be better advised to foster greater sharing of these tasks, or should we encourage the enhancement of women's ability to pay for substitute childcare? These issues are significant for a woman with children, but assume particular importance when she becomes sole provider for her family. It is to this issue that we now turn.

LONE PARENTHOOD

It is increasingly likely that women and children will spend some period of their lives in a one-parent family. The majority of lone parents are women, since after divorce the majority of children live with their mothers. Only one single parent in seven is male. While lone mothers face the same disadvantages as other women in the labour market, these are compounded by their single-handed responsibility for child-care.

This section compares the economic activity and hours worked of lone mothers and lone fathers with those of parents in two-parent families. These comparisons raise a number of interesting questions about whether income support policy for lone parents should be based on financial benefits, or measures designed to improve their employment situation, such as training or child-care provisions. They also go some way to explain the relatively high risk of poverty for lone parents compared to two-parent families, and the high dependence of lone mothers on state benefits.

Two cautions should be noted: first, the number of cases on which some of the analysis is based is rather small, particularly for lone fathers; second, the analysis is limited to lone-parent *households*, thereby excluding lone parents living with others. Those living with others are more likely to be single (unmarried) mothers, and other evidence such as the study by Nixon (1981) of lone mothers on Family Income Supplement (FIS) suggests that their employment patterns are affected by their household circumstances – notably, having others in the household who can provide child-care. In general, single unmarried mothers are younger than divorced, separated or widowed mothers, and are more likely to have young children. They are in consequence also more likely to be dependent on benefits and to experience higher rates of unemployment (Martin and Roberts, 1984a, p. 109).

Economic activity of lone parents

Any analysis of the employment behaviour of lone mothers is likely to compare their behaviour with that of mothers in two-parent families. The similarities and differences that arise, however, have different implications for the families involved. Lone mothers are far more likely to be the chief economic supporter for their family than are married mothers, and their employment patterns should therefore be compared with those of fathers in two-parent families.

First however, let us look at lone mothers in comparison to married mothers. As Figure 3.4 shows, in 1981 lone mothers were rather less likely to be economically active than married women in two-parent families, although they had been *more* likely to be so in 1968 and 1974. They were also more likely to be unemployed.

These differences in participation probably reflect the age of the children involved. As shown above, participation rates are lower when children are under 5, and the Women and Employment Survey analysis found significantly lower participation rates for single (unmarried) mothers. Once the age of the youngest child was taken into account, these differences disappeared (Martin and Roberts, 1984, p. 110).

However, the overall differences in participation between 'lone mothers' as a group and married mothers are not substantial. They are different, however, to the behaviour of lone fathers, and to fathers in two-parent families. While only 61 per cent of lone mothers were economically active in 1981 (and 47 per cent were working) this was true of 98 per cent of fathers in two-parent families, and 86 per cent of lone fathers. Indeed, lone mothers are far less likely to be either economically active or working than lone fathers, over 80 per cent of whom were working at all four dates. Limited though it is, this analysis is valuable in showing clearly that it is the difference in behaviour between men and women that is significant rather than the family situation of lone mothers.

Hours worked

When hours are examined, an interesting picture emerges. As is to be expected, lone mothers are far more likely to work part-time than are lone fathers: around two-thirds of lone mothers worked part-time at the four dates we investigated, whereas this was true of only a third of lone fathers at most. Again, predictably, lone fathers were much more likely to work more than forty-eight hours per week, although the extent to which they did so fell significantly over the period in line with the trends for all men. But when we consider lone mothers and married mothers it is clear that the latter are far more likely to be working part-time than the lone mothers. Indeed, lone mothers are almost *twice as likely* as other mothers to be working over forty hours a week, despite their sole responsibility for child-care. This analysis confirms the findings of other surveys. The Women and Employment Survey, for example, showed that half of all lone mothers worked full-time, compared with only one-third of married mothers (Martin and Roberts, 1984a, p. 110).

The picture that emerges, then, is that like other women, lone mothers are far less likely to work full-time than their male counterparts. And over the period they became less likely than other mothers to be economically active. When they do work, however, they are more likely to work full-time, a somewhat paradoxical situation given what might be presumed to be greater child-care responsibilities.

How can these working patterns be explained? The Finer Committee (1974) suggested that at least part of the explanation lay in the structure of the benefit system. Lone parents were particularly at risk of the 'poverty trap', a situation whereby means-tested benefits (such as FIS) are withdrawn as earnings rise, leaving net incomes virtually unchanged over a wide band of earnings.

Certainly, it still seems to be the case that in order to improve their living standards, lone mothers need to work full-time. Information from the Women and Employment Survey shows that lone parents who worked full-time had significantly higher incomes than those who worked part-time, and both groups had higher incomes than non-working lone parents. Twenty-six per cent of lone mothers working full-time had net incomes of over £80 per week, compared with only 9 per cent of those working part-time, and none of the non-working mothers (Martin and Roberts, 1984a, p. 111, Table 2.28). There have been a number of changes in the benefit system, but it seems unlikely that they have made the combination of part-time work and receipt of benefit a more attractive option than it was previously. The 'choice' facing lone parents remains either to work full-time to become independent of the benefit system or to rely wholly on benefits.

UNEMPLOYMENT AND THE FAMILY

The emerging interest in the impact of unemployment on the families of unemployed workers is a welcome counterweight to a focus solely on those individuals who are registered as unemployed. With more than 3 million people unemployed, perhaps two or three times as many will be in families directly experiencing unemployment. When husbands, wives, mothers and fathers become unemployed, their families suffer with them, both in terms of reduced income and in terms of the psychological and social impact of unemployment. In this section we develop a family perspective on unemployment. We consider how far unemployed workers are able to rely on the safety net of their partner's earnings, or whether unemployment is concentrated within particular families, and the relative incidence of unemployment in families with children.

Between 1961 and 1981 the numbers registered as unemployed rose from around 300 000 to over two and a half million, or from 1.3 per cent to 10.4 per cent of the workforce. The major increase, however, occurred from 1979 onwards, when unemployment stood at 1.3 million (5.3 per cent of the workforce) but subsequently rose by nearly two million in two years. In the FES households on which we are focusing, unemployment rose from just over 1 per cent for men in 1968 and under 1 per cent for women, to nearly 10 per cent for men and around 5 per cent for women in 1981. Such a snapshot disguises an important trend, that of an increase in long-term unemployment, which became more important at the end of the period.

For most people unemployment means a significant drop in income. Families in general have become more likely to have two earners, but what of the unemployed? How far are family incomes buttressed by those of other earners when the head of household is unemployed?

Husbands and wives

Somewhat contrary to expectations, unemployed married men are *less* likely to have available a wife's earnings as a safety net to their own unemployment than those who are employed. This is true whether it is the 'stock' of employment that is considered, as in the analysis of the 1971 census (Smee and Stern, 1979) or the 'flow' analysed in detail in the 'cohort study' of unemployed men entering unemployment in 1978 (Moylan, Millar and Davies, 1984). Smee and Stern's study showed that, on average, the wife of a man out of work in the 1971 census was only two-thirds as likely to have a job as the wife of a man in work. Seven years later, the 1984 cohort study showed that in the week prior to their husband's registration only about one-third of the wives of unemployed men were in employment, compared to more than half of all wives. While some of this difference is accounted for by factors such as the age of the wives in this study and the greater likelihood of them having dependent children, these did not fully explain the differences in employment levels.

This picture is confirmed by our analysis of the FES. In 1979, for example, when 54 per cent of childless employed men had employee wives, this was true of only 36 per cent of unemployed men, and in 1981 the difference was 66 per cent to 51 per cent. For men with children the same differential exists: again in 1979, 34 per cent of employed fathers had employed wives, whereas this was true of only 23 per cent of unemployed men. In contrast, 71 per cent of unemployed fathers had wives who were not in employment, compared to 54 per cent of employed fathers.

At the beginning of the period the lack of a second earner is explained by the fact that wives of unemployed men were more likely to be outside the labour force than the wives of employed men, rather than being unemployed themselves. But towards the end of the period the level of unemployment for these wives is also significantly higher than their counterparts with employed husbands. This confirms the evidence of the DHSS cohort study, where among the economically active wives in the study some 16 per cent were unemployed – both registered and unregistered – compared to just 2 per cent for wives as a whole (3 per cent of all economically active married women).

There are several possible explanations for this concentration of unemployment and inactivity in particular families. Job opportunities for both men and women may be poor in a particular area, or wives may respond to their husband's unemployment by withdrawing from the labour force. Married women in the DHSS cohort study of the unemployed were far less likely to be working part-time than comparable women with employed husbands. There is also strong *prima facie* evidence to suggest that the supplementary benefit system, by reducing benefit pound for pound as the wife's earnings rise above a low disregard level, reduces the incentive for the wives of unemployed men to retain or take up paid employment. The proportion of cohort wives in the families receiving supplementary allowances who left employment was far higher than those in families dependent on unemployment benefit, whose additional earnings are not treated in the same way (Moylan, Millar and Davies, 1984, ch. 10).

Other workers

An increasingly important issue is the unemployment of young people within the family. Rates of unemployment among young men aged 18–19, for example, rose from 8 per cent in 1979 to 17 per cent in 1981 (OPCS, 1984b), and have subsequently risen to over 23 per cent.

In our household categorisation the majority of the third adults in three-adult households are sons or daughters of the head of household (four out of five). In these households, too, if the head of the household is employed, then the (adult) child is likely to be employed, whereas if the head of household is unemployed there is a much higher likelihood that the (adult) child will be so too. Other surveys give a similar picture. An analysis of the 1983 Scottish school-leavers survey, for example, found that having an unemployed father severely reduced the probability that a school-leaver in the survey was in employment, by a factor of some 26 percentage points (Main, 1984).

The situation of children in families affected by unemployment is often overlooked. The incidence of unemployment among family heads with children is higher than for family heads without children; and the unemployment rate is higher for fathers in large families than in small families. Clearly the explanation of these facts is complex, and reflects the impact of social class and the structure of the benefit system. But the implication is that the proportion of children affected by unemployment is higher than the proportion of households affected.

In 1981, census data showed that just over 8 per cent of dependent children in Great Britain lived in households where the head was unemployed, suggesting over 1 million children (Central Statistical Office, 1983). In 1985 the figure is likely to be about 1.3 million. Thus, significant numbers of our children are experiencing the deprivation and restrictions which unemployment brings.

In general terms it appears that unemployment is concentrated in particular families, and that this trend is becoming more severe as the level of unemployment rises. The General Household Survey shows that 7 per cent of households in 1976 contained two or more unemployed people, while by 1982 this had risen to 13 per cent (Central Statistical Office, 1983).

What are the implications of these findings? Unemployment means a significant drop in living standards, which fall further as the duration of unemployment increases. In 1981 49 per cent of families in which at least one member had been unemployed for thirteen weeks or more had incomes at or below supplementary benefit level. But for families with dependent children where the father is unemployed, the risk of poverty increases significantly. Some four-fifths of families of this type had incomes at or below supplementary benefit level, and a further 14 per cent had incomes within 40 per cent of this level (Central Statistical Office, 1983, p. 187). While it has become increasingly less likely for unemployed heads of household to have another worker in the household, it has become more likely for the employed.

Thus the rise of the two-earner household in combination with an increase in unemployment is leading to a polarisation of families in terms of income: the gap between the average gross incomes of households with unemployed heads and those households with employed heads has widened over recent years.

POLICY ISSUES

This chapter has documented the significant increase in married women's participation in the paid labour market between 1968 and 1981. In common with many other social changes, the implications of this trend have been only partially recognised, and in many areas policy is lagging. Here we discuss a few of the policy issues that are raised, and which (as far as employment is concerned) will loom large on policy agenda for the remainder of the decade.

The increasing reliance of families on two earners should be viewed in the context of a significant decline in the value of child support through transfer payments (and tax allowances). This, it can be shown, has often been offset by the increased employment of mothers. Piachaud (1982), for example, has argued that 'the most important single change in the economic circumstances of families since the war has not been any changes in benefits for children but rather the growth in two earner families'. He also observed that 'the increase in the extent of married women working has meant that, for some families, incomes before taxes and benefits have increased faster than average earnings'.

Piachaud's work raises the issue of the balance between collective support for children and the extent to which families with children support themselves at adequate standards of living by relying on two earners. The cost to families if mothers stay at home to care for their children is substantial: fewer material benefits in both the short and long term, and restricted employment opportunities for mothers when they return to employment.

Just how substantial these costs are has been shown by Joshi (1985a). She estimates that the cost of career breaks, the greater likelihood of part-time work and of downward occupational mobility depress women's lifetime earnings on average between 25 and 50 per cent. In these terms alone the cost of a two-child family is put at some £50,000.

On the other hand, if women return to employment while they have young children they may often have to organise and pay for a complex network of substitute care, the quality of which varies greatly. The level of provision is well below that which mothers say they would prefer, and is unlikely to increase while the level of unemployment remains high.

With child-care provision at its present level few women have a genuine choice about whether or not to go out to work. This in itself reflects, at least in part, a continuing ambivalence of attitudes. Too often working mothers are seen as putting materialism above the interests of their families, and it is still possible to ask 'why do women work?' – a question seldom asked of men (Martin and Roberts, 1984a).

It is clear that many women work for financial reasons, and a high proportion of these say they work to pay for basic essentials (Martin and Roberts, 1984a) and are in this way contributing to the welfare of their family. In any event, the high level of part-time working by mothers, and the importance they in particular attach to 'convenient hours of work' (Martin and Roberts, 1984a, p. 78) demonstrate women's concern about their domestic responsibilities.

Part-time work is the way in which the majority of mothers mesh their home and working lives. Few fathers work part-time, or are even able at present to work reduced hours. Hence it is on women's paid employment that the main effect of children is felt.

More generally these issues turn on the division of domestic labour, and the extent to which the unequal sharing of tasks affects participation in the paid labour market. There is much controversy about whether public policy should seek to influence the decisions which couples make about the shares of paid and unpaid work they undertake. But in reality much public policy is still framed on the assumption of unequal sharing, and those who wish to practice greater sharing – parenting rather than mothering – find their ability to do so limited. Chapter 6 considers these issues in more detail in relation to the situation around childbirth, but they arise with similar force right through the period when there are dependent children, and in relation to care of the elderly or handicapped.

One example of the assumptions about paid and unpaid work is a discussion of changes to the tax system. Over recent years there has been a frequently voiced concern about the situation of one-earner families who, some argue, are treated less favourably than two-earner families in the tax system. The former are currently eligible for the married man's tax allowance (MMA), which is equivalent to one and a half times the single person's allowance (SPA), while the latter can qualify for up to two and a half times the SPA. Some see this as an unwarranted subsidy to two-earner families, and favour redressing the balance. A universal system of two allowances for a two-parent family has been mooted, as have measures designed to give a financial incentive for women to stay at home.

The concern shown in the 1980 Green Paper, *The Taxation of Husband and Wife* (HMSO, 1980), for the situation of the one-earner couple (and in its 1986 successor, *The Reform of Personal Taxation* (HMSO, 1986), was not matched by an analysis of who such couples might be. Clearly there are two main groups: couples where one partner is unemployed, disabled or retired, and couples where one partner – normally the wife – does no paid work from 'choice'. In this latter category there are again two main groups: those where the wife is over 45, has not worked for a number of years and is unlikely to do so again, and those where there are young children or other dependants being cared for. How numerically significant are these two groups?

In the cases where women are currently not working the Women and Employment Survey has shown that 62 per cent are women with dependent children, and 6 in 10 of these have a preschool aged child (Martin and Roberts, 1984a). Only about a quarter of non-working women are over 50 years of age, without dependent children. Given that these older women are likely to have different employment histories to the younger cohorts, it is likely that this group of women will decline in number and in proportionate terms in the years ahead. Thus, while some transitional arrangements might need to be made, the majority of one-earner, two-parent families could be compensated for any loss if MMA were abolished by a corresponding increase in child benefit. Furthermore, in recognition of the greater likelihood that one-earner couples have young children, the idea of an under-fives premium is attractive (Rimmer, 1984).

The other major group of one-earner families is the one-parent group. Although there are potentially two earners available to contribute to the support of the family – both the custodial and the non-custodial parent – the reality is that few lone parents can rely on maintenance from their former spouse. Among lone mothers in the Women and Employment Survey, for example, only 29 per cent of single mothers received maintenance, as did 42 per cent of the divorced or separated mothers (Martin and Roberts, 1984a).

Even when maintenance payments are made regularly, they are often at a very low level. All these factors imply that lone parents' earnings potential is crucial. Yet the current emphasis on policy is towards transfer payments, rather than on increasing their earnings potential and addressing the deskilling around childbirth. This is particularly important for lone mothers, who are the group at greatest risk of poverty. A more active approach to their support would involve giving lone parents priority on training and re-training courses, and ensuring adequate and flexible child-care facilities.

Such measures, however, would still fall short if the level of women's earnings in general remains well below that of men. The high activity rates of lone fathers compared to lone mothers emphasise that the relative levels of men's and women's pay is crucial. Although there have been some advances in the wake of the Equal Pay act, with women's earnings rising from 63 per cent to 75 per cent of those of men between 1970 and 1977, this advance has since slowed and even reversed. In 1981, the full-time hourly earnings of women relative to men dipped below 75 per cent, falling slightly to about 74 per cent in 1983. Until there is greater equality in the labour market, lone mothers will continue to rely heavily on state benefits.

Again more generally, the issue of maintenance raises the question of the economic dependence of women on their husbands. As we have seen, although women are likely to have earned incomes of their own for perhaps the majority of their married lives, their earnings are limited both by part-time working and by the relative wage levels of men and women. Only about one woman in six has equality with her husband in terms of earnings. Clearly the level of women's economic independence can be overstated, especially where mothers are concerned. The achievement of greater economic independence requires action on a number of fronts: child-care, access to training and re-training, and the greater sharing of household and caring tasks analysed above.

The impact of unemployment should also be recognised. As unemployment rises and persists at high levels, the calls for women to 'go back to the home' and leave the jobs for men become more frequent and less guarded. As noted above, unemployment is also creating a number of one-earner families where previously both partners worked. Even more worrying, the evidence analysed here shows that the concentration of unemployment is increasingly creating 'no-earner' families. The standard of living of such families is moving further away from that of their two-earner equivalents.

Were unemployment to be evenly distributed throughout the working population, then each one of us could expect to be unemployed on average once every six years. In reality unemployment is borne disproportionately by the old and the young, by the unskilled and by those in minority groups. Women's registered unemployment rates, often lower than men's, disguise substantial unregistered and therefore hidden unemployment, in addition to which women are still disadvantaged in the benefit system.

Forty years on from the 1944 White Paper on employment policy, its commitment to full employment has been overtaken by the goal of reducing inflation, and is threatened in the longer term by the uncertain impact of new technology. While the 1944 White Paper was concerned primarily with the cyclical fluctuations in demand, the current situation demands a fundamental re-appraisal of the role of paid employment and unpaid work, of the length and patterns of working life, and of the integration of the worlds of family and employment. These issues form the agenda for the next decades. They are central to the issue of equality between men and women in the labour market.

4 Family Formation, Occupational Mobility and Part-time Work

Peter Elias

INTRODUCTION

The proportion of part-time workers in the labour force is higher in the United Kingdom than in almost every other industrialised country in the world. Not only is the proportion of part-time workers high in the UK, but the remarkable growth in the number of part-time jobs over the last twenty years has been sustained through the recessions of 1974–5 and 1979–81. This chapter investigates the relationship between the growth of part-time employment, its role within women's working lives, and the associated changes of occupation accompanying movements into and out of part-time work.

Earlier work by two of the contributors to this book (Elias and Main, 1982) established that the majority of part-time workers aged 30 years and older are women who have children, and that part-time jobs are highly concentrated within a few low-status, low-paid occupational categories. This raised the question of whether or not the process of family formation has serious repercussions in terms of a potential constraint on the choice of occupations facing those women who wish to combine a reduction in weekly hours of paid employment with non-paid domestic/family responsibilities. If a woman decides to opt for part-time work following a spell out of paid employment associated with child-birth, does she have to accept work which underutilises her prior work experience or qualifications? If so, does such a period of employment influence her future employment prospects, whether in full-time or part-time work?

Elias and Main (1982) offered some preliminary support for the former proposition by examining the types of jobs held by men and women who had 'occupation-specific' professional qualifications, in nursing and teaching. An analysis of the distribution of occupations held by women with such qualifications who worked part-time showed that a substantial proportion were working in low-paid jobs. However, such a restricted analysis of occupational mobility probably raised more questions than it sought to answer. For instance, we have no indication of the extent to which qualified women who work part-time in low-status jobs do so because they *prefer* such jobs. Furthermore, we have little knowledge about the effect of working part-time in a low-paid job on a woman's future working life. Does the labour market operate in such a way that women are segregated into occupations with limited prospects, or stigmatised by the very nature of their part-time employment? These are the questions investigated in this chapter.

The chapter is presented in four sections. Following this introduction, the second section reviews the evidence on occupational movement, part-time working and family formation. The next section considers further evidence on the link between qualifications and occupations. The fourth section presents a cohort analysis of the 'average' occupational status of women in full- and part-time jobs, according to whether or not they have had children.

FAMILY FORMATION AND OCCUPATIONAL DOWNGRADING

One of the first large-scale surveys to provide information on the link between occupational structure, family formation and part-time working in Great Britain was the 1975/6 National Training Survey. Through an analysis of the outline work histories contained in this survey, Stewart and Greenhalgh (1982) showed that, for women aged 45–54 years, the proportion in high-level non-manual occupations was 25 per cent for women with an uninterrupted work history, and 13 per cent for those with two or more breaks from paid employment. Conversely, the proportion of women in personal service occupations was 14 per cent for 'continuous' workers and 29 per cent for women with two or more breaks in their working lives. For women in this age range with just one break in their working lives, the length of that break was correlated with their current occupational category. Lower occupational status was associated with longer breaks from employment.

Given that breaks in employment are primarily associated with family formation, it is tempting to infer from these results that the more breaks from paid employment that a woman takes, or the longer the period of time spent out of paid employment, the more likely it is that she returns to a job in a lower occupational category. Equally, however, it could be argued that women with little or no academic qualifications and fewer skills experience more interruptions to their paid employment and that such women are likely to be concentrated within lower level occupations. Stewart and Greenhalgh attempt to control for such effects by examining the occupational level of women at the time of the survey, conditional upon their occupational position ten years earlier. The two most significant variables which determine if occupational levels were maintained were whether or not a woman was employed full-time at the time of the survey and the number of years worked in the ten-year period.

These findings were the first to demonstrate a significant link between family formation, occupational status and part-time work. Job continuity and full-time working were found to be conducive to the preservation of occupational position, yet discontinuous employment and part-time working are associated with family formation. Further work in this area, using the same source of information, was pursued by Elias and Main (1982). Rather than classifying occupations in an ordinal sense, Elias and Main devised a classification based on occupational skill content. In an examination of the distribution of women's current occupations by full-time and part-time status, it was noted that nearly two out of five part-timers were concentrated in an occupational group which was comprised of low-skilled catering and cleaning occupations. Further, part-time work was shown to be associated with family formation, and a substantial proportion of women working part-time in this low skill content occupational category were found to have clerical, commercial, nursing or teaching qualifications. However, to reiterate the point made in the introduction, there is no way of determining the dynamics of the underlying process from this limited cross-sectional analysis of occupations and qualifications. For example, a reduction in the demand for qualified teachers, coupled with an oversupply of trainees from the educational sector, could yield a general surplus of persons with teaching qualifications across many occupations. The limited work history information available in the National Training Survey gave no indication of the extent to which this apparent mismatch between qualifications and occupations is a temporary state of affairs for individual women, rectified as they move back from part-time into full-time employment following a period of family formation.

The link between family formation, occupational mobility and part-time work has been the subject of more recent studies, utilising the rich and detailed work history information in the 1980 Women and Employment Survey (WES). Martin and Roberts (1984a) conducted an investigation of occupational movement between the last job a woman held before her first birth and her most recent job, examining such occupational mobility for women who returned to full-time or part-time work in their first job following their first birth, and also by whether they were working full-time or part-time at the time of the survey. In this analysis the occupational classification is ordered with reference to a social class stratification of occupations. *Any* movement between the ordered aggregate occupational categories is classified as movement into a 'higher' or 'lower' level occupation, regardless of the skill content of that occupational category. Using this approach, Martin and Roberts note that 40 per cent of women with children were in a different occupational category from that which they were in prior to their first birth. Of this group, the majority had moved to a lower category. Downward mobility was strongly associated with a return to part-time work after childbirth. Women who returned initially to full-time work but subsequently worked part-time were most likely to have moved down the occupational hierarchy. Conversely, women whose most recent job was full-time were likely to have regained or exceeded the point they had reached in the occupational hierarchy prior to their first birth.

In a related study, as an adjunct to her analysis of women's earnings, Joshi (1984) ranked the occupation groups identified within the Women and Employment Survey with reference to current earnings and cross-classified the ranked groupings of current or most recent occupation by the 'top' or highest occupation group reported in a woman's paid employment history. This cross-classification indicated that 18 per cent of women whose highest occupational category in her work history was identified as 'teaching', held their most recent or current occupation in a lower-ranking occupation group. Of women with their highest occupation as 'nursing or other intermediate non-manual', 39 per cent had a current or most recent occupation in a lower-ranked occupation group. As Joshi notes, however, movement to a lower-ranked occupation group, where groups are ranked by current pay, does not necessarily imply a reduction in earnings for the individual. The broad occupational grouping system employed in the WES does not enable one to distinguish different grades within an occupational category. For example, a young nurse might, later in her life, be employed in a higher-paid secretarial job. Second, we are observing women at different stages in their work histories/family life-cycle. If the typical cycle involves a period of work in a lower-paid category, and if this represents a temporary state of affairs associated with the desire to combine child-care responsibilities with paid employment, then the fact that Joshi includes incomplete work histories in her analysis will overstate the importance of downward occupational mobility over a woman's working life.

Further evidence on the link between occupational mobility and family formation was obtained by Dex (1983). Again using WES data, she established a typology of occupational profiles. This typology was used to generate a limited set of occupational transitions which could be regarded as *downward* occupational movements. For those women who had children and who were aged 40 years and over, Dex's analysis showed that just over 60 per cent experienced at least one downward occupational transition in their work history. Interestingly, though, a similar percentage of these women had also experienced at least one upward occupational transition. For those women aged 40 years and over who had never had children a smaller proportion (48 per cent) had experienced at least one downward occupational change, while 63 per cent recorded at least one upward movement. Dex studies the timing of these movements for women with children over each woman's life-cycle, showing that the majority of the downward occupational changes occurred during or immediately after a period of family formation. In contrast, upward occupational movement was typical of what Dex terms the 'initial work phase' or the 'final work phase'.

In Chapter 8 of this book, Dex and Shaw use a multivariate approach to examine the correlates of downward occupational movements across the first break from paid employment associated with childbirth. The most significant factor correlated with downward occupational movement was a *part-time* job following childbirth. It is also interesting to note that women who are in the professional occupations (management, teaching, nursing) are less likely to experience a major downward occupational shift on their return to work. Using similar work history information from the USA, they show that this 'part-time' effect is a particularly British phenomenon.

These studies indicate that there is a clear relationship between family formation, part-time working and downward occupational mobility. British women who have children are likely to return to part-time employment. In doing so, a considerable proportion will experience a major downward shift relative to their previous occupational status and earnings. For those who have professional qualifications, many will be working in job in which they will not be able to utilise these qualifications. There are, however, a number of issues which remain to be resolved. First, we have little evidence which compares men with women. For example, it would be of interest to examine the occupational movements of men who experience a prolonged spell of unemployment, to see if this can be compared in any way with the break in employment for childbirth and subsequent return. Second, we have little information about the *net* effect of these occupational movements over a woman's working life. If there is a rapid recovery in occupational status in what Dex terms the 'final work phase', it might be more appropriate to regard the observed downward occupational movements as a temporary phenomenon. In Chapter 2, Main indicates that many older women who are working full-time have previously worked part-time. Dex (1983) observed upward occupational changes in the later stages of a woman's working life. If, on the other hand, the effect of part-time working is to segregate women into low-skilled, low-paid occupations, and if such segregation has repercussions in terms of a woman's future occupational status, further consideration must be given to the policy implications of such a barrier to occupational mobility.

SKILL UTILISATION AND OCCUPATIONS

Before returning to these issues, it is worthwhile examining the occupational distribution of male and female employment, using a much larger survey which employs a more disaggregated system of occupational classification than that used in the Women and Employment Survey. To this end, the 1981 Labour Force Survey has been analysed to provide information on gender segregation by occupation in the labour market and its relationship with part-time work.

In their analysis of the National Training Survey, Elias and Main (1982) developed an eighteen-fold classification of occupations based upon the skill content and training requirements for particular jobs.

This grouping of occupations was applied to the detailed occupational categories obtained from the 1981 Labour Force Survey. Figures 4.1 and 4.2 show the relevant proportions of men and women in these occupational groups and, for women, their full-time or part-time employment status. Using the information available in this survey on labour force status one year earlier, the histograms for women also record the proportion in either full-time or part-time employment in 1980.

Some evidence of the extent of occupational segregation can be gained from an examination of these distributions. Male occupations

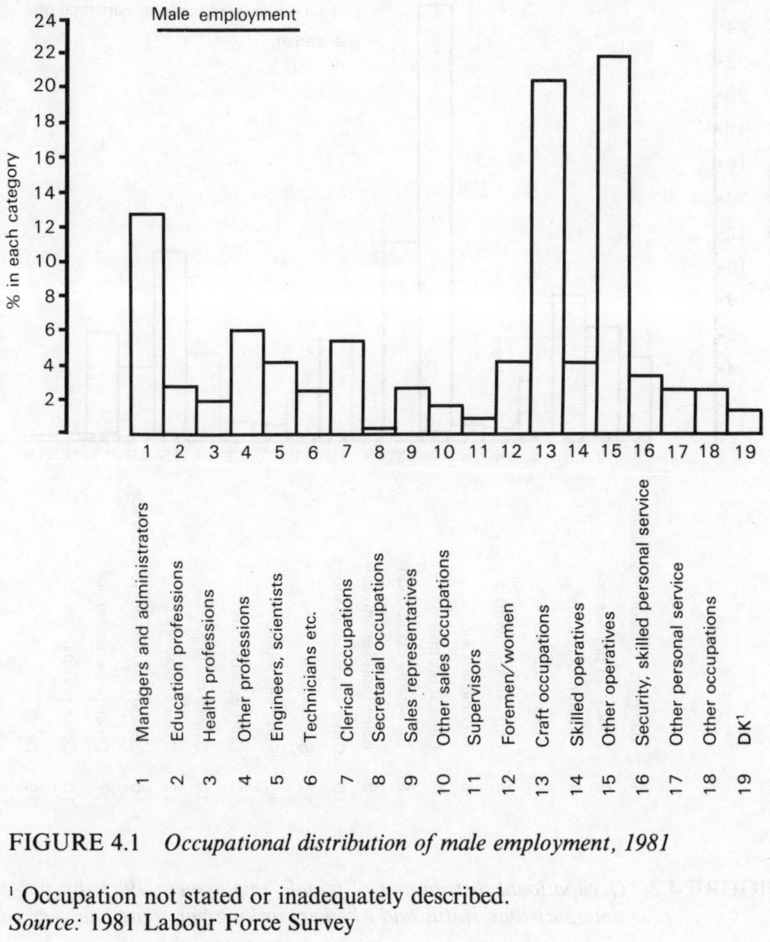

FIGURE 4.1 *Occupational distribution of male employment, 1981*

[1] Occupation not stated or inadequately described.
Source: 1981 Labour Force Survey

are distributed across the range of categories used in this classification, with the exception of secretarial work. Three categories account for more than one-half of male employment: managerial jobs, craft occupations and the semi-skilled 'other operative' category. On the other hand, female occupations are concentrated within three broad groups: health and education professions; clerical, secretarial and

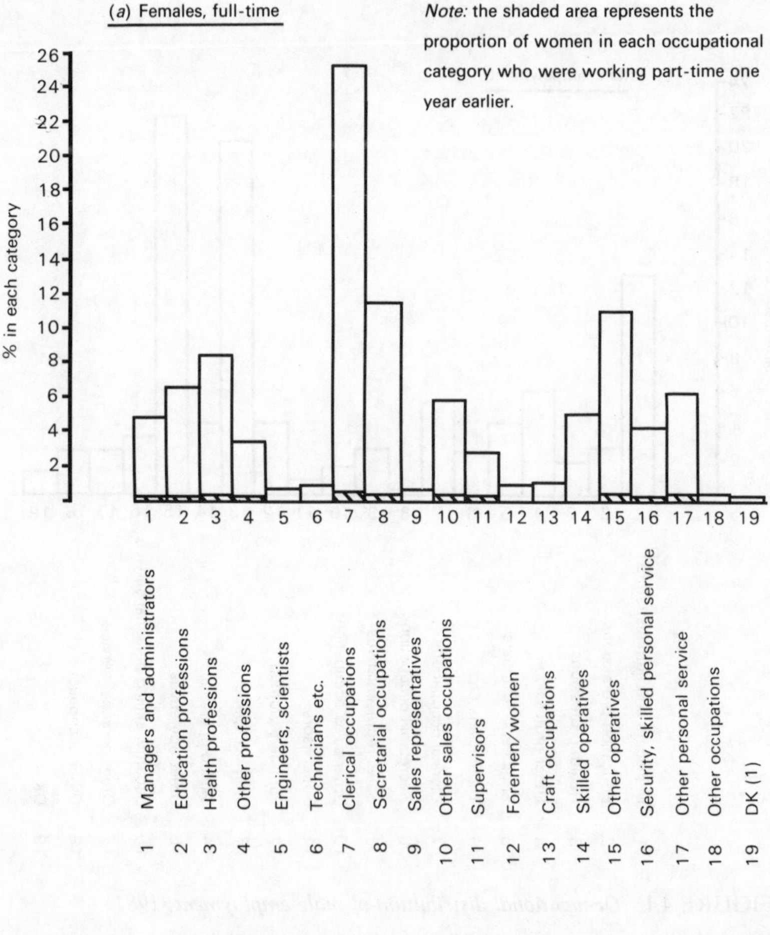

FIGURE 4.2 *Occupational distribution of female employment 1981, by full-time/part-time status and whether working part-time one year earli*

sales jobs; semi-skilled operative: and 'other personal services'. There is a remarkable difference in the female occupational distributions between full-time and part-time workers. More than one-third of women working full-time are employed in clerical and secretarial jobs,

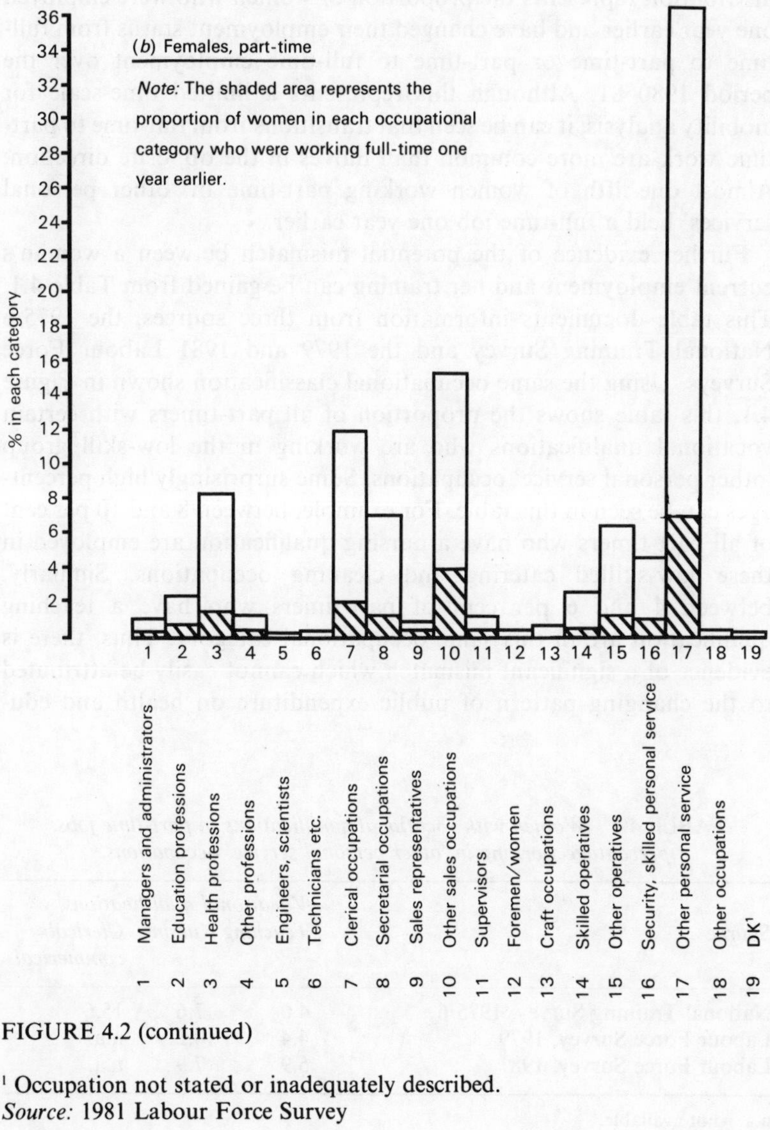

FIGURE 4.2 (continued)

[1] Occupation not stated or inadequately described.
Source: 1981 Labour Force Survey

whereas over one-third of female part-timers are found in the low-skill category 'other personal services', which consists of occupations such as waitresses, barmaids, kitchen assistants, counterhands, school meals assistants, cleaners and service workers in catering and cleaning occupations 'not elsewhere classified'. The shaded area of each distribution represents the proportion of women who were employed one year earlier and have changed their employment status from full-time to part-time or part-time to full-time employment over the period 1980–81. Although this represents a limited time-scale for mobility analysis, it can be seen that transitions from full-time to part-time work are more common than moves in the opposite direction. Almost one-fifth of women working part-time in 'other personal services' held a full-time job one year earlier.

Further evidence of the potential mismatch between a woman's current employment and her training can be gained from Table 4.1. This table documents information from three sources, the 1975/6 National Training Survey and the 1979 and 1981 Labour Force Surveys. Using the same occupational classification shown in Figure 4.1, this table shows the proportion of all part-timers with certain vocational qualifications who are working in the low-skill group 'other personal service' occupations. Some surprisingly high percentages can be seen in this table. For example, between 8 and 10 per cent of all part-timers who have a nursing qualification are employed in these low-skilled catering and cleaning occupations. Similarly, between 4 and 6 per cent of part-timers who have a teaching qualification are in this same occupational category. Thus, there is evidence of a significant mismatch which cannot easily be attributed to the changing pattern of public expenditure on health and edu-

TABLE 4.1 *Women with vocational qualifications in part-time jobs: percentage working in 'other personal service' occupations*

Source	*Vocational qualifications:* Teaching	Nursing	Clerical/ commerical
National Training Survey, 1975/6	4.0	7.6	15.6
Labour Force Survey, 1979	4.4	10.2	n.a.
Labour Force Survey, 1981	5.9	7.9	n.a.

n.a. = not available.

cation. For instance, if there was a sudden decline in the demand for qualified teachers, it would come as no suprise to find a proportion of persons with teaching qualifications working in jobs which did not utilise these skills. However, the decline in the demand for teachers did not commence until after 1979, whereas the proportion of part-timers who were qualified teachers working in 'other personal service' occupations has increased steadily throughout the latter half of the last decade. For nurses, there has been a steady increase in the demand for qualified nursing staff, with the number of nurses employed in the UK growing from 440 000 in 1978 to 493 000 by 1981, yet the proportion of qualified nurses working part-time in 'other personal services' remains higher in 1981 than in the mid-1970s.

These results are indicative of a potential mismatch between vocational training and occupations and suggest that the mismatch is associated with part-time working. Given the limited areas of vocational training selected for analysis, namely nursing and teaching qualifications, the extent of the problem may be understated. These qualifications cover only 9 per cent of employed women. It is quite possible, therefore, that other vocational qualifications lie underutilised within a large proportion of all part-time jobs.

In an attempt to overcome this partial analysis, information is utilised from two surveys which have adopted a more direct approach to the issue. Questions related to the use of skills in a woman's current job were included in both the 1965 Survey of Women's Employment and the 1980 Women and Employment Survey. Comparisons between the replies to these questions are made difficult by the fact that the 1965 survey asked the respondent about the use of prior *training and qualifications* in the current job, whereas the 1980 survey referred to the use of *work experience and abilities*. The 1980 question is, therefore, considerably broader in scope. Women without formal training and qualifications who responded to this question in the 1980 survey may have considered that they had acquired certain abilities which were not fully utilised in their current job. The exact wording and coding of the question is shown at the end of this chapter. Tables 4.2 and 4.3 show an analysis of the response to these questions by age group and by whether a woman was currently working full-time or part-time. Because of these differences in wording, comparisons are limited to the differential response between women in full-time and women in part-time jobs in each year, shown as the third row in each table. This difference can be viewed as a measure of the extent to which perceived skills, abilities and training lie underutilised in part-

TABLE 4.2 *Working women not using all of their previous training/qualifications in their present job, by age groups and full-time/part-time status, 1965 (%)*

	16–19	*20–24*	*25–29*	*30–34*	*35–39*	*40–44*	*45–49*	*50–54*	*55–59*	*60–64*
Full-time (FT)	15.1	20.6	18.7	22.7	18.4	18.8	19.2	15.7	13.6	10.4
Part-time (PT)	(57.1)	25.6	36.5	34.0	26.8	28.3	24.4	17.4	16.4	12.8
Difference (FT-PT)	(42.0)	5.0	17.8	11.3	8.4	9.5	5.2	1.3	2.8	2.4
Base (=100%)	466	397	269	305	399	493	491	413	351	214

Source: Survey of Women's Employment, 1965.

TABLE 4.3 *Working women not presently making full use of work experience/abilities, by age groups and full-time/part-time status, 1980 (%)*

	16–19	*20–24*	*25–29*	*30–34*	*35–39*	*40–44*	*45–49*	*50–54*	*55–59*	*60–64*
Full-time (FT)	36.7	39.0	37.6	34.9	32.0	27.1	24.4	22.5	18.9	(20.0)
Part-time (PT)	(50.0)	59.0	68.4	55.7	49.8	42.1	35.1	24.9	25.3	(16.7)
Difference (FT-PT)	(13.3)	19.1	30.8	20.8	17.8	15.0	10.7	2.5	6.3	(3.3)
Base (=100%)	212	347	319	410	409	404	385	371	311	32

Source: Women and Employment Survey, 1980.

time as opposed to full-time jobs. It is immediately apparent that there is a major difference in the response to these questions between women in full-time employment and part-timers. From both surveys it can be seen that this difference reaches a peak in the 25–29 age group, the prime years for family formation, declining quickly thereafter up to the 45–49 age group. For women in the older age groups there is little appreciable difference between full-timers and part-timers in terms of their perceived under-utilisation of training/qualifications (1965) or experience/abilities (1980).

These results appear to indicate that the under-utilisation of skills associated with part-time jobs occurs *during* a period of family formation and that the types of part-time jobs in which women work in the period *following* family formation makes better use of prior skills or training. Equally, it could be the case that the longer a woman works in a low-skill, part-time job, the less likely she is to perceive that she is under-utilising her work experience gained prior to a period of family formation. The analysis presented in the next section attempts to shed further light on this issue via a cohort analysis of occupational work histories and the relationship between such occupational profiles, part-time working and family formation.

A COHORT ANALYSIS OF OCCUPATIONS AND PART-TIME WORK

The detailed work history information contained in the 1980 Women and Employment Survey enables a cohort analysis of occupational histories to be constructed. This section focuses upon three cohorts of women born in the five-year periods 1921–5, 1931–5 and 1941–5. Five-year age groups were selected to overcome problems associated with the sample size of each cohort. The three five-year periods were chosen to represent three cohorts of women in the Women and Employment Survey who had completed their family formation and whose employment experiences spanned a twenty-year period. It is, of course, possible that further children will be born to the youngest of these cohorts, women aged 35–39 in 1980, but the small numbers involved are unlikely to influence the analysis.

Figure 4.3 displays the employment profiles for the three older cohorts (55–59 year-olds, 45–49 year-olds and 35–39 year-olds) by whether or not the cohort members have ever had any children (natural, fostered, adopted or stepchildren). While the number of cohort members in the childless category is fairly low, it is quite clear that the typical 'u-shaped' profile of employment evident in such cohort employment diagrams (see Figure 2.12 in Chapter 2) is associated with family formation. For women who have never had children, the proportion of the cohort in employment remains high throughout the life-cycle. Compared with the oldest cohort (aged 55–59 years in 1980), employment rates for the younger age groups are about ten percentage points higher for women aged over 30 years. In sharp contrast, employment rates for women who have had children decline rapidly over the first ten years of their working lives, with a remarkably similar employment experience across the three cohorts as they move into the family formation period. The return to work, shown by Main in Chapter 2 to be associated with the growth of part-time employment, reveals a major difference in behaviour between the three cohorts of women who had children. Approximately two-thirds of 35–39 year-old women with children were employed in 1980, compared with just over 40 per cent of the 55–59 year olds at this same point in their life-cycle twenty years earlier.

The next stage of this analysis investigates the occupational status of the employed members of each cohort for each year in their working lives. Occupational profiles are represented in a fairly simplistic fashion. Using the analysis of grouped occupational earnings differentials undertaken by Joshi (1984), the twelve-fold classification of earnings used in the WES is collapsed into two categories, those with above-average earnings and those with below-average earnings after controlling for the effect of personal characteristics. In the former category are professional occupations, teachers, nurses, etc., intermediate non-manual occupations, and clerical jobs. The latter group consists of sales, skilled and semi-skilled manual jobs and unskilled occupations. Further details on the occupational pay differentials and some information on the stability of pay differentials through time are given in the appendix at the end of the chapter.

The proportions of women in employment shown in Figure 4.3 are split into four groups, by whether or not a woman is working in an 'above-average earnings' occupation group or 'below-average earnings', and by whether or not she is a full-time or part-time worker. This approach reveals the changing occupational status of women as they move through the family building years, and identifies whether or not the growth of part-time employment is related to such occupational changes. It must be stressed that the technique used here portrays the average experience of a member of the age group as time

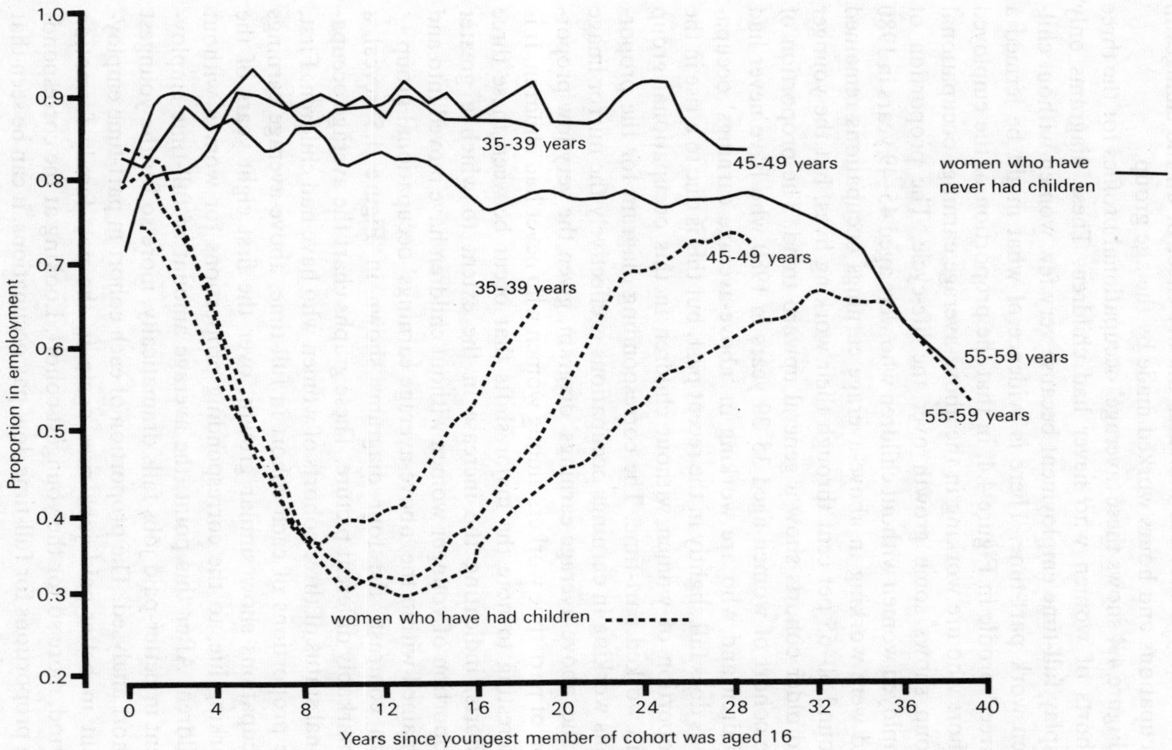

FIGURE 4.3 *Employment rates for three cohorts of women, by whether or not they ever had children*

passes. It does not reveal the variety of occupational changes that one woman may make, but indicates the net effect of all the changes in occupations and hours worked made by the age group.

Figure 4.4 shows these 'average' occupational profiles for the three cohorts of women who never had children. These diagrams only display full-time employment because very few women without children work part-time. There is evidence of what might be termed a 'career' profile in Figure 4.4, in that the proportion of the employed cohort who are working in the above-average earnings occupational group shows some growth over the life-cycle. The proportion of employed women without children who were aged 45–49 years in 1980 and were working in above-average earnings occupations remained around 60–65 per cent through their working lives, but the younger and older cohorts show a general upward trend. The proportion of the cohort of women aged 35–39 years in 1980 who have never had children and who are working in 'above-average earnings' occupations does fall slightly in the recent past, but this is due to a rise in the proportion of women without children in this occupational group who worked part-time. The corresponding diagram for the proportions working in earnings occupations is effectively the mirror image of the 'above-average earnings' diagram, given the very low proportion of part-time workers among women who never had children. It is interesting to note the major shifts that occur between these three cohorts, indicating the increase in the extent to which a greater proportion of younger women without children have moved into and remained within the 'above-average earnings' occupational group.

In contrast, the four diagrams shown in Figure 4.5 reveal a remarkably different picture. These graphs chart the average occupational status of three cohorts of women who have had children. First, the proportions of each cohort in full-time, above-average earnings occupations show similar growth, over the first eight years of the working life, to the corresponding proportions for women without children. After this point, the average amount of full-time employment in better-paid jobs falls dramatically, more so for the youngest cohort analysed. The proportion of each cohort in part-time employment in better-paid jobs rises again in the post-family formation period, more so for the youngest cohort. Looking at the corresponding proportions for full-time, low-pay occupations, it can be seen that this growth in part-time better-paid jobs is reflected in terms of a decline in full-time employment in low-pay occupations, with virtually no change in the proportion of each cohort employed *part-time*

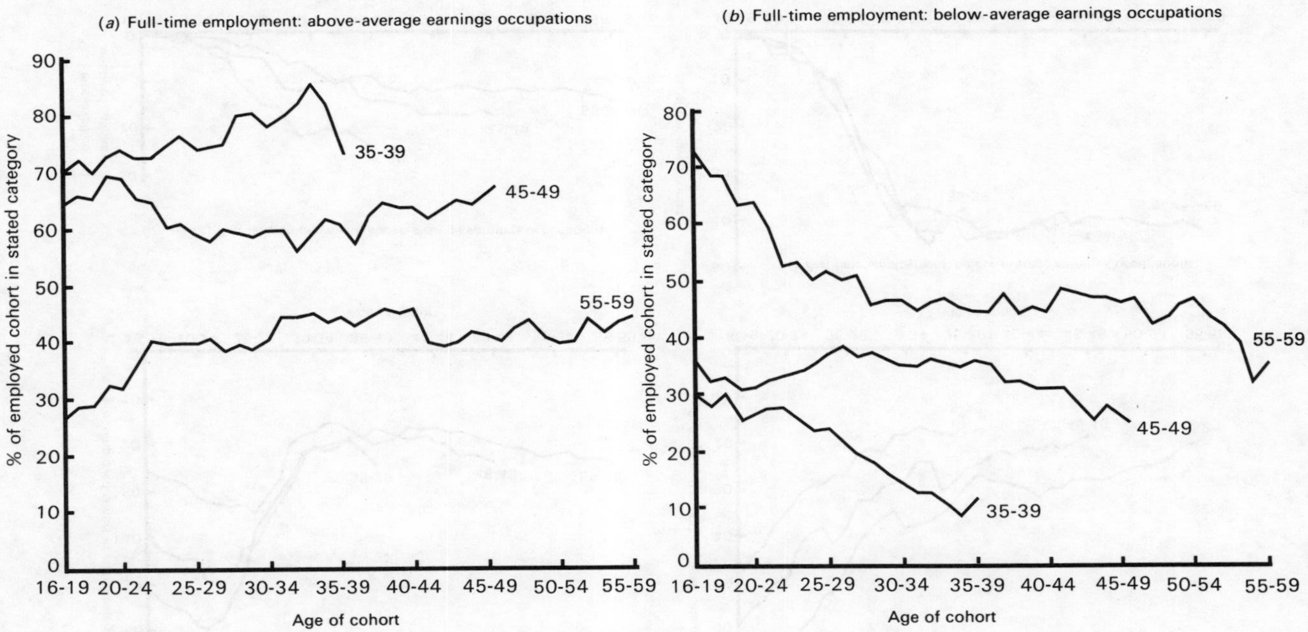

FIGURE 4.4 *The occupational and employment status of three cohorts of women who have never had children*

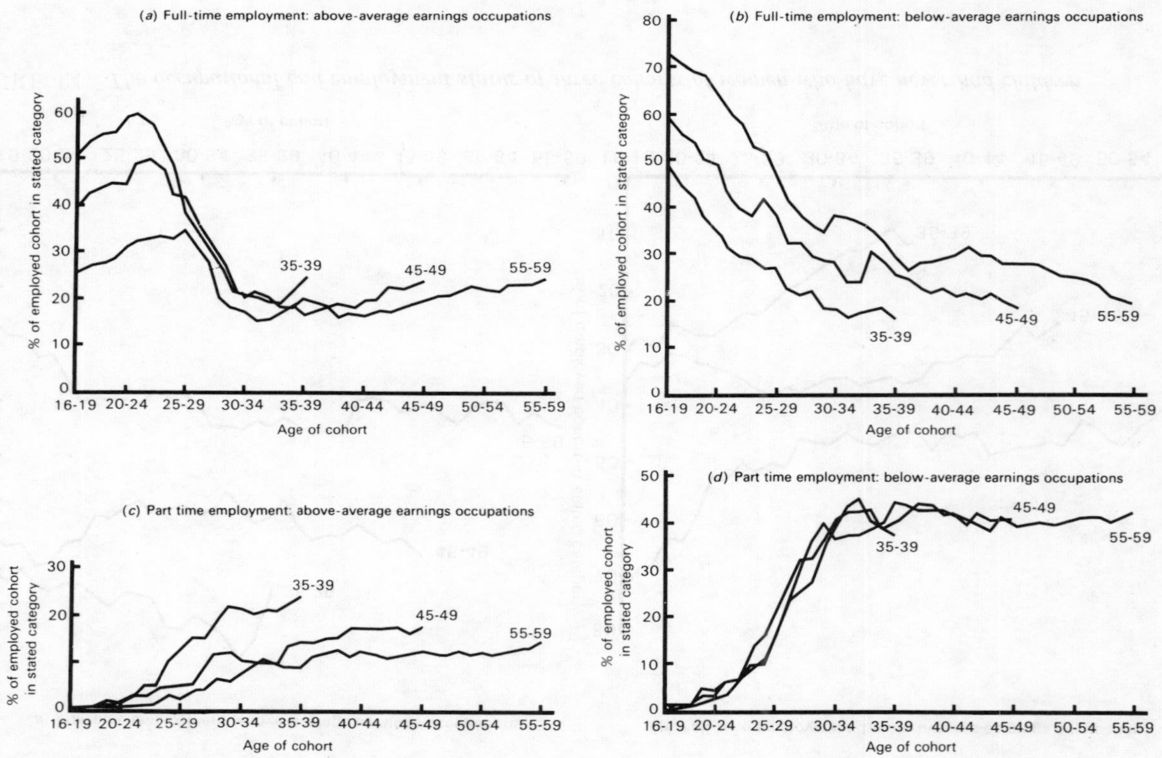

FIGURE 4.5 *The occupational and employment status of three cohorts of women who have had children*

in low-pay occupations. Indeed, the proportion of employed women working part-time in below-average earnings occupations has remained virtually constant over the twenty-year period spanned by the analysis of the three cohorts.

On balance, those women who have had children display substantial downward occupational mobility over the family formation period. There is some evidence to suggest that the youngest cohort analysed is staging a modest 'occupational recovery' in part-time, but not full-time, employment, but this recovery is nowhere near sufficient to restore the cohort to the growth path in occupational status it established prior to family formation. It is quite remarkable to note that the proportion of employed 35–39 year-olds who were working part-time in low-paid jobs in 1980 is virtually identical to the same proportion for the oldest cohort when they were aged 35–39 years in the early 1960s.

SUMMARY

There is evidence that many women experience severe occupational downgrading during their working lives and that such downward occupational mobility is associated with a period of family formation. An analysis of occupational work histories indicates that there is only a limited amount of occupational 'recovery' following a period of downward mobility. Women who have had children do not, on average, regain their occupational status prior to childbirth; nor does the increased proportion of employed women in part-time jobs paying above-average earnings, exhibited by the youngest cohort analysed, compensate for the decrease in occupational status between ages 20 and 30 years which is associated with childbearing. Remarkably, it has been shown that, for women who have had children, the proportion of employed women in their late thirties in 1980 who were working part-time in occupations with below-average earnings is, at 40 per cent, virtually identical to the proportion for women who were in the same age group twenty years earlier.

This finding derives from the segmented nature of the labour market for full-time and part-time workers. Part-time jobs are concentrated within a narrow range of occupations, principally in the area of low-skill personal service work. Where part-time jobs occur in other occupation groups, they are generally at the lowest hierarchical level within the vertical structure of an occupation group and carry a relatively less attractive set of 'fringe benefits' (disproportionately fewer paid holidays, sick pay, access to occupational pension schemes, training and opportunities for promotion). For many women with young children, the lack of facilities for the care and education of their pre-school children and their assumed domestic responsibilities leave them with little choice but to opt for *part-time working* upon their return to work. Employers have not been slow to recognise the financial advantages of tapping into such a cheap, well-educated and flexible labour reserve, but at what price to women's occupational status has such flexibility been obtained? The evidence presented in this chapter shows the negative impact this will have on women's occupational status while working part-time and subsequently on their occupational status throughout the remainder of their working lives.

APPENDIX

Perceived use of training/qualifications/experience/abilities in current job: the 1965 and 1980 surveys

In the 1965 Survey of Women's Employment, all women who were 'gainfully employed' (i.e. working for pay, unemployed and seeking work or sick and intending to return) were asked: 'If you consider you have any training or qualifications that fit you for particular jobs, do you feel that you are using it/them all in your present job?' Replies were coded into the following categories:

—no training/qualifications
—using all
—using some/using part only
—Using none

Replies coded to the last two categories are shown in Table 4.1.

In the 1980 Women and Employment Survey, all women who held a paid job during the seven days prior to their interview (or who were away from a paid job due to temporary illness, holiday or maternity leave) were asked: 'Do you feel your present job makes full use of your work experience and abilities?' Replies were coded Yes/No.

An edited version of the 1965 Survey was not available. Instead, the Institute for Employment Research gained access to an unedited copy of the original card-deck. These data were reconstructed to match the original edited version as closely as possible. In the original edited survey, age details were recorded for 3885 working women. In the reconstructed survey, age information was found for 3773 working women. The tabulated results obtained from the 1980 Survey are based on a similar sample of 3200 working women.

Occupations and earnings in the Women and Employment Survey

The work history data collected in the Women and Employment Survey (WES) do not include historical information on earnings. A crude indicator of earnings can be obtained by using *occupation* as a proxy variable.

Occupations in WES are coded into thirteen groups. These are:

1 Professional occupations
2 Teachers
3 Nursing, medical, social occupations
4 Other non-manual occs.
5 Clerical occupations
6 Shop assistant and related sales
7 Skilled occupations
8 Childcare occupations
9 Semi-skilled factory work
10 Semi-skilled domestic work
11 Other semi-skilled occs.
12 Unskilled occupations
13 Unclassifiable

Joshi (1984) regressed current hourly earnings on this set of occupation categories, controlling for age, education and work history. Her estimated proportional differentials between the occupational groups are:

Occupation group	*Proportional differential*	
1	104%	these are defined as occupations with above-average earnings
2	90%	
3	37%	
4	39%	
5	26%	
6	—	these are defined as occupations with below-average earnings
7	11%	
8	−15%	
9	12%	
10	–	
11	9%	
12/13	reference group	

The classification of occupations into two groups, 'good' (above-average earnings) and 'poor' (below-average earnings) is based upon the relationship between occupational categories and hourly earnings that existed in 1980. The use of this classification to categorise earning potential from an historical analysis of occupations requires a degree of stability in relative earnings by occupation. Some indication of such stability can be gained from an analysis of relative earnings by occupation, noting that the classification of WES occupation codes into two groups corresponds well with the New Earnings Survey (NES) categories 'non-manual' and 'manual'. In 1968, the first year of the NES, the differential between female hourly earnings in non-manual and manual occupations was 38 per cent. By 1983, fifteen years later, this differential had declined to 31 per cent. On average, therefore, the classification used in WES will represent a sharper distinction between 'above-average' and 'below-average' earnings in the late 1960s than was the case by 1980.

5 Women's Hourly Earnings: the Influence of Work Histories on Rates of Pay

Brian G. M. Main

INTRODUCTION

Despite the effects of the Equal Pay Act and the Sex Discrimination Act in the mid-1970s, there remains a marked difference between the average hourly earnings of men and those of women. Of course, the variation in the average hourly rate of earnings of men and women in full-time jobs, shown in Table 5.1, is only one source in the variation of earnings between men and women. McIntosh (1980), reporting on a survey of employers, emphasised the importance of men's longer hours of work and their greater propensity to work overtime and shiftwork. Further, Joshi (1982) has emphasised a less direct influence, whereby the lower hourly earnings available to women encourage breaks from employment which in turn reduce a woman's eventual pension rights.

This chapter restricts itself to the specific topic of average hourly earnings, but picks up a thread of the Joshi analysis by investigating the extent to which a woman's employment record, or work history, can be said to influence her hourly rate of pay. An earlier attempt to examine this phenomenon was made by Zabalza and Arrufat (1985). Controlling for measurable differences in personal characteristics, these authors found that as much as two-thirds of the difference in average hourly earnings between married men and married women could be attributed to what they label the 'depreciation' effect of non-

TABLE 5.1. *Average hourly earnings for males and females in full-time employment, 1970–83*

Year	*Males*	*Females* (*pence per hour*)	*Females/Males* (*percentage*)
1970	66.7	42.0	63
1971	74.4	47.4	64
1972*	83.4	53.8	64
1973	94.3	60.5	64
1974	107.6	70.8	66
1975	139.9	98.5	70
1976	166.8	122.6	74
1977	181.1	134.0	74
1978	204.3	148.2	73
1979	232.2	166.0	72
1980	288.2	207.0	72
1981	332.0	241.8	73
1982	365.6	263.1	72
1983	423.0	310.3	73

Source: New Earnings Survey, various years.
* Figures for 1972 represent an average of two reported figures describing firstly those not affected by absence (basis for 1973 and later) and secondly all persons irrespective of absence (basis for 1970 and 1971). Females include all those aged 18 years and above, and males include those aged 21 and above. Overtime earnings are included.

participation. In a companion paper, Zabalza and Tzannatos (1985) estimated the effect of the implementation of the Equal Pay Act of 1970 to be a 19 per cent increase in the hourly earnings of women. This gain would represent, by their calculations, somewhere between one-half and three-quarters of that part of the gap between male and female wage rates that cannot be explained by differences in experience or education. By assuming that that part of the difference in wage rates that cannot be explained by personal characteristics represents the effects of discrimination, Zabalza and Arrufat concluded that the Equal Pay Act eliminated between a half and three-quarters of the effects of sex discrimination.

An important element of this argument is that a great deal of the difference in average hourly earnings between the sexes can be ascribed to the different patterns of work history followed by men and women. As will be seen below, this line of argument is not new. The purpose of this chapter is to use the detailed work histories available in the 1980 Women and Employment Survey to investigate this hypothesis.

One problem faced by Zabalza and Arrufat (1985) was the lack of accurate work history data. They solved the problem by an imaginative backward-projection technique which essentially estimated women's past work histories by observations on their current employment status. The Women and Employment Survey has the advantage of a detailed work history for each of the 5000 or so women involved, although unfortunately it lacks a suitable sample group of males for direct comparison. The main report on the Women and Employment Survey is available in Martin and Roberts (1984a), and some relevant secondary analysis has been conducted by Joshi (1984). Both of these will be discussed below.

The second section of the chapter extends the discussion of the influence of work histories on rates of pay by reviewing some of the relevant literature. Empirical results obtained by regression analysis are presented in the third section, where an attempt is also made to deal with the problem of sample-selection bias. The fourth section offers an interpretation of the findings of the regression analysis in terms of the influence of work histories on hourly earnings. Conclusions and policy considerations are presented in the final part of this chapter.

THE INFLUENCE OF WORK HISTORIES

The basic idea, that periods of employment induce an increase in the potential wage rate and that periods of non-employment lead to a depreciation in the potential wage rate, is generally associated with the work of Mincer (1974), and particularly with Mincer and Polachek (1974). Adopting what is referred to as a 'human capital' approach to earnings, Mincer argued that a person's wage rate is related to his or her productivity, and that productivity is a function of both formal education and on-the-job training, including the acquisition of additional skills through experience. It is argued that the opportunity to acquire such training comes with employment experience and that periods out of employment lead to an obsolescence or depreciation of the training acquired to date. The theoretical basis of this approach has been critically reviewed by Blinder (1976), and a series of articles by Sandell and Shapiro (1978), Mincer and Polachek (1978), Corcoran (1979), Mincer and Ofek (1982), Corcoran *et al.* (1983) and Shaw (1983a) have offered varying empirical estimates of the 'depreciation' effect for the US economy.

To view average hourly earnings as a function of work history does not, of itself, necessitate the adoption of this 'human capital' approach whereby hourly earnings are related to personal productivity and training. The empirical specification is equally appealing to institutional economists who view hourly earnings as dependent on access to certain areas of the labour market and, within any enterprise, to the more highly paid jobs which it is argued are secured by those who generally have long employment records. Thus, institutional economists such as Applebaum (1981) have also used the approach.

In the UK the work by Zabalza and Arrufat (1985) has attracted considerable attention but, unfortunately, their data, derived from the General Household Survey, lack precision on the nature of work histories.[1] Stewart and Greenhalgh (1984) use data from the National Training Survey, which has detailed work history information on all individuals. However, the earnings data in that survey records only into which of ten groups a person's weekly earnings fall,[2] and, to complicate matters, no information is available on hours of work. Their exercise was therefore an investigation of weekly earnings rather than hourly earnings and, in that sense, it was impossible to separate the hours of work decision from the market rate of pay.

Joshi (1984) has already investigated hourly earnings as reported in the Women and Employment Survey. However, the wage equation which she derived was based on rather limited work history information[3] and the exercise was undertaken only as part of the estimation of a labour supply function. The decision to participate or not in the labour force is, of course, influenced by the wage rate that could be earned if a person was in a job, and it was to obtain information on such potential wages that Joshi estimated her wage equation.

The general relationship between hourly earnings and length of time in current job shown by the Women and Employment Survey has been commented on by Martin and Roberts (1984a). Table 5.2 presents the average hourly earnings of women in full-time and part-time employment in the Women and Employment Survey[4] compared with data from the 1980 New Earnings Survey. The Women and Employment Survey reports low hourly earnings, particularly among part-time employees, the difference being greater the lower the average wage of the group. This finding is consistent with expectations, since the New Earnings Survey is based on a sample of employees who fall within the Inland Revenue tax net. Many low-paid employees whose earnings are below the minimum for tax reporting

TABLE 5.2. *Average hourly earnings by age group, 1980 (£ per hour)*

	New Earnings Survey			Women and Employment Survey		
Age group	*Males Full-time*	*Females Full-time*	*Females Part-time*	*Females Full-time*	*Females Part-time*	*Females All*
16–17	1.18	1.18	1.24	1.10	1.03	1.10
18–20	1.82	1.57	1.55	1.46	1.16	1.45
21–24	2.32	1.94	1.71	1.82	1.61	1.78
25–29	2.75	2.27	1.74	2.21	1.65	2.01
30–39	3.05	2.31	1.72	2.23	1.70	1.93
40–49	3.08	2.19	1.70	2.13	1.62	1.86
50–59	2.89	2.13	1.64	1.95	1.61	1.77
60–64	2.63	1.97	1.56	—	—	—
65 +	2.64	1.95	1.53		—	—
All	2.77	2.03	1.68	1.94	1.65	1.81

TABLE 5.3. *Average hourly earnings by time spent not in employment (£ per hour)*

Years of working life not spent in employment	*Women in employment at the time of the survey*			*Percentage of working life not spent in employment*	*Women in employment at the time of the survey*		
	Full-time	*Part-time*	*All*		*Full-time*	*Part-time*	*All*
0–4	1.96	1.83	1.93	0–9	1.99	1.93	1.98
5–9	2.04	1.57	1.75	10–19	1.93	1.80	1.87
10–14	1.89	1.62	1.72	20–29	1.98	1.58	1.76
15–19	1.72	1.54	1.60	30–39	1.95	1.63	1.75
20–24	1.68	1.52	1.57	40–49	1.88	1.56	1.68
25–29	1.27*	1.34*	1.33	50–59	1.69	1.55	1.60
30–34	1.18*	1.35*	1.30*	60–69	1.69	1.53	1.57
35–39	1.36*	1.30*	1.33*	70–79	1.83*	1.48	1.61
40–44	0.81*		0.81*	80–89	1.34*	1.30*	1.31*
				90–99	0.75*	1.48*	1.19*
All	1.94 (1629)	1.65 (1277)	1.81 (2906)	All	1.94 (1629)	1.65 (1277)	1.81 (2906)

* Less than 25 women in group.
Source: Women and Employment Survey (1980).

purposes are excluded from the New Earnings Survey. The majority of such employees will be women working part-time in jobs of low skill content. Table 5.3 records the average hourly earnings for women in employment in 1980, firstly by the *number of years* of working life spent out of employment, and secondly by the *proportion* of working life spent out of employment. For both those women working full-time and those working part-time at the time of the survey, the relationship is clear. Those with a long period out of paid employment, in absolute or proportionate terms, receive a lower rate of hourly earnings. The next section attempts to specify this relationship in a more detailed fashion.

REGRESSION ANALYSIS OF HOURLY EARNINGS

Hourly earnings are to be explained as a function of labour market experience. The number of explanatory variables is kept deliberately small to produce what is essentially a reduced form relationship[5] where only the most basic variables descriptive of labour market experience are used. It is necessary to supplement these variables with information describing the educational experience and qualifications which each woman has, in this instance the total number of years of post-compulsory education she experienced[6] and the highest level of educational credential she achieved. The entire Women and Employment Survey sample had an average of just over one year of post-compulsory education. Just under 13 per cent had achieved credentials above A level, including degrees, teaching, nursing and social work credentials and professional qualifications. Only 3 per cent had university degrees. The next group, some 22 per cent of the sample, possessed school-leaving credentials at A and O level, while 14 per cent of the sample held CSEs, clerical qualifications or trade apprenticeships (the latter mainly hairdressing). Lastly, around 1 per cent had foreign credentials. Thus, some 50 per cent of the sample had no educational credentials at all. Table 5.4 gives some idea of how hourly earnings relate to these educational credentials.

Work histories are described by the length of time (in years) spent in full-time employment in the current spell, and the length of time spent in full-time employment in each of the three previous employment spells. The fifth such variable describes the number of years spent in full-time employment in all earlier employment spells. A similar set of five variables records, in exactly the same way, the years

TABLE 5.4. *Gross hourly earnings by educational qualifications (£ per hour)*

Highest level of qualification	*Full-time*	*Part-time*	*All*
Degree or equivalent	2.91	2.47	2.78
A levels or O levels	1.82	1.61	1.76
CSEs, clerical qualifications, trade apprenticeship	1.69	1.66	1.67
Other or foreign	1.90	1.43	1.66
None	1.66	1.52	1.58
All	1.94	1.65	1.81

Source: Women and Employment Survey, 1980.

spent in part-time employment over the work history. The non-employment part of the work history[7] is described by four variables. The first describes the length of time (in years) in the last spell of non-employment until the fourth such variable describes the length of time spent in the fourth and all earlier spells of non-employment. As a further refinement to the analysis, a dummy variable is also included to indicate whether current employment is in a full-time job. Additionally, a variable is included to express the length of time that each woman has been with her current employer.

The first column in Table 5.5 gives the results of a regression of the logarithm of hourly earnings on the descriptive variables introduced above. The estimated coefficients can be interpreted as the approximate percentage change in hourly earnings that can be expected from a unit change in the relevant descriptive variable.

It is interesting to digress a little at this point to discuss a potential problem with the statistical procedure, although the non-technical reader may prefer to proceed directly to the discussion of results which commence in the next section. As it stands, column 1 of Table 5.5 offers a relationship between hourly earnings and work histories for those women currently in employment. However, it is not clear that it would be appropriate to apply this information to women currently out of employment to generate their potential hourly earnings. This is due to the problem of *sample selection bias*, whereby those women in employment may have different unmeasured characteristics from those not in employment. If the correlation between the measured and unmeasured characteristics differs between the two groups, a possible bias emerges. The problem is discussed in Smith (1980), who argues that unmeasured characteristics which cause a

TABLE 5.5 *Regression of log of hourly earnings on work history descriptors*

Descriptive variables	*First-stage wage equation* *Coefficient*	(*t-stat*)	*Second-stage wage equation* *Coefficient*	(*t-stat*)
Years as full-time in current spell	.0115	(9.63)	.0114	(9.48)
Years as full-time in last spell	.0067	(4.76)	.0069	(4.84)
Years as full-time in 2nd last spell	.0055	(2.73)	.0056	(2.79)
Years as full-time in 3rd last spell	.0080	(2.50)	.0080	(2.50)
Years as full-time in 4th last and all other prior employment spells	.0029	(0.72)	.0031	(0.79)
Years as part-time in current spell	.0053	(3.02)	.0051	(2.91)
Years as part-time in last spell	.0029	(0.99)	.0030	(1.03)
Years as part-time in 2nd last spell	.0093	(1.30)	.0095	(1.32)
Years as part-time in 3rd last spell	.0031	(0.28)	.0031	(0.29)
Years as part-time in 4th and all other prior employment spells	−.0023	(0.27)	−.0019	(0.22)
Years in last non-employment spell	−.0026	(2.04)	−.0025	(1.96)
Years in 2nd non-employment spell	−.0003	(0.16)	−.0003	(0.16)
Years in 3rd non-employment spell	.0019	(0.51)	.0018	(0.49)
Years in 4th and other prior non-employment spells	−.0006	(0.13)	−.0006	(0.14)
Years with current employer	.0021	(1.19)	.0020	(1.13)
Current employment is full-time	.0613	(3.73)	.0550	(3.17)
Years of post-compulsory education	.0667	(13.08)	.0660	(12.82)
Degree of equivalent	.2945	(10.83)	.2881	(10.37)
A, O levels or equivalent	.0470	(0.18)	.0449	(2.44)
CSEs or equivalent	.0338	(1.73)	.0321	(1.64)
Other or foreign qualifications	−.0157	(0.23)	−.0153	(0.23)
LAMBDA			−.0304	(1.13)
Constant	.2311	(11.17)	.2520	(9.08)
Mean of dependent variable	0.51		0.51	
$\overline{R}^2$	0.31		0.31	
Standard error of regression	0.34		0.34	
F-statistic	61.93		59.18	
N	2906		2906	

woman to have a higher wage rate will also make it more likely that she is found participating in the labour market. A two-stage method of correcting for this source of bias is outlined in Heckman (1979), and this will be adopted here.

The essence of Heckman's procedure is to enter an additional term (lambda)[8] into the wage equation. This term reflects the probability that a woman will be in employment at any time. Estimates of the probability that a woman is in employment at any time are presented in Table 5.6. The fact that a woman is either in employment or not in employment at the time of the survey leads to a binary dependent variable which is best treated by some non-linear statistical estimation technique such as probit.[9] The last column in Table 5.6 presents an interpretation of these estimates that is similar to that obtained from a linear regression.[10] The descriptive variables used in Table 5.6 are self-explanatory and relate principally to the age, marital status and family formation experience of each woman. In addition, the estimated potential level of hourly earnings is calculated from the estimates in the first column of Table 5.5 as an approximate measure of the opportunity cost of a woman's non-participation.

Estimates obtained in Table 5.6 are not dissimilar to those reported by Layard, Barton and Zabalza (1980) in a similar exercise. Having an unemployed partner clearly exerts a strong negative influence on the probability of a woman being in employment. It is also clear that the younger any children are, the stronger is their influence on the probability that a woman will be observed not in paid employment. The estimated potential hourly earnings also have a strong influence in the opposite direction. The mean of the potential hourly earnings over the entire sample was £1.63 per hour. The coefficient of 0.969 reported in Table 5.6 therefore suggests a wage elasticity of around 0.9, which is rather high compared with some other estimates, but consistent with estimates produced by Joshi (1984).[11]

The second column of Table 5.5 uses the estimates of the probability of being in employment presented in Table 5.6 to correct for potential sample-selection bias by the inclusion of the term 'lambda'.[12] The coefficient on the lambda term (and hence the correction) was not found to be statistically significant.[13] Nevertheless, the logic behind this correction is so strong that it is this second version of the wage equation that is used to analyse the effect of work histories on women's potential hourly earnings. In a similar exercise, Zabalza and Arrufat (1985) do find a statistically significant value for the coefficient on lambda, as do Dolton and Makepeace (1984).

TABLE 5.6 *Maximum likelihood estimate of the probability of being in employment*

Descriptive	*Estimated probit coefficient*	(t-*stat*)	*OLS interpretation*
Single	−.0612	(1.14)	−.023
Partner unemployed	−.7475	(5.78)	−.276
Youngest child aged 0–2 years	−1.6940	(17.88)	−.625
Youngest child aged 3–4 years	−.9159	(8.5)	−.338
Youngest child aged 5–10 years	−.2672	(2.93)	−.099
Youngest child aged 11–15 years	.1326	(1.66)	.049
Total number of children under 16	−.0600	(1.76)	−.022
Own age under 25 years	.2863	(3.66)	.106
Own age 25–34 years	.0501	(0.83)	.018
Own age 45–54 years	−.2753	(4.28)	−.102
Own age 55–59 years	−.7806	(9.91)	−.288
Estimated potential hourly earnings (£)	.9691	(16.76)	.357
Constant	−.7094	(6.16)	
Mean of dependent variable		.630	
Chi-squared statistic		1414.6	
N		5318	

IMPLICATIONS OF THE REGRESSION ANALYSIS

The regression coefficients presented in the second-stage equation in Table 5.5 suggest that hourly earnings are significantly influenced by the length of time spent in the current spell of employment. The effect is twice as strong for full-time employment (with an increase in hourly earnings of around 1.1 per cent for each year of full-time work experience) as for part-time employment (with an increase in 0.5 per cent per year of part-time experience). Full-time experience in earlier spells of employment exerts a positive and significant influence, but part-time experience does not.

Years spent with the current employer, as distinct from the current employment phase, have no significant independent effect upon a woman's current earnings. This is a surprising finding, as such a measure might have been expected to indicate an accumulation of skills particular to the current employer. Joshi (1984) found such a variable to be significant, although her results also indicate an interaction with part-time working. Table 5.5 indicates that currently being in full-time as distinct from part-time employment adds an estimated 5.5 per cent to hourly earnings.

As expected, time spent out of employment exerts a downward influence on hourly earnings. The effect is only just statistically significant for the most recent spell of non-employment, where every year decreases hourly earnings by approximately 0.3 per cent. Earlier spells have no significant influence. Taken together these results suggest that, apart from full-time employment experience, the labour market has a relatively short 'memory'. Major influences on hourly earnings are seen to be associated with the current employment spells and the immediately prior period of non-employment, if any.

Labour market experiences apart, educational experience and qualifications are seen to play an important role in determining hourly earnings. For every year of post-compulsory education, expected hourly earnings increase by 6.6 per cent. Educational qualifications also exert a positive influence ('other or foreign qualifications' excepted), with a degree-level qualification leading to hourly earnings that are approximately one-third higher[14] than for someone with no educational qualifications. This last finding confirms the simple analysis of Table 5.4, where those with a degree-level qualification were seen to have hourly earnings that were 75 per cent (full-time) to 63 per cent (part-time) higher than those with no qualifications. Much of the remaining difference is explained by the extra years of post-compulsory education involved.

Rather than interpreting these regression results in a partial way, variable by variable, it is possible to use the estimated coefficients to predict what the women in the Women and Employment Survey could have expected by way of hourly earnings had they followed a different work history. This can be done for the women who were in jobs at the time of the survey by redefining their recorded work histories up to that point in time. Table 5.7 reports the results of an extreme form of such an experiment where each woman is assumed to have worked continuously in full-time employment with the same employer since ending full-time education. Results are reported by age groups corresponding with those in Table 5.2.

In this experiment the average hourly earnings of the women who were in employment at the time of the survey would rise to £2.18 from the observed average of £1.81. This represents an increase of 20 per cent. Interestingly, women in full-time employment at the time of the survey had average hourly earnings of £1.94 and those in part-time

TABLE 5.7 *Average hourly earnings expected if continuously employed in a full-time job (£ per hour)*

Age	All women in survey	Women in employment at the time of the survey Full-time	Part-time	All in employment
16–17	1.42	1.43	1.46	1.43
18–20	1.52	1.53	1.53	1.53
21–24	1.72	1.78	1.73	1.77
25–29	1.92	2.12	1.88	2.03
30–39	2.06	2.16	2.00	2.07
40–49	2.34	2.45	2.29	2.36
50–59	2.67	2.68	2.70	2.69
All	2.15	2.13	2.23	2.18
N	5318	1629	1277	2906

Note: Each woman assumed to have been continuously employed in a full-time job with the same employer since she left full-time education.

employment only £1.65. The rise to £2.18 would therefore represent a much more marked increase for those in part-time employment than for those in full-time employment. According to the regression analysis in Table 5.5, being in full-time rather than part-time employment results in an increase in average hourly earnings of only 5.5 per cent. The remaining difference must therefore be due to the different work histories and/or educational histories of women in part-time employment when compared with those in full-time employment. To shed more light on this, Table 5.7 divides the results of the experiment into those who were in full-time and those in part-time employment at the time of the survey. Thus, for the full-timers, the hypothetical work history would raise average hourly earnings from the £1.94 reported in Table 5.2 to the £2.13 reported in Table 5.7, an increase of 10 per cent. The comparable increase for part-timers is as much as 35 per cent.

These increases can be placed in perspective by noting the observed percentage difference between the average hourly earnings of men and women as reported from the New Earnings Survey of 1980 in Table 5.2. Full-time male employees are seen to earn an average of £2.77 per hour compared with the £2.03 per hour for full-time female employees and £1.68 per hour for part-time female employees.[15] This represents a male advantage of 36 per cent over full-time female employees and 55 per cent over part-time female employees. Thus, while the hypothetical work history outlined above goes some way to closing this gap (10 percentage points and 35 percentage points respectively for full-time and part-time employees), a large proportion of the gap remains unexplained. If the extreme assumptions of continuous employment in a full-time job with the same employer since leaving full-time education can be taken as removing what Zabalza and Arrufat (1985) have labelled the 'depreciation effect' from women's working lives, then only 28 per cent (full-timers) and 64 per cent (part-timers) of the gap is explained. As reported above, Zabalza and Arrufat (1985) found that as much as two-thirds of the difference in wage rates between males and females could be ascribed to differences in work histories.

The results reported here do not seem to be totally incompatible with the Zabalza and Arrufat (1985) findings,[16] but they do highlight the importance of treating part-time employment in an explicit manner. It is women in part-time employment who are more likely to suffer from the effects of a broken employment history. The results of Table 5.5 emphasise that the level of average hourly earnings owes less to being in full-time (as against part-time) employment at the time of the survey than to having a record of continuous full-time employment. Continuous part-time employment is less advantageous but, according to Table 5.5, still quite effective, suggesting that those in part-time employment are unlikely to have a long continuous employment record. On the face of things, these findings contrast with those of Stewart and Greenhalgh (1984), who attribute a greater importance to current part-time status than a history of part-time working. As mentioned above, however, their analysis is based on less complete work history information and is concerned with weekly earnings, which means that hours of work play an important part.

To illustrate the relationship between continuous full-time employment and hourly earnings, consider a woman of age 40 who, having left school at age 17 with some school-leaving credentials, works for eight years, then has eight further years of non-employment, to be followed by seven years of employment where she is found at age 40.[17] If the first employment phase was full-time and the second part-time (but spent with the same employer) then the expected hourly earnings according to Table 5.5 would be £1.67. If, however, the final employment phase was all in full-time employment, expected hourly earnings would be £1.85. Finally, if the woman had maintained a continuous employment phase, all in full-time employment with the same employer since leaving school, then the expected wage would be £2.21.

Thus, work histories have a clear bearing on average hourly earnings.[18]

One phenomenon which is not addressed here is the decline in earnings potential at older ages, which is evident in Table 5.2. This decline is often claimed to be due to the approach of retirement, shortening the period remaining in the labour market and, hence, the period over which any investment in training can be repaid. One possibility is that the amount of training and updating of skills will decline to such an extent that the market wage declines. It is also possible, however, that the decline is a function of 'vintage' effects whereby younger generations of workers are more productive and hence command relatively higher wages. To address the problem would require the introduction of quadratic terms in labour market experience into the analysis of Table 5.5. To avoid complications, these investigations are left to a later paper.

CONCLUSIONS

The work histories of women do appear to have a strong association with their average hourly earnings. The regression results of Table 5.5 indicate the influence of each aspect of a work history on average hourly earnings. To see the full implications of these results it is necessary to vary the work histories of women in the sample and to observe the predicted effect. This is done in Table 5.7, where each woman is given the strongest labour market attachment imaginable – continuous full-time employment with the same employer since leaving full-time education. These results should then suggest an upper bound on the earnings potential available to women by following a 'male-like' work history.

The procedure indicated that women's hourly earnings would be 20 per cent higher if they followed such a work history. It is among those currently in part-time employment, however, that the increase is most marked. The results suggest that women currently in full-time would enjoy a 10 per cent increase overall in average hourly earnings, but that those in part-time employment would enjoy a 35 per cent increase. Such increases, which it must be repeated are the *maximum* attainable by altering work histories, would go only part way to closing the gap between women's hourly earnings and those of men. Based on the information from the New Earnings Survey for 1980 presented in Table 5.2, to reach the level of hourly earnings of full-time male employees, women's hourly earnings would have to rise 36 per cent and 65 per cent for full-time female employees and part-time employees respectively.

As Table 5.7 sets out the results of making women's working lives look 'more like men's than men's', the unexplained gap must be due to the different levels of educational experience and qualifications which men and women bring to the labour market and the different rates at which experience and education are rewarded. Unfortunately, the absence of male respondents in the Women and Employment Survey is problematic, for unless women can be compared directly with men of equivalent experience and education it is impossible to distinguish the effects of discrimination from the effects of different levels of education and experience brought to the labour market. It is clear that women with degree-level qualifications do relatively well in the labour market (Tables 5.4 and 5.5). If the 40 year-old women in the example introduced in the preceding section had left university at age 21 and worked continuously for nineteen years in full-time employment with the same employer, her expected average hourly earnings would be £3.48. However, the available data do not allow this to be compared with what a man of similar qualifications and experience could be expected to earn.

The main conclusion of this paper must therefore rest on the comparison of women with women. It does seem clear from these results that the low wage rates of part-time female employees are in large part due to the type of work history which such a status implies, rather than the phenomenon of actually being in part-time employment at any point in time. Full-time employment leads to a higher growth of earnings than part-time employment. Employment experience in earlier phases is heavily discounted. On the other hand, only the immediately previous spell of non-employment has any statistically significant depreciation effect on potential earnings.

The policy implications of this paper stem from the finding that there is a limited, albeit non-trivial, potential for women to increase their average hourly earnings by following work histories similar to those of men. If greater equality in male and female earnings is to be achieved, there is ample scope for action through increased training, particularly for training of the type that occurs on-the-job. There also seems to be potential for increasing the skill content of part-time employment. While there may be limits to the extent of skill upgrading possible in existing part-time jobs, it is undoubtedly the case that many more highly skilled jobs could be made available on a part-time basis. The area of part-time employment is dominated by women, but it seems difficult for them to increase their earnings potential through such employment experience within the range of part-time jobs now available.

NOTES

1. Zabalza and Arrufat use the 1975 General Household Survey. Two work history variables are used. The first, 'potential experience', is computed as age minus the age when left school. The second, 'actual experience', is computed as the sum of the probability of participating in the labour force in each year since the person left school. An allowance is made for cohort effects by borrowing results from Joshi and Owen (1981).
2. A technique suggested by Stewart (1983) was used to adjust for the grouping of the earnings data.
3. Joshi (1984) uses months in current job, and months ever worked divided into part-time working and full-time working. Little attention is paid to the way this employment is divided up into spells, save to include the total number of spells of 'non-work'.
4. Average hourly earnings are computed as the 'usual weekly earnings' (gross) in a woman's main job divided by the 'usual hours worked' in that job.
5. The relationship is essentially a reduced form in the sense that other variables which might explain and be explained by wage rates such as occupation or industry are deliberately excluded. In a similar sense personal variables such as age are too closely related to work experience to be useful.
6. Allowance is made for the fact that the minimum school-leaving age varied through time. It changed to 15 in 1945–6 and to 16 in 1972–3.
7. No attempt is made to distinguish involuntary periods of non-employment due to unemployment or illness from voluntary periods of non-employment.
8. The term 'lambda' is equal to (f/F), where F is the value of the standard normal cumulative distribution function that corresponds to the estimated probability that an individual is in employment. The term f is the value of the standard normal density function that corresponds to F. See Heckman (1979) for details.
9. Non-linear methods such as probit are extensively discussed in Maddala (1983).
10. The last column of Table 5.6 actually gives the slope of the expected probability of being in employment evaluated at the mean of the regressors. See Maddala (1983, p. 23) for a full explanation.
11. A comparison of Joshi's own results with the results of others working in this area can be obtained from Joshi (1984, Table 9).
12. Derivation of the lambda term has been discussed in note 8.

13. Not significant being judged at the 95 per cent confidence level and hence a *t*-statistic of 1.96.
14. With a coefficient as large as 0.2881 it is necessary to take anti-logs to interpret the coefficient. This suggests that a degree level credential increases hourly earnings by a factor of 0.33 compared to a woman with no credentials.
15. It should be noted that these reported averages are based on all those over 16, which includes women over 60 who are not included in the Women and Employment Survey.
16. It should be emphasised here that Zabalza and Arrufat (1985) were comparing married women and married men. Results from analysis of the Women and Employment Survey are based on the experience of both married and single women.
17. Main (Chapter 2) found this approximately 8–7–8 year pattern to be the most common at age 40 among the women aged 40–44 in 1980.
18. Nothing has been done to allow for the fact that work histories themselves may reflect earnings potential, although education and credentials have been controlled for and an attempt has been made, through 'lambda', to allow for those in employment being different from those not in employment at the time of the survey.

6 Parental Employment and Family Formation

Shirley Dex and Ed Puttick

INTRODUCTION

The majority of adults in Britain today enter parenthood with a partner. What are the interactions between their economic and domestic responsibilities as parents? This chapter will address this question by collecting together the information that is now available, from published sources and from our own analyses, about the various choices and constraints that couples face over the period of family formation. In particular we are interested in documenting the influences on couples' decisions to have children, their number and spacing, on whether the woman should take maternity leave, on whether the man will share responsibility for the children, on the extent to which parents are engaged in paid work through the period of family formation, and the way decisions to return to work are made by those who give up paid work over childbirth. In all cases changes have been occurring, although it is not always clear to what extent. The information available is far more extensive for women and wives than it is for men or husbands, partly because new data have been collected on women's employment patterns, for example in the Women and Employment Survey.

The focus of other studies of family formation has tended to be either on women's participation in the labour force and its determinants (Joshi, 1984) or on trying to understand women's changing patterns of fertility and birth spacing, without reference to men. This chapter seeks to tackle the issues in two different ways from earlier studies. We take a life-cycle approach by examining the decisions and choices in the order in which they are likely to arise. We will also focus on couples rather than on women, since the vast majority of women with children are married, and decisions about childbearing and childrearing must be assumed in some sense to be joint decisions. In this chapter we examine the changes in the behaviour of both parents as far as data permit. It might be assumed that men's behaviour has changed very little, but we do not wish to prejudge that issue at this stage. Certainly such a view has meant that less data are available about men's behaviour over the family formation period so that one often has no way of knowing the extent to which this assumption is correct.

Ultimately we are interested in drawing policy implications from this review of the changes. Our review will focus on what is known and can be documented about parental choices over family formation. In practice, of course, couples and individuals make choices which are constrained in various ways: for example, by finance or by employment opportunities. In attempting to document the influences on decisions that are made over the family formation period we hope to clarify more of the ways in which couples' choices are constrained at this time.

How couples actually behave only leads us part of the way in trying to determine what they would like to do, and how they would like to see improvements in their lives. We have some details about the preferences people express, although we would not expect people always to be aware of the full range of options that could be made available, when they are not currently available. However, it seems reasonable to argue that the direction of any changes exhibits something about people's preferences. Thus an identification of the constraints people face, plus some general deductions about their preferences as exhibited in their changing behaviour, permit us to draw certain policy implications from our analysis. We will make policy suggestions specifically intended to widen individuals' and couples' range of choices.

Our description of changes that have been occurring in parenting and the allocations of parental responsibility is derived from a variety of sources: demographic sources document the changes in fertility and birth spacing for women; surveys of labour force behaviour for men and women document the patterns of economic activity and childbearing (e.g. the 1980 Women and Employment Survey and the Labour Force Survey); additional information on parental leave-taking comes from specific smaller scale surveys. This mixture of published sources combined with some new analysis of the Labour Force Survey is used to document what is known about decisions in a life-cycle framework. The sections of this paper consider the particular decisions as they arise for couples who first approach and then pass through the period of family formation.

THE AGE OF FIRST CHILDBEARING

The first decision a couple make about their family formation is when to have their first child. This decision, in the vast majority of cases, follows a period of full-time work for the woman (and the man), and the woman's pregnancy with the first child acts as a boundary to her initial phase of full-time work (Hunt, 1968; Martin and Roberts, 1984a). Over time we have seen a raising of the school-leaving age as well as a voluntary increase in staying on at school. This means that the length of time spent working before the first childbirth may have decreased, since this duration will depend upon both the school-leaving age and the age of the woman at the first childbirth. Dex (1984a) demonstrated that the trend was for women's duration of working before childbirth to have decreased over the post-Second World War period, even after school-leaving age was taken into account. Also, the duration of this initial working spell was related to completed family size after controlling for age; the longer the duration of working prior to childbirth, the smaller the family size (Dex, 1984a).[1]

Werner (1983) documents the recent trends in women's ages at first childbirth from 1938 to 1982. The average age of women on having their first legitimate birth declined markedly between 1938 and 1969. The average age at first birth within marriage fell from 26.4 years in 1938 to a minimum of 23.9 years in 1969, but by 1981 it had risen again to 25.3 years. Werner points out that the trend seems to be continuing upwards. A study of a cohort born in 1946 found that, by the age of 32 years, 84 per cent of women and 74 per cent of the men were parents. Women had their first child at an earlier age than men, and the median age of women at their first birth was 23.0 years, whereas for the men the equivalent age was 25.9 years (Kiernan and Diamond, 1983). The longitudinal study pointed out that the results for women in this 1946 cohort matched those of other studies of women born in the 1930s and 1940s in that there was a peaking and concentration of first births when women were in their early twenties.

The most recent figures on fertility (OPCS, 1985) confirm that these trends are persisting. Fertility distributions for men have rarely been computed, although Kiernan and Diamond (1983) note that the age distribution of men at their first childbirth is more dispersed than it is for women; after the peak for men at the age of 25 there was a rapid decline after age 28. We are unable to say whether the changes visible in women's ages of childbearing are closely matched by their husbands' ages – given a gap for the husband's older average age.

Some suggestions have been offered about why women's age of childbearing has increased since 1969. Werner (1983) points out some other concomitant demographic changes. From the 1930s to the 1960s marriages were tending to be earlier and, at the same time, the age of the women at their first childbirth was falling. Now the picture is being reversed, and there has been a rise in the mean age of women at their first marriage. The growth in the number of women who are divorced from their first husband without having children but who remarry and have children by their second husband, helps to raise the age of women at first childbirth. Werner also suggests that there is a tendency for newly married women to delay starting a family in order to remain in employment for a longer period, but here his supposition must be speculative, although not necessarily incorrect.

What determines the age at which parents decide to have children? Several studies cast some light on this decision, although they do not focus on why ages have changed over time. In addition to the age at which couples marry, family of origin, education and social class were found to be important determinants of parents' ages at childbirth (Kiernan and Diamond, 1983). In particular, the age at which the parent's mother got married influenced men's and women's ages at their first childbirth. Men and women whose parents had married at younger ages were more likely themselves to have become parents earlier. The age at which men's mothers left school was influential in the men's ages at the birth of their first child, but the same effect was not visible for the women; the earlier the mother of the man left school, the earlier the man had children. The size of the family of origin and the social class of the origin family did not influence the ages at first birth of the parents after the parents' own education was taken into consideration. The type of school attended and the level of interest shown by their parents in their secondary education was important for women. The study by Kiernan and Diamond found that a woman started her childbearing at an older age when her parents had been interested in her education.

The education of both parents influenced the age at which they had their first child: the higher the education, the later the first childbirth, and this was found to be the single most influential predictor of the age of childbearing. To some extent we might expect this result because of the institutional arrangements involved: if a person takes a degree, for example, they are likely to be 21 at least before they start to consider childbirth. Additionally, an important economic mechanism is at work here for women because the higher the woman's education, the higher her potential earnings and the less likely she is to want to stop work. Studies of women's participation in the labour market have confirmed that this mechanism operates to keep higher-earning women in the labour market more than lower-earning women (Joshi, 1984). It is not surprising, therefore, that we see the economic mechanism reflected in delaying childbirth. In addition, for men, Kiernan and Diamond found that their level of ambition in adolescence had a direct bearing on their age at the birth of their first child: higher ambition delayed the first childbirth. Lastly, the social class of the last or current full-time occupation (at age 26) influenced the age at first birth of both sexes; the higher the social class, the older the parent when the first child is born. Werner (1984) confirmed this relationship between social class and the mother's age at first birth.

A study of the duration of the period of women's paid work prior to their first childbirth by Dex (1984a) provides some additional insights into the timing of the first childbirth for women. If women stayed in their first job longer, they tended to have a delayed first childbirth, whereas if they took maternity leave, other things being equal, they had an earlier first childbirth. All of these results could be argued to be supporting the economic incentive effect found in Kiernan and Diamond. They also suggest that women who are more attached to work delay their childbearing.

In summary these results show that there is some transmission of norms between generations as far as reproductive behaviour is concerned. There is also an important economic mechanism at work, however, and it influences both parents. In the case of men it looks as if having young children may hinder a man's career advancement in its early stages (Kiernan and Diamond, 1983). The economic effects of earnings foregone from childbirth are highly influential on women's decision to have their first child; but these effects can be mediated to some extent by taking maternity leave.

As couples approach parenthood, several decisions need to be made: whether the woman should take maternity leave; whether the man should take any time off work; whether the woman should give up her paid work for a period to have all the children the couple intend ever to have. These decisions are not necessarily made all at once, or all at the beginning of the family formation period. In fact, we know very little about the timing or order in which decisions of this sort are made, or changed. This lack of information means that the consideration of these choices in the following sections of this chapter will not necessarily be in the order in which most people make them. The decisions about whether to take maternity leave or parental leave are considered first; the spacing of births and women's patterns of working and childrearing over the period are considered subsequently.

MATERNITY LEAVE

Maternity leave became a statutory right for women only in 1977, although employers were given notice in 1975 that this would come into force. Some private maternity schemes were available long before then. We might expect that the statutory provisions would have increased women's take-up of maternity leave in the later 1970s, although we suspect that it may be too early to see the full effects of these changes. We have already noted that the 'take-up' of maternity leave recorded for women in the Women and Employment Survey (WES) was associated with a younger age of family formation on average, other things being equal. Of the childless women in the WES who expected to have children in the future, 27 per cent stated that they would continue working following a period of maternity leave after the birth of a child. Martin and Roberts (1984a) also noted that 14 per cent of all women with children returned within six months of their first childbirth. Other work has shown that taking maternity leave is associated with shorter periods out of paid work, by approximately three years on average (Dex, 1984a). We can consider two further issues in this section: what determines whether women take maternity leave, and is there any evidence that maternity leave take-up has increased as a result of the legislation?

We might expect the decision to take maternity leave to be related to the woman's occupation, especially if we are considering the period prior to the legislation. Since the legislation stipulates an eligibility requirement in terms of the length of time in a job, we might expect that maternity leave take-up would also be related to job tenure. Dex and Shaw (1986) examined these issues using two age cohorts from the Women and Employment Survey. Of the younger group (aged 26–36 in 1980), 6.2 per cent took maternity leave at their first childbirth and 4.3 per cent of the older cohort (aged 44–58 in 1980) took maternity leave. This is not a very large difference in the proportion taking maternity leave over time, but it is likely that the full effects of the statutory provisions are not reflected in these younger women's experiences, given that they were interviewed in 1980, only three years after their introduction. Rowland (1981) confirms that only a small proportion of eligible women actually took maternity leave. Daniel (1981) found that 46 per cent of women did not qualify.

There are some occupational differences, however, between women who take and those who do not take maternity leave, as the percentages in Table 6.1 from Dex and Shaw (1986) illustrate. The effect of occupation can be seen in both younger and older cohorts. Women

TABLE 6.1 *Comparison of occupations before childbirth of British women who did or did not take maternity leave for first childbirth (%)*

	Younger women (aged 26–36)		*Older women (aged 44–58)*	
Occupation group of last job before first batch	*Women who took maternity leave for first birth*	*Did not take maternity leave (but had children)*	*Women who took maternity leave for first birth*	*Did not take maternity leave (but had children)*
Professional	—	1	2	—
Teacher	14	5	7	3
Nurse	7	7	2	4
Intermediate non-manual	7	3	7	1
Clerical	36	37	15	30
Sales	7	13	8	12
Skilled	14	8	20	8
Child care	—	1	—	1
Semi-skilled factory	8	20	17	27
Semi-skilled domestic	6	2	5	5
Other semi-skilled	3	3	17	6
Unskilled	—	1	2	2
Base (= 100%)	73	1100	60	1382

Source: Women and Employment Survey 1980

who took maternity leave were far more likely to be teachers or skilled workers and far less likely to be in semi-skilled factory work or sales. These results highlight the unevenness of maternity leave provisions between occupations and, in particular, the low level of take-up in semi-skilled factory work. Daniel (1980, pp. 104–5) has similar findings. Rowland (1981) confirmed that the take-up of maternity leave was related to a woman's occupation: 68 per cent of women who returned to work after maternity leave were at or above the intermediate non-manual level, compared with only 18 per cent of non-returners. This finding has serious implications, given that at least two-fifths of working women are currently employed in manual work.

Dex and Shaw's (1986) analysis of the relationship between maternity leave and job tenure revealed that older women who had taken maternity leave (prior to the legislation) had been in their first jobs longer than those who did not take maternity leave, but only by seven months on average. The job tenure before childbirth of younger women who took maternity leave was hardly different from younger women who did not take the leave. These findings confirm that there is a sizeable group of women who were eligible to take maternity leave but who did not do so. Presumably this group do not choose to return to work after childbirth to fulfil the conditions required by the leave. They are making this decision in the context of a number of constraints and preferences relating to child care: the availability of part-time work, the economic consequences of not returning to work soon after childbirth, and the extent to which men are prepared to share child-care and other domestic responsibilities.

On the issue of whether the legislation has made significant differences to women's take up of maternity leave, the WES data of 1980 provide some relevant information. Table 6.2 displays, for a selection of age cohorts, the proportions taking maternity leave and the proportion of maternity leaves as a proportion of births over the 1970s decade. This analysis is not restricted to first births only. For younger cohorts the whole set of yearly data points is not available.[2]

There are sizeable fluctuations in the proportions taking maternity leave in each year through the 1970s, as there are in the proportion of maternity leaves as a percentage of all births in that year. The information in Table 6.2 is not easy to interpret. The different age cohorts will be at different stages of their life-cycle when the legislation occurred. We might expect to see smaller effects, from the introduction of the statutory provisions, on women who are towards the end of their childbearing years than those who are towards the

TABLE 6.2 *Take-up of maternity leave for different age cohorts, 1970–9 (%)*

Year	*Age of cohort in 1980* 20–24		25–29		30–34		35–39	
	Ml[1]	*ML/B*[2]	*ML*[1]	*ML/B*[2]	*ML*[1]	*ML/B*[2]	*ML*[1]	*ML/B*[2]
1970					0.5	4.0	1.1	7.7
1971			0.3	3.5	0.9	5.2	1.2	9.0
1972			0.1	1.4	0.4	2.7	0.6	4.8
1973			0.0	0.0	1.0	6.6	0.2	2.2
1974			0.3	0.3	1.0	7.4	0.0	0.0
1975			1.2	8.5	1.2	7.6	0.3	4.4
1976	0.0	0.0	0.7	5.4	1.4	13.3	0.2	3.1
1977	0.3	5.4	0.9	6.7	1.6	14.8	0.3	7.4
1978	0.3	2.8	0.9	5.9	0.8	8.3	0.0	5.9
1979	0.7	5.6	1.2	8.6	1.2	11.8	0.5	15.0

Notes: [1] *ML* = percentage of cohort taking maternity leave during the year.
[2] *ML/B* = percentage of those women with a birth during the year taking maternity leave.
Source: Women and Employment Survey.

beginning. In the case of the younger cohorts the birth is likely to relate to the first childbirth, whereas in the older cohorts it is highly unlikely to be the first childbirth that is being recorded. Whether women are equally likely to take maternity leave for their last child as they are for their first, when they may not have had the option of maternity leave for their older children, is difficult to discern. Certainly we have no information on this issue, although the results suggest that these events are not equally likely. In addition, the picture may be complicated by social class or other effects: for example, women in higher social class groups delay childbirth, and if they were more likely to take maternity leave we would see an increase in take-up over time not because of the legislation, but possibly coincident with it. Women in higher social class groups also have smaller families (Werner, 1984). Given this set of complications, our conclusion must be tentative.

The information obtained from the Women and Employment Survey suggests that the experience of maternity leave has been on the increase. In the 30–34 age group, a very large increase, from 7.6 per cent of births being accompanied by maternity leave to 13.3 per cent, took place in 1976, coincidental with the announcement of the legislation, although it is not consistently high in all years thereafter; in 1978 the proportion dropped to 8.3 per cent. There is a similar increase in the 35–39 age group, but it was much smaller and occurred between 1976 and 1977. In this latter 35–39 age group, large proportions of maternity leaves of all births are also visible in 1970 and 1971 when the group were closer to their peak childbearing age.

Whilst our conclusions must be tentative, there is some evidence from the Women and Employment Survey that maternity leave has increased since the statutory provisions were announced. Given that the take-up fluctuated, however, there are clearly other factors which have influenced women's decisions to take maternity leave. A woman's occupation is one of these factors; the other possible influences are at present unclear.

PATERNITY LEAVE

Paternity leave is beginning to receive more attention and discussion on unions' collective bargaining agendas. Traditionally, childbirth and family policies have been viewed as women's issues. Women and children have been seen as needing protection, sometimes to supplement, at other times to substitute for, the economic breadwinning support of the husband. Discussions about paternity leave are a recognition that both parental roles need to be considered as part of family policies. There is evidence that men are more fully involved in the family than used to be the case, that they no longer see their role only as breadwinner but also see themselves as fathers with domestic responsibilities within the family. Some of this evidence comes from the fact that increasing numbers of men are now attending childbirth, supporting their wives in the immediate post-natal period, and are helping with childrearing and child-care (Cleary and Shepperdson, 1981; McKee, 1980, 1982; McKee and O'Brien, 1982).

At present in Britain there are thought to be relatively few paternity leave schemes, although no census or comprehensive survey of such provisions exists. A survey by Incomes Data Services (1980) did inquire about paternity leave. Certainly paternity leave is not a statutory right. We do, however, know something about the father's paternity leave-taking in practice from a recent survey on this topic (Bell, McKee and Priestley, 1983). In addition this survey asked fathers about their preferences concerning paternity leave.

Perhaps the most surprising finding of the Bell *et al.* study is that, contrary to the undomesticated stereotype of men, they found 'a strong cultural commitment to the idea of men being at home for at least a short time, around the time of childbirth, and especially when the mother and child came home from hospital' (p. 6). Large numbers of men take time off work during their wives' childbirth, even though, in many cases, their employers do not sanction it. Holiday entitlement was used up by some men in order to be at home at this time, while others resorted to unofficial and informal leave-taking practices. Manual workers in particular were liable to lose pay.

Men could be differentiated mostly, not on the basis of whether they wanted time off paid work, but according to how they achieved time off and how much time off they took. Bell *et al.* suggest that the factors that determined time off for men were the hours and pattern of work of the men, and further details of the man's work situation (e.g. ability to leave work without permission, relationship with supervisor, volume of work, cover arrangements, etc.) The man's occupational category did not sufficiently reflect these distinctions and was therefore not a good proxy of a man's time off paid work at the time of childbirth.

In view of the commitment to taking time off and the *ad hoc* arrangements which exist to facilitate this behaviour for fathers, it is not surprising that 91 per cent of all fathers expressed a desire to see a statutory paternity leave scheme introduced; 73 per cent wanted a period of leave of 1–2 weeks. The sample was divided between those who wanted a block period of leave and those who wanted flexible arrangements. We conclude, along with Bell *et al.*, that the present paternity leave arrangements severely constrain men's participation in childbirth and childrearing and that, given the stated preference of husbands to participate in these events to a greater extent, choices at present are severely restricted, for both men and women.

BIRTH SPACING AND WOMEN'S PAID EMPLOYMENT

The majority of couples have more than one child, so that after the birth of the first child decisions arise about whether to have more children and, if so, when. Women also make a decision about whether to return to paid work between their childbirths. Of course, if they previously decided to take maternity leave at their first childbirth, unless they change their minds about post-natal employment, which some women obviously do, these women are committing themselves to work between childbirths. The cross-sectional (and often aggregate level) studies of women's participation in the labour market over family formation have left a number of unresolved issues concerning the changes that have been occurring.

The cross-sectional picture is consistent with several possible changes: the increased employment of women with children may be associated with delays in second and subsequent childbirths which facilitate intervening periods of work. Alternatively, women could have had their childbirths closer together than in the past, thus permitting them to return sooner after completing their childbirths. Of course, it may be the case that both these changes have occurred to different groups of women. The information displayed in Chapter 2 in this volume shows that a number of these changes have been occurring simultaneously.

Britton (1979) and Ni Bhrolchain (1983) have both shown that birth spacing has altered. The median interval between first and second births has fallen steadily for women with two or three children since the beginning of the century, although more recently it may have been increasing again. Britton and Ni Bhrolchain differ on the timing of the turning point of this series. There is further dispute about what has been happening to the intervals between second and third, and third and fourth births. The best we can say about these intervals is that they seemed to decline before the 1950s, and they may now be more stable. Britton adds that these changes have contributed to a gradual shortening, for any given completed family size, of the interval between marriage and the last childbirth. The problem with all of these results is that one is never quite sure, except when viewed from a considerable distance, whether childbirths are complete. The intervals between successive births for economically active women have been generally shorter than those of non-economically active women (Ni Bhrolchain, 1983). In some cases, the difference in size is quite large.

The Women and Employment Survey provided more detailed information about women's work history activity over the period of family formation. The types of working and not working patterns of different generations, and their durations, are documented in Dex (1984a). The results suffer from the fact that the family formation period of many women was incomplete. Dex (1984a) compared actual patterns of family formation with those which women said they intended to have, in an attempt to give at least an impression of the final frequencies of patterns. Not surprisingly, a mixture of patterns of combining childbirth and economic activity were visible in all age groups, although changes appeared to have been occurring over time.

The dominant family formation pattern among older women was clearly to have a single break from paid work in which they had all their childbirths. In the 40–49 age group, approximately 46 per cent of women with children had this pattern. Younger women also had this sequence pattern but not to the same extent. In the 20–29 age group, 36 per cent of women with children had had or intended to have this pattern, although this frequency was most likely to be an over-estimate.[3] The duration of time spent out of work had also fallen for the younger women. Younger women seemed to be turning increasingly to a pattern of working between childbirths; this had been a minority experience for the older women. Of the 40–49 age group, 15 per cent worked after every birth, whereas 30 per cent of the 20–29 year group had or intended to have this experience (Dex, 1984a). The durations of time out of work in this pattern had also fallen in the younger age group. An analysis of the determinants of the sequence patterns of women over family formation suggested that perceived financial hardship was encouraging women to work between births. The deaths of children and break-ups of marriage, plus the decision to take maternity leave, also contributed to the choice of a 'working between births' pattern. Family size was of little importance (Dex, 1984a).

Whilst the evidence is incomplete, it would appear that a complicated mixture of changes in women's birth spacing and employment patterns has been taking place. More women now work between childbirths, and there is no evidence that the intervals between births have increased to facilitate such activity. Women who have a single period of fertility have been reducing their time out of paid work by returning to work sooner, although nearly all women have experienced a decline in their period of unpaid work over childbirth, irrespective of the type of pattern of working and childbirth they have chosen.

WOMEN'S RETURN TO WORK

Unless women take maternity leave they may face the choice, at some stage after childbirth, of whether or not to return to work. Martin and Roberts (1984a) found that 78 per cent of women with children had returned to work at some time since their first birth. A much higher proportion (90 per cent) were likely to return at some point, the difference consisting of women with very young children who had not made their first return to work by the WES interview in 1980. When this proportion is examined by cohort it was found to be increasing: of women whose first birth had occurred in 1940–4, 87 per cent had made a return, whereas 95 per cent of women whose first birth had been in 1960–4 and whose children were all 16 or over had returned to paid work at some stage. A life table technique demonstrated that there was a rise in the proportion of women with first births in successive five-year periods who had made an initial return to work by any given interval. Of the women whose first birth was in 1950–54, half had made an initial return by 9.7 years after their first birth, whereas for women with first births in 1975–8, half had returned within 3.7 years. Main also displays similar trends in Chapter 2.

A multiple regression analysis of the timing of women's first return to work on the sample of those who had returned found that the timing was influenced by women's past working experience, their past job mobility, their opportunity cost of not working (as measured by occupation and education), family finances, and labour market conditions (Dex, 1984a). Women were more likely to bring forward their return to work if they had more previous working experience and a large number of jobs prior to childbirth, if their opportunity cost of not working was higher, if their family finances were lower, and if unemployment was lower when they were looking for work.

For women who worked between their childbirths, their first spell of working after returning to work fluctuated slightly over the generations, but not in a systematic way (Dex, 1984a, Table 26). For example, women who were 50–59 in 1980 who had returned to work between childbirths spent an average of approximately six years working after their first return to work, the same average as the 20–29 year-olds; the 30–39 and 40–49 year-olds spent between three and four years on average working at this time. Of the women who had returned to work twice, their second period or working after a second spell out of paid work because of childbirth had progressively declined from just over four years in the 50–59 year group to two years in the 20–29 year group. The intervening periods of not working all showed a similar decline over time, as we noted earlier. It is possible that this picture may change in some respects when the rest of the younger age groups have completed their experiences of family formation. In this respect, it is instructive to examine the cross-sectional picture, since it can provide another perspective on the final outcomes. The Labour Force Survey provides such a picture for both husbands and wives in 1981, after some data rearrangements.[4]

The employment rates of couples where the wife is between the ages of 25 and 34, the peak fertility years for women, were examined by the age of their youngest child and their family size. For purposes of comparison, the employment rate of couples with no children is also provided as a baseline. Figure 6.1 displays these rates using histograms. We note first that there is only a small gap between the employment rates of husbands and wives of this age who have no children: 93 per cent of husbands were in paid employment in 1980, compared with 82 per cent of wives.

Women's employment rates fall drastically when they have children to around 17 to 27 per cent in the first three years after childbirth, and then gradually increase to 75 to 80 per cent when the child of a one-child family is aged 11–15. The proportion of women unemployed also varies with the age of the child, with the largest percentage being when the youngest child is under one year old. Men's economic activity rates exhibit little variation with the age of the youngest child. They fluctuate mostly between 96 and 98 per cent. Husbands with children were unemployed in around 5–6 per cent of these households, which is slightly higher than that of childless men of this age.

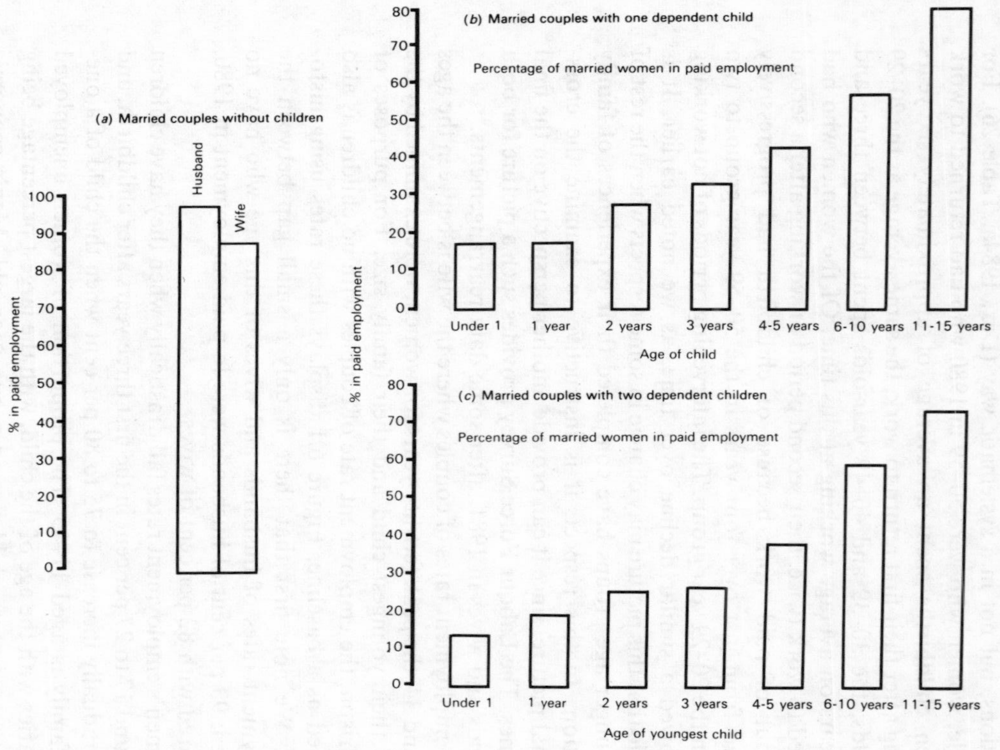

FIGURE 6.1 *Percentage of men and women in paid employment, for married couples without children and, for married women aged 25–34 years, by number of dependent children and age of youngest dependent child*

The employment rates of men in the two-child families were high for all groups, and similar therefore to the one-child groups. Although not displayed in this figure, unemployment rates were also parallel. Women's employment rates differed, however, according to whether they had one or two children, after controlling for the age of the youngest child. The two-child families are displayed in part (c) of Figure 6.1. The employment rates for women with two children are are generally lower than those for women with only one child.

An increase in employment rates occurs for women with two children, similar to that for women with one child, as the younger child's age increases. Also, as the younger child gets older the gap between the one- and two-child families narrows. For example, in the one-child family where the child is 3 years old, the activity rate of the women was 32 per cent, whereas in the two-child family with the younger child of the same age, the parallel activity rate was 26 per cent. When the child was 6–10 years old, women with one child had an activity rate of 56 per cent, whereas for women with two children the rate was 59 per cent. Although not shown on this figure, an examination of women's unemployment rates showed that the percentages of women with two children who were unemployed were slightly lower than for those with one child, irrespective of the age of the youngest child. The women with one child may be slightly more likely to be unemployed, possibly because they are slightly younger on average than women with two children, although it is likely that having two children is a greater constraint than one child on a woman making herself available for work.

We examined families with three and four children, although the results are not displayed here. Women's participation rate continued to fall as family size increased for each youngest child age category. The only different result worthy of comment was that men with four or more children had far higher unemployment rates than men with smaller families. We presume that this finding reflects a relationship between family size and social class level of the husbands, with large families being more likely among the unskilled, who are also more likely to be unemployed. For this group the 'poverty trap' relationship between low-paid jobs, unstable employment and the tax and social security benefit regimes is likely to complicate the picture substantially.

The general results overlap with those found in other data and other analyses (Joshi, 1984): that childbearing and family size do affect women's activity rates. This information from the Labour

Force Survey suggests that husband's activity rates are relatively uninfluenced by family size and the age of the youngest child. This conclusion runs slightly contrary to a regression analysis of men's activity rates by Greenhalgh (1979), which found that the presence and age of children did influence men's participation; in fact children aged 0–4 increased men's participation rates. The difference may be a result of differences in the samples, since we have been considering here husbands of couples only, rather than a sample of all men. It would be useful to have the Greenhalgh finding confirmed using micro rather than aggregate date.[5]

We need to ask why women's participation rates fall with the increase in family size, after controlling for the age of the youngest child. Unfortunately we can only speculate on this matter. Possibly the number of children does make it more difficult for women to organise work and child-care. Certainly the costs of child-care would usually increase as the numbers of children increased, whereas women's earnings from working would stay constant. It may also be the case that women are more often ineligible to take maternity leave to have their second or third child, especially if they took maternity leave for their first child but went over to part-time work after fulfilling the minimum return requirements. All of these factors could play a role in explaining women's lower activity rates.

WEEKLY HOURS OF WORK FOR RETURNERS

Women who return to work after childbirth often return to part-time jobs. The Women and Employment Survey showed that approximately two-thirds of women's first return jobs were part-time, that is, thirty hours or less per week. Thereafter women hold a variety of jobs, some continuing in part-time work, some moving into full-time jobs, and others moving between these statuses on more than one occasion (see Chapter 2). The same variety of patterns is also possible after a full-time first return to work (Dex, 1984a). Less is known about men's hours of work when they have children, although some have argued that the presence of young children increases men's hours of work (for example, Moss, 1980). The Labour Force Survey data permit a detailed examination of the hours of work of both husbands and wives. We can again control for family size and the age of the youngest child. A selection of the histogram distributions of the women's hours of work are set out in Figures 6.2 and 6.3. The men's

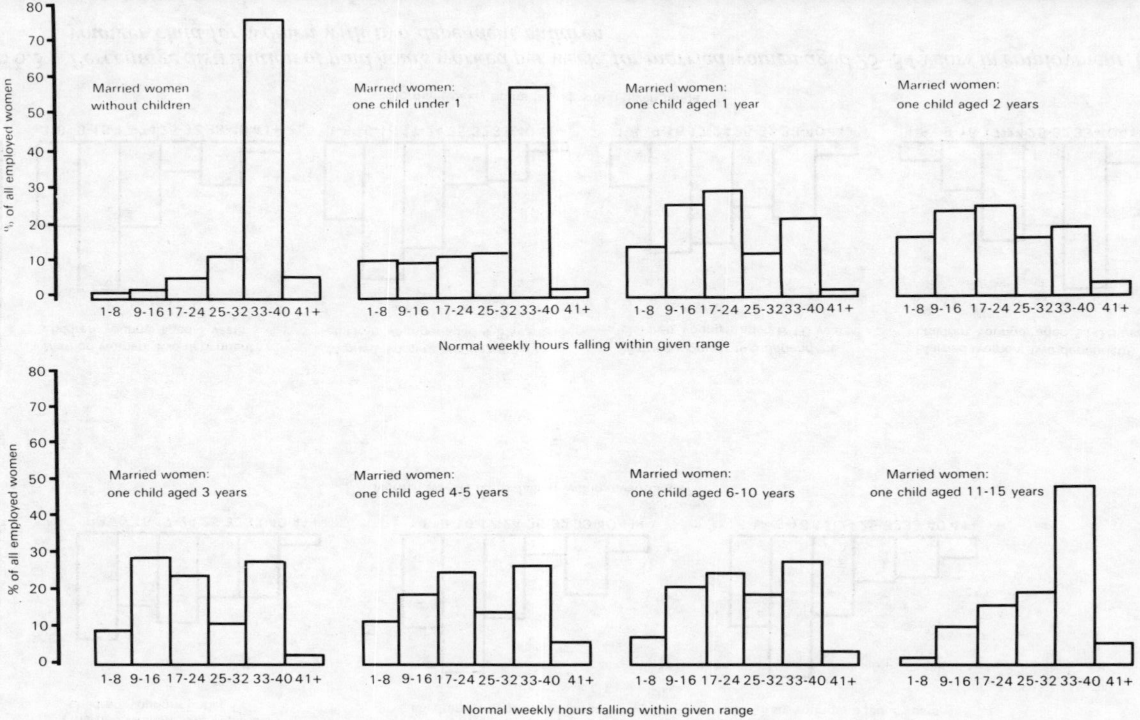

FIGURE 6.2 *Percentage distribution of paid hours worked per week, for married women aged 25–34 years in employment and by age of child for women with one dependent child*

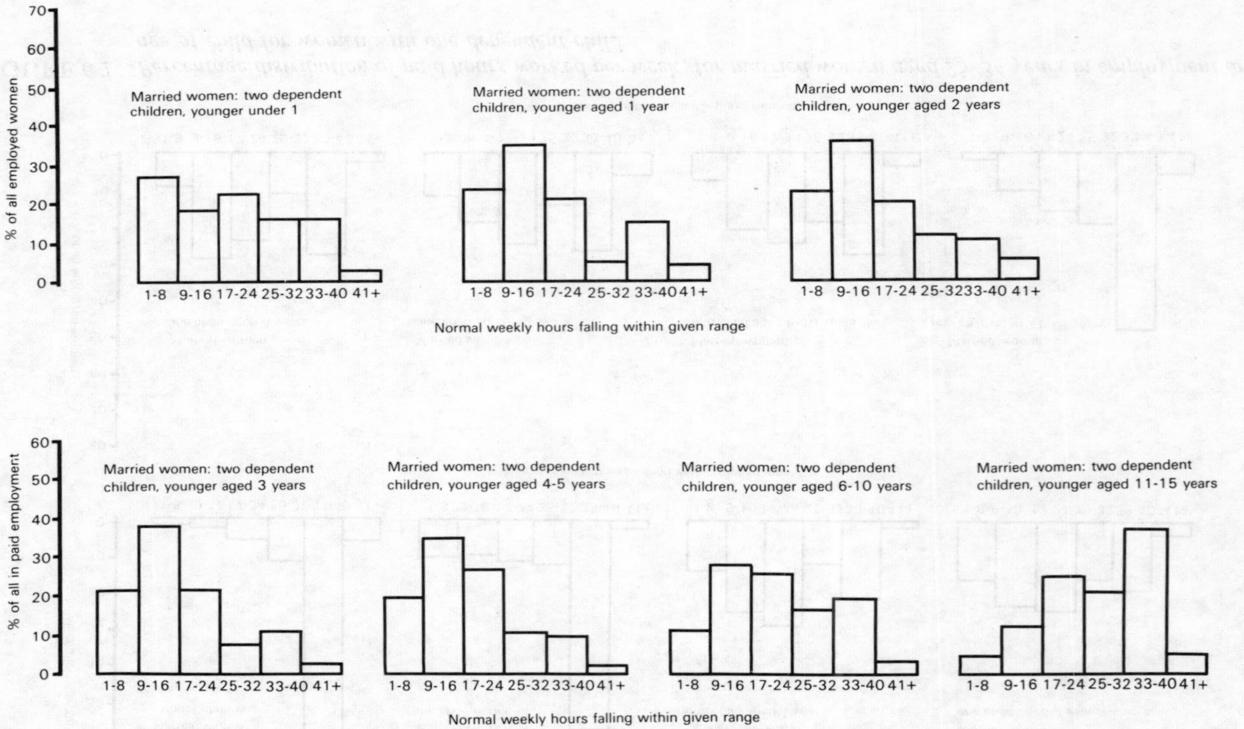

FIGURE 6.3 *Percentage distribution of paid hours worked per week, for married women aged 25–34 years in employment, by age of younger child for women with two dependent children*

hours distributions were also examined and are described in the text, although they are not displayed in the figures.

The distributions for husbands and wives who are without children have the similarity that the modal category is the same in both cases, 33–40 hours per week. Very few women work more than 40 hours, although nearly 30 per cent of men were found in these higher hours categories. The presence of children clearly has marked effects on women's distributions of hours of work in the way we would expect: the frequencies of women employed in the part-time hours categories all increase. There are variations according to the age of the youngest child and the family size, however. In the one-child families, wives with a youngest child of less than one year have a notably different distribution from other women with either older children or more children; a large proportion (56 per cent) of this group whose youngest child is less than one year are working between 33–40 hours. By the time the child is one year old the proportion in this full-time hours group has fallen to 21 per cent and the modal category is 17–24 hours per week. From then on the pattern of the distribution changes predictably, with the proportions in the lower part-time categories, especially 1–8 hours, gradually declining, and the proportion in the 33–40 hour category increasing, although not by very large amounts. The most obvious explanation of this anomalous frequency when children are under one year old is that many of the women who take maternity leave return to full-time work to fulfil the requirements of their leave but then switch to part-time work, possibly because they find it more difficult than they had imagined to care for a young baby and work full-time. This finding has not been evident in other studies, probably because they have not examined such small age bands.[6] The fact that the same effect is not visible in the hours distributions for women with two children may suggest that one consequence of taking a part-time job after the first childbirth is that women are no longer eligible for maternity leave for subsequent childbirths. Also, the child-care costs are likely to increase as family size increases, although women's earnings from working stay the same.

Women with two children are far more often located at the lowest end of the hours distribution. Whilst the youngest child is under one year old the modal hours category for women is the 1–8 hour group, but this changes to the 9–16 hour category when the youngest child is between the ages of 1 and 5 years. A peak in women's hours distributions, just under 16 hours, has been noted by other studies (Martin and Roberts, 1984a). The point has been made that 16 hours per week is currently a threshold for the employment protection legislation. Women who work less than 16 hours do not have the same levels of employment protection as those who work more hours, nor are they likely to have the same access to employer-provided fringe benefits. Husbands' hours of work fluctuate far less than their wives' hours; approximately 65 per cent work between 33 and 40 hours in all the family size and age of youngest child samples. There is some variation among the other 33 per cent of husbands such that the hours worked appears to increase as the age of the youngest child increases. In the case of the one-child family approximately 14 per cent of husbands work 49 hours or more when the child is under one year old. This percentage stays the same when the child is between the ages of 1 and 3 years. When the child is 4–5 years, 21 per cent of men work 49 hours or more, although the percentage falls back again when the child is aged 6–10 years. In the case of the two-child families, the proportions of men working very long hours is slightly higher, in every band for the age of the younger child, than it was for one-child families. When one examines women's and men's hours together, as children get older, women's hours of work were increasing and men's hours were decreasing. A redistribution of hours of work over the family formation period appears to take place, therefore. We suspect, however, that household income is maintained or possibly grows concomitant with the redistribution.

A separate analysis was carried out, for all these relationships, on the samples of wives who had working husbands and the husbands who had working wives. There were hardly any differences between the hours distributions of these sub-samples and the whole samples of wives and husbands respectively. This finding suggests that, for those who are working, women's working hours behaviour is not influenced by the husband's participation in the workforce to any great extent, nor are the husband's hours influenced by the woman's labour force participation. However, husbands and wives may well influence each others' participation in the labour force; for example, women with unemployed husbands may be less likely to be employed than those with employed husbands. It could still be the case, however, that wives and husbands affect each other's hours of working. We have not been able to examine this issue, although some women in the Women and Employment Survey did indicate that their own working hours were constrained by their husbands' hours.

Over the period of family formation, women's and men's hours of work changed, although women's hours changed to a far greater extent than those of men. Women took part-time jobs on returning to work after childbirth, but many increased their hours as their children grew older. The changes in women's and men's hours of work over this stage in the life-cycle confirm that women are still taking major responsibility for child-care but that as children get older, a small amount of redistribution in the hours of work may be taking place between parents, possibly alongside a redistribution of child-care responsibilities.

CHILD-CARE

Husbands' and wives' hours distributions together confirm that the overall child-care responsibility falls primarily on women and that part-time work is a way in which women in Britain manage to combine child-care with a measure of economic activity. This choice of the part-time work option has the consequence that many mothers' occupational status tends to be diminished, as the chapters by Elias and Dex and Shaw demonstrate. Couples face constraints on their working behaviour, therefore, when they become parents.

Traditionally women have been assumed to be responsible for child-care. Now that more women work, their working hours have to be fitted around the child-care provision which is available and affordable. There is no evidence that husbands have reduced their working hours to facilitate women going to work. It is certainly the case that most of the jobs that men do and most of the higher-paid, secure 'career' jobs are currently defined by employers as full-time, where hours reductions are not considered to be an option. The study of paternity leave demonstrated that there are some men who would like to spend more time in child-care than they do at present, especially in relation to the birth.

Husbands are involved in child-care currently, however. Martin and Roberts (1984a) found that 50 per cent of women who work part-time with pre-school children relied on their husbands for child-care; 57 per cent of all working women and 63 per cent of part-time workers, both with school-aged children, also relied on husbands for child-care. Presumably the husband's child-care is fitted in around his normal weekly hours. Martin and Roberts (Table 4.11) also show that women's hours of work and time of day of working are clearly linked to the child-care arrangements they make. Among women working part-time, those who worked mornings or in the middle of the day were least likely to need to make arrangements for school children; 80 per cent of women with evening jobs had to make arrangements for child-care, and in 90 per cent of these cases the husband provided the care. It would seem to be the case that for many women, work is fitted in around child-care and the availability of the husband to care for the children.

CHOICES AND CONSTRAINTS

The focus of our discussion so far has been mostly on the actual patterns of behaviour which couples can be seen to have. As we stated at the outset, we are also interested in the preferences people might have but are not able to attain, with respect to working and parental responsibilities. Identifying constraints which people face is one step towards finding out more about their preferences. A number of constraints have been identified in our analysis and we can summarise these here.

Women are going out to work more and spending less time economically inactive over the period of family formation, partly for financial reasons. Many women give their main reason for working as wanting money to buy necessities, and they frequently give this as a reason for choices made in the past to go out to work. Women also appear more likely to prefer to be employed outside the home nowadays. Many are constrained by the need for alternative child-care if they want to work. Given the inadequate provision of pre-school care, discussed below and in Chapter 9, the most common solution is to fit a part-time job around child-care and the husband's availability to provide child-care while the wife is at work. Taking a part-time job means downward occupational mobility for many women and low pay; we presume that this is not part of an ideal solution for these women but one they accept given the constraints they face. Joshi (1985b) has estimated that the costs to a mother of taking responsibility for children are high: at least six to seven years of labour force membership and about twice as many years' worth of average earnings. This is not counting the effects of any downward occupational mobility which often comes from taking part-time jobs. The option of part-time work is a particularly British solution to reconciling women's economic activity and parental responsibility. In the USA relatively higher earnings and possibly the tax credits for child-care expenses contribute to American women choosing to return to work full-time after childbirth and paying for child-care, as Dex and Shaw in this volume document. It might well be the case that British women would prefer this option as an alternative to low-paid part-time jobs, if the help with child-care expenses or higher earnings for women were available in Britain. Joshi (1985b) suggests the best policy would be for employers to be given tax incentives to provide child-care facilities.

At present, 11 per cent of women who work part-time say that they would prefer to work more hours (Martin and Roberts, 1984a); women who are working full-time say that they would prefer a job with fewer hours, in 31 per cent of cases (Martin and Roberts, 1984a). The Labour Force Survey found that of unemployed married women aged 16–24, 50 per cent preferred a full-time job and 50 per cent a part-time job; in the 25–49 age group, 31 per cent preferred a full-time job and 69 per cent a part-time job. For non-married women, the vast majority of women up to the age of 49 preferred a full-time job (OPCS 1984a). These women's responses are clearly set in the context where they are effectively responsible for two jobs and cannot afford to pay for domestic help or child-care provision. When unemployed men have been asked about their hours of employment preferences, most appear to prefer full-time hours, especially up to the age of 49.[8] Households could benefit at certain points in their family cycle from the increase in availability of part-time work, therefore. It would be more of an unequivocal benefit if part-time employment did not predominantly consist of low-status, low-skilled jobs. Protecting part-time work from being disadvantageous might involve a thorough restructuring of the organisation of work. It is argued in the final chapter of this book that such restructuring could have positive benefits for employers in the long run.

The evidence on the low take-up of maternity leave suggests that the eligibility requirements may be too restrictive. However, the evidence suggests that a change in the eligibility requirements would not be sufficient in themselves to bring about a large increase in take-up. The reasons for low take-up are much more complex, as documented by Daniel (1980).

Firstly, the considerable variation in take-up of maternity leave and return to work by women in different occupations and industries would indicate that the organisation of work, the degree of support and positive encouragement towards women returning to work and towards equal opportunities in general varies between different employers, industries and trade unions. For example, Daniel (1980) found a much higher return to work amongst teachers and nurses than civil servants and women working in nationalised industries.

Secondly, both Daniel (1980) and Martin and Roberts (1984a) suggest that the right to return to work is only a symbolic right if the necessary infrastructure to facilitate returning to work is not provided. The 'right' of a mother to return to work when her baby is six months old is meaningless if she does not have access to good quality child-care at a price which she and her partner can afford. There is overwhelming evidence that in order to offer most women a real rather than a symbolic choice about returning to work, they require access to child-care either from their partner or a nursery and the right to return to work part-time in their old job.

Thirdly, maternity leave and mother's employment is still seen by our society as a mother's problem rather than a household issue. Thus, men do not have an equal opportunity to participate in the care and raising of their children. Despite evidence that men do want paternity leave in order to be at home at and around the time of childbirth, it is not part of the political agenda, and has only been raised in Parliament as a private member's bill. Similarly, the EEC directive on 'Parental Leave and Leave for Family Responsibilies' which would extend the time for which *both* parents could share the care of their young babies has been strenuously opposed by the current government. Such a measure would facilitate real equality of opportunity between parents who choose to make use of parental leave.

Finally, women's current earnings potential must have a significant impact upon the household distribution of paid and unpaid work. The fact that the majority of women are not exercising their right to return to work after childbirth but are waiting until they can get a part-time job which 'fits in' whilst their partner works full-time, is in part a reflection of men's earnings compared to women's. In the long term, desegregation of jobs and equal pay for work of equal value may be as important as the rules surrounding maternity, paternity and parental leave in facilitating real choices for parents in their distribution of paid and unpaid work within the household.

There is evidence, therefore, that both women and men face constraints in the present circumstances as they seek to combine paid work and parental responsibility. In certain areas they have expressed the desire for change when asked; for example, women in their hours of work, men in their entitlement to leave at childbirth. The fact that women feel the strains of combining paid work and the responsibility for child-care, as things stand, suggests that they would prefer a different set of arrangements. Widening couples' choices through enacting the policy proposals outlined in this volume can only be beneficial to parents and children.

NOTES

1. Dex (1984a) did not control for class or education differences, which could well be influencing this result.
2. The Women and Employment Survey data also provide information about maternity leave for older women for the years prior to 1970. We examined this time series but found it had nothing to add to the discussion.
3. Dex (1984a, Appendix E) describes the procedure for reallocating women between categories. It is not possible to be precise about this reallocation, given the interview responses available. The frequencies in the 'return after all births' group are likely to be overestimates as a result.
4. The Labour Force Survey is a survey of households, but the data are stored for individuals since the usual analyses are of individuals. Some rearrangement was required therefore to regroup the individuals into their households. This rearrangement was performed by Peter Elias at the Institute for Employment Research, University of Warwick.
5. Greenhalgh (1979) uses group activity rates for men. One could repeat the model using a dichotomous dependent variable of whether an individual was economically active or not, and thus conduct the analysis on micro or individual-level data.
6. Joshi's (1984) analysis of women's participation in paid employment took 0–2 years for the youngest child's age band, for example.
7. See Martin and Roberts (1984a), Tables 8.5 and 8.6); 15 per cent of all working wives said that their husband's employment affected their own, and of these 51 per cent said that their husband's hours of work were inconvenient and constrained their own hours.
8. OPCS Monitor (OPCS,1984a) displays these results from the Labour Force Survey. Of the unemployed men aged 16–24 and 25–49, 98 and 99 per cent respectively said they would prefer a full-time job, although only 90 per cent of the 50-and-over group preferred full-time hours.

7 The Effects of Caring for the Elderly and Infirm on Women's Employment

Audrey Hunt

INTRODUCTION

Present government policy is directed towards providing care for the elderly and infirm by the community, as distinct from increasing the contribution made by national and local government services. The inadequacies of these government services at present have been shown by many studies over the last twenty years, including some official surveys (Harris, 1968 and 1971; Hunt, 1970 and 1978). The effect of current government policy will therefore be to place even heavier burdens on the shoulders of the families, in particular the women in the families, of the infirm and elderly.

This chapter examines one aspect of the problems faced by women with caring responsibilities, namely the effect of such responsibilities on the employment of women. For the sake of brevity, people with such responsibilities are referred to as 'carers' throughout this chapter. This definition excludes those people with paid caring responsibilities (e.g. nurses, home helps, etc.)

A number of recent studies (Charlesworth, Wilkin and Durie, 1983; EOC, 1980a, 1981 and 1982; Briggs, 1983; Rossiter and Wicks, 1982; Rimmer and Popay, 1982; Finch and Groves, 1983) have provided valuable information about the personal, financial and social problems faced by carers. This chapter seeks to supplement the qualitative information provided in these studies with detailed statistical evidence of the recent past, present and possible future extent of the effects on women's employment of caring for the elderly and infirm. This evidence is based mainly on data derived from two large-scale surveys: *A Survey of Women's Employment* (Hunt, 1968) and the Women and Employment Survey (Martin and Roberts, 1984a). These are referred to throughout the remainder of this chapter as 'the 1965 survey' and 'the 1980 survey'.

The present attitudes of society are such that if there are domestic responsibilities, whether for children, the sick or the elderly, these responsibilities are almost automatically expected to belong to women. Seldom, if ever, in quantitative surveys about employment are working men asked about the care of their children or whether they have to look after sick or elderly people. As a consequence, there is at present no information about men carers comparable to that provided about women by the 1965 and 1980 surveys. Consequently few reliable comparisons can be made between the effects of caring on men's and women's work.

Evidence from some of the studies previously cited indicates that roughly one in four of carers are men. Although this emphasises the preponderance of women in the caring role it also shows that, contrary to popular opinion, the number of men who have caring responsibilities is not negligible. Whitehorn (1984), quoting from a survey by the Harris Research Centre, stated that 32 per cent of men, compared with 68 per cent of women, would be prepared to give up work to care for an elderly parent. A study of the Home Help Service (Hunt, 1970) showed that among 'male housewives' (i.e. men responsible for domestic arrangements in their households) 10 per cent had a person in their households who needed special attention and 10 per cent gave some help to an elderly or infirm person living elsewhere. For female housewives the figures were 14 per cent and 18 per cent respectively. These findings are not directly comparable with any in the present chapter, because they relate solely to housewives, including those over 64 years of age, but they provide another indication that caring is not exclusively a woman's concern.

Another aspect not covered in this chapter is that of the difficulties of carers who are themselves over retirement age. Most people above this age would, of course, be retired from paid employment. The women who are investigated in this study are below the retirement age and, if they have caring responsibilities, they are more likely to be caring for people older than themselves, for their parents and persons of their parents' generation. In the 1965 survey, 2 per cent of dependants were aged under 16, 16 per cent were aged 16–64, 28 per cent were aged 75–84, and 54 per cent were 85 and over. People above retirement age will have decreasing responsibility for the older generation but increasing responsibility for spouses and, possibly, siblings and others. It is in this age group that male carers are most likely to be found.

The home help study (Hunt, 1970) estimated that, between the ages of 35 and 64, roughly half of all housewives can expect at some time or another to give help to elderly or infirm persons. Given that most women will have domestic responsibilities for at least part of their lives, this implies that the issue of care for the elderly and infirm will impinge upon the majority of families in Great Britain at some stage in their life-cycle. The present chapter deals only with the situation at two points in time, and therefore underestimates considerably the percentage of women who may be affected by caring responsibilities during their lifetimes. However, within these limitations it is hoped that this chapter will provide a useful statistical framework and possibly give some indication of the future dimensions of the problem of caring for the infirm and elderly within the community. It will also provide a basis for comparison with the effects on women's employment of their other major caring role, the responsibility for children.

DEFINITIONS AND COVERAGE

In the 1965 survey 'carers' were defined as those answering 'yes' to the question:

> Are there any elderly persons or invalids that you have to look after to any extent, living here or elsewhere?

In the 1980 survey 'carers' were defined as those answering 'yes' to the question:

> Apart from looking after the family in the usual way, some women may have extra responsibilities for looking after a sick or elderly friend or member of the family. Is there anyone like this who depends on you to provide some regular services for them?

It has to be recognised that different wordings of similar questions may produce different answers from respondents. However, our analysis will show that these questions have identified the same kind of women in each survey and that the increase in the percentage of carers shown between 1965 and 1980 does in fact represent a real increase.

The definitions of carer used in the two surveys are broader than those used in some other studies. It might be argued that they include women who do not have very heavy responsibilities. It is worth examining the extent of these responsibilities. In 1965, 32 per cent of the dependants of employed carers and 35 per cent of those of non-employed carers were bedfast or housebound. Employed carers had to perform all duties for 18 per cent; the corresponding figure for non-employed carers was 33 per cent. Only 7 per cent of all carers performed only occasional services. In 1980 carers were asked how many hours a week they spent in looking after their dependants. Only 26 per cent of employed carers and 14 per cent of non-employed carers spent less than five hours a week, whereas 7 per cent of employed carers and 7 per cent of non-employed carers spent thirty hours a week or gave constant attendance. The significance of these time commitments should not be underestimated. Even five hours a week on top of working hours and carers' own domestic responsibilities cannot be regarded as negligible.

Dependants lived with carers in 41 per cent of instances in 1965 and in 24 per cent in 1980. It is hard to compare quantitatively the pressure of caring for infirm people living in one's home with that of caring for those living elsewhere. Possibly living with an invalid imposes greater mental stress, but helping one who lives elsewhere may involve more physical effort in going back and forth. It seems, therefore, that the definition may include a small proportion whose caring responsibilities are not particularly onerous, but that the great majority of those identified in both years have a considerable amount of additional work and potential stress by virtue of their caring function.

In the 1965 survey, women aged 16–64 years were interviewed, but in the 1980 survey those aged 60–64 years were not included. Therefore women in this age group have been omitted from the 1965 figures, or shown separately where they appear to be of interest. In 1965, full-time students were not asked about responsibility for elderly or infirm persons, although they were in 1980. They have been omitted from the 1980 figures. For the sake of conciseness we have referred to these modified samples as *all women* in both cases. They number 6632 in 1965 (7260 when the 60–64 group is included) and 5161 in 1980.

The classification of women as full-time or part-time employees was based in both surveys on the women's own opinion, which showed very little difference from the standard definition of part-time as 'not more than thirty hours a week'. Both surveys include as employees those temporarily unemployed or sick. The 1965 survey also included as employees a small group who worked regularly but not all the time, e.g. seasonal workers.

For the sake of conciseness, women without caring responsibilities are referred to as 'others'.

COMPARISON OF CARERS IN THE 1965 AND 1980 SURVEYS

Details of the proportions of carers found in each age group in the two surveys are shown for women of different employment status in Tables 7.1 to 7.4 and in Figures 7.1 and 7.2.

The percentage of women defined as carers rose from 11 per cent of all women in the 1965 survey to 14 per cent in 1980, a statistically significant increase. Each employment group showed an increase, the smallest being among part-time employees (from 15 per cent to 16 per cent). Almost all age groups in all employment status groups showed an increase, the most marked increases being in the 45 or over age group, except in the case of part-time employees, where the 45–49 age group showed a slight decrease. It must be borne in mind that the proportion of part-time employees in 1980 was considerably higher than in 1965. The effect of this is discussed later. The sharp rise in the incidence of carers between the 30–34 and 40–44 age groups is common to all employment groups in both surveys, as can be seen in Figures 7.1 and 7.2. The figures also show that in 1980 the proportion of carers is consistently higher among part-time employees than in any other employment group, including the non-employed, from age 35 onwards. This was not the case in 1965, when the percentage of carers among the non-employed was higher for many age groups, particularly the oldest. It can be seen that, in both years, there is a decrease in the percentage of carers in all employment groups after the age of 50, probably as a consequence of the deaths of elderly dependants when carers are about this age.

There was an overall increase in the percentage of economically active women from 55 per cent of those aged 16–59 in 1965 to 65 per cent in 1980, almost entirely due to an increase in part-time employ-

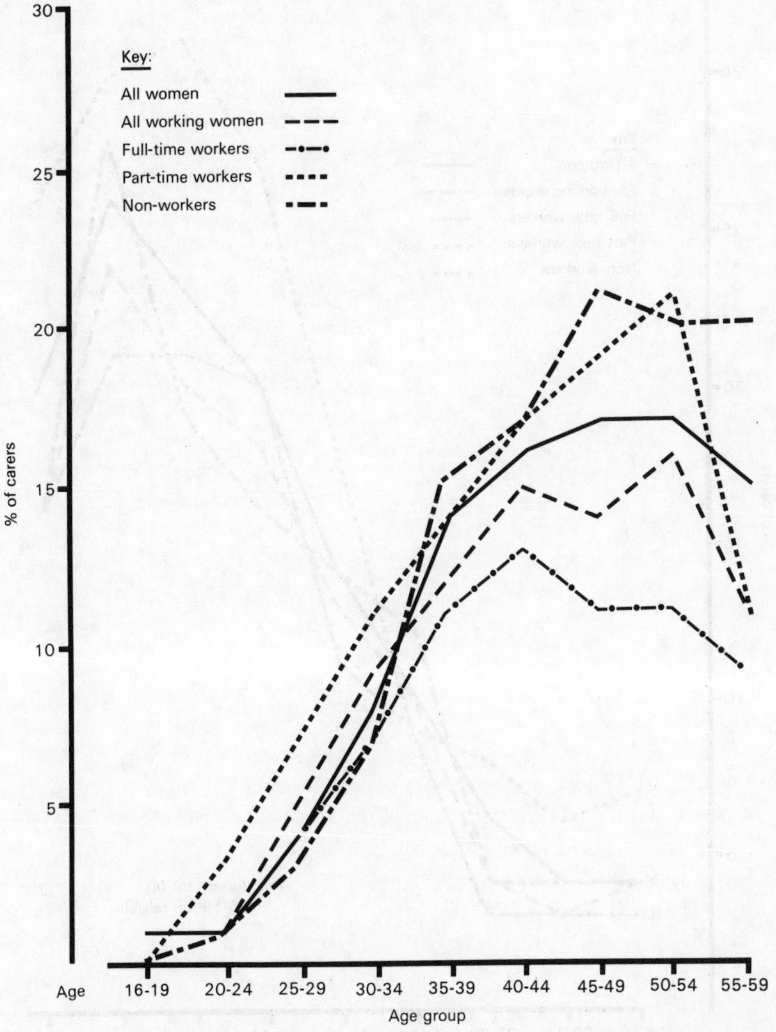

FIGURE 7.1 *Percentage of carers among women of different employment status, 1965*

ment. However, the percentage of carers who were employed full-time rose from 21 per cent to 28 per cent, while the total percentage of employed carers rose from 48 per cent to 59 per cent. It can be seen from Tables 7.3 and 7.4 that the increases in the percentages of carers

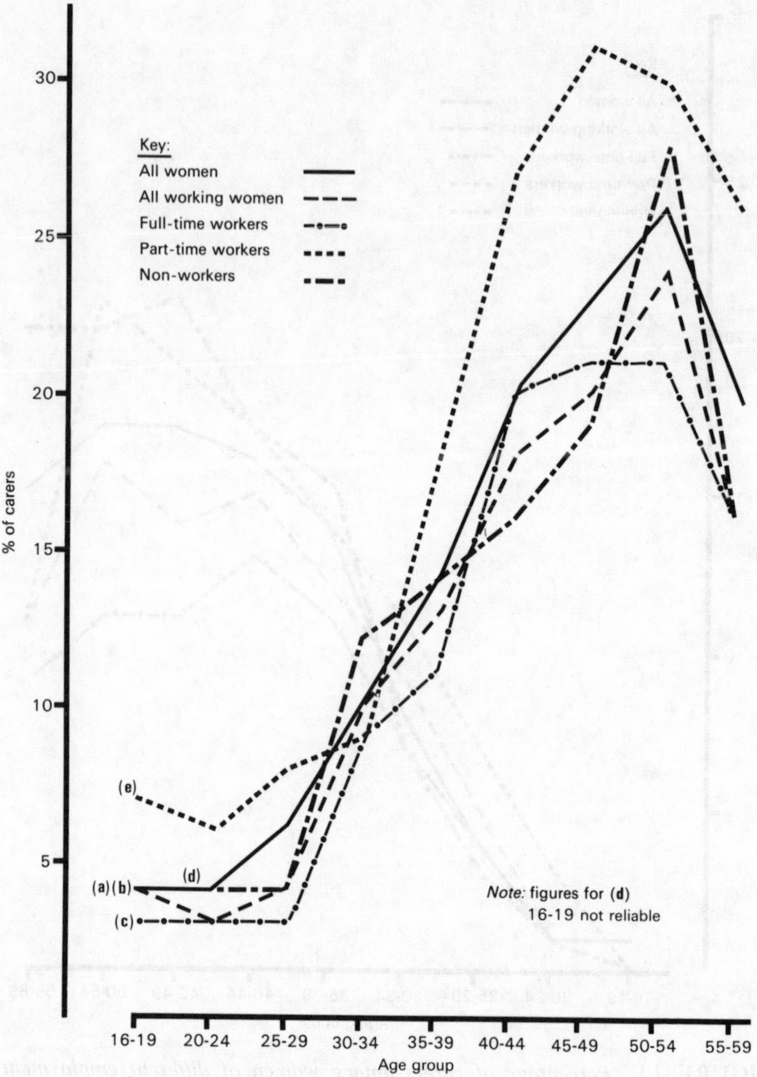

FIGURE 7.2 *Percentage of carers among women of different employment status, 1980*

TABLE 7.1 *Percentage of carers among all women (excluding full-time students) and among full-time workers, part-time workers and non-workers, by age group, 1965*

	Total	*Total excluding 60–64*	*16–19*	*20–24*	*25–29*	*30–34*	*35–39*	*40–44*	*45–49*	*50–54*	*55–59*	*60–64*
Percentage of careers among:												
All women	11	11	1	1	4	8	14	16	17	17	15	13
All working women	10	10	1	1	5	9	12	15	14	16	11	13
Full-time workers	7	7	1	1	5	7	11	13	11	11	9	9
Part-time workers	15	15	—	3	5	11	14	17	19	21	12	17
Non-working women	13	13	—	1	3	7	15	17	21	20	20	13

Source: Survey of Women's Employment 1965

TABLE 7.2 *Percentage of carers among all women (excluding full-time students) and among full-time workers, part-time workers and non-workers, by age group, 1980*

	Total	*16–19*	*20–24*	*25–29*	*30–34*	*35–39*	*40–44*	*45–49*	*50–54*	*55–59*
Percentage of carers among:										
All women	14	4	4	6	10	14	20	23	26	20
All working women	13	4	3	4	10	13	18	20	24	16
Full-time workers	11	3	3	3	9	11	20	21	21	16
Part-time workers	16	*	4	4	12	14	16	18	28	16
Non-working women	16	7	6	8	9	18	27	31	30	26

*There were only three part-time workers in this age group, of whom two were carers.
Source: Women and Employment Survey, 1980.

TABLE 7.3 *Employment status of carers and others by age group, 1965*

	Total	*Total 60–64*	*16–19*	*20–24*	*25–29*	*30–34*	*35–39*	*40–44*	*45–49*	*50–54*	*55–59*	*60–64*
All women												
Employment status												
Working: full-time	33	35	87	53	24	20	24	30	38	30	27	15
part-time	18	18	1	6	12	20	24	26	23	22	20	17
others*	2	2	2	2	2	3	3	2	3	3	2	2
Total working	54	55	92	62	38	43	51	58	64	55	49	35
Not working	46	45	8	38	62	57	49	42	36	45	51	65
Base (= 100%)	7260	6632	513	650	746	745	805	877	783	775	722	628
Carers												
Employment status												
Working: full-time	21	22		50		17	20	24	25	19	16	11
part-time	24	24		12		29	24	28	26	27	15	22
others*	2	2		—		5	2	1	4	2	3	1
Total working	48	49		62		51	46	54	55	48	35	35
Not working	52	51		38		49	54	46	45	52	65	65
Base (= 100%)	807	726		43		59	111	138	130	135	110	81
Non-carers												
Employment status												
Working: full-time	35	36	87	53	24	20	25	30	40	32	29	16
part-time	17	18	1	6	11	20	24	26	22	21	21	17
others*	2	2	3	2	2	2	3	2	3	3	2	2
Total working	54	56	92	62	37	42	52	58	65	56	52	35
Not working	46	44	8	38	63	58	48	42	35	44	48	65
Base (= 100%)	6453	5906	507	641	718	686	694	739	653	640	612	547

*Temporarily unemployed or sick; regular casual.
Source: Survey of Women's Employment 1965.

TABLE 7.4 *Employment status of carers and others, by age group, 1980*

	Total	*16–19*	*20–24*	*25–29*	*30–34*	*35–39*	*40–44*	*45–49*	*50–54*	*55–59*
All women										
Employment status										
Working: full-time	36	74	56	31	23	30	34	37	35	28
part-time	30	1	9	18	33	37	41	40	36	30
Total working	65	75	65	49	57	67	75	76	71	58
Not working	35	25	35	51	43	33	25	24	29	42
Base (= 100%)	5161	343	563	680	759	635	576	534	529	542
Carers										
Employment status										
Working: full-time	28			30	20	22	34	35	28	22
part-time	32		12		39	37	33	32	39	24
Total working	59		42		59	59	67	67	67	46
Not working	41		58		41	41	33	33	33	54
Base (= 100%)	728		77		76	92	115	121	138	109
Others										
Employment status										
Working: full-time	38	75	57	32	24	31	34	37	38	29
part-time	28	*	9	18	33	38	44	42	35	32
Total working	66	75	66	50	56	69	77	79	73	61
Base (= 100%)	4433	328	541	640	683	543	461	413	391	433

Source: Women and Employment Survey, 1980.

employed full-time and part-time is common to all age groups, except for those aged 16–29 years, where the numbers of carers are very small.

The age composition of carers had changed to some extent. In 1965 71 per cent of carers were aged 40–59, but by 1980 this had fallen to 67 per cent. This was accounted for by a fall from 71 per cent to 61 per cent in the percentage of non-employed carers in that age group. It appears possible that caring responsibilities are beginning to fall on women at an earlier age.

COHORTS IN THE 1965 AND 1980 SURVEYS

Part of the populations sampled in 1965 and in 1980 were common to the two surveys: those aged 16–44 years in 1965 would be 31–59 years in 1980. It is thus possible to compare five five-year age groups from the two surveys. These constitute two samples of the same population taken at a fifteen-year interval. The effects of natural wastage and migration are unlikely to be significant. The comparison between these cohorts is shown in Table 7.5. This demonstrates clearly the extent to which caring responsibilities have increased over the years for these groups of women. In the cohort aged 20–24 in 1965, 1 per cent had caring responsibilities in that year. By 1980 (when this cohort

TABLE 7.5 *Percentage of carers in each cohort, 1965 and 1980*

Age group	*1965* *1980*	*20–24* *35–39*	*25–29* *40–44*	*30–34* *45–49*	*35–39* *50–54*	*40–44* *55–59*
Carers						
Working full-time	1965	1	1	1	3	4
	1980	3	7	8	7	4
Working part-time	1965	*	1	2	3	4
	1980	5	7	7	10	5
Not working	1965	*	2	4	7	7
	1980	6	7	7	9	11
Total	1965	1	4	8	14	16
	1980	14	20	23	26	20
n	1965	665	748	745	805	878
	1980	635	576	534	529	542

* = less than 0.5 per cent.
Sources: Survey of Women's Employment, 1965.
Women and Employment Survey, 1980.

would be aged 35–39) the proportion had risen to 14 per cent. This is the same as for the cohort aged 35–39 in 1965. However, in the cohort aged 25–29 in 1965, the percentage rose from 4 per cent in 1965 to 20 per cent in 1980 (when they were aged 40–44). Among women aged 40–44 in 1965 the percentage of carers was 16 per cent, significantly less. This seems to indicate that the effects of the growth in the elderly population in recent years (discussed in a later section) had begun to affect women in their early forties by the year 1980. It seems that if present trends continue, many women will have only a few years between the time of family formation and the incidence of other caring responsibilities.

Presenting the figures in cohort form enables us to see more clearly the effects of both increased caring responsibilities and changes in employment patterns. The upper part of Table 7.6 shows the increase

TABLE 7.6 *Employment status of carers, 1965 and 1980 (%)*

Age group	*1965* / *1980*	*20–24* / *35–39*	*25–29* / *40–44*	*30–34* / *45–49*	*35–39* / *50–54*	*40–44* / *55–59*
Percentage of:						
Full-time workers with caring responsibilities	1965	1	5	7	11	13
	1980	11	20	21	21	16
Part-time workers with caring responsibilities	1965	3	5	11	14	17
	1980	14	16	18	28	16
All workers with caring responsiblities	1965	1	5	9	12	15
	1980	13	18	20	24	16
Non-workers with caring responsibilities	1965	1	3	7	15	17
	1980	18	27	32	30	26
Percentage of:						
Carers working full-time	1965	*	36	17	20	24
	1980	22	34	35	28	22
Carers working part-time	1965	*	14	34	25	30
	1980	37	33	32	39	24
Carers not working	1965	*	50	49	54	46
	1980	41	33	33	33	54
Total	1965	*	100	100	100	100
	1980	100	100	100	100	100
Bases (for lower part of table only)	1965	9	28	59	111	138
	1980	92	115	121	138	109

*There were only 9 carers in this group, so percentages would be unreliable.
See Tables 7.3 and 7.4 for individual bases for top part of table.
Sources: see Table 7.5.

in caring responsibilities in each cohort and in each employment group. The changes are less marked in the oldest cohort, where caring responsibilities had already begun to make themselves felt in 1965. The lower part of Table 7.6 shows the difference between what might have been expected had employment patterns in general remained the same between 1965 and 1980. For example, the cohort of carers aged 25–29 years in 1965 might have been expected in 1980 to correspond with those aged 40–44 years in 1965, namely 24 per cent employed full-time, 30 per cent part-time and 46 per cent not employed. In fact, the 1980 composition was 34 per cent employed full-time, 33 per cent employed part-time, and 33 per cent not employed. A contributory factor to this particular difference may be the increasing tendency of women to return to work after having children. In 1965 two-fifths of non-employed carers had children under 16 in addition to their infirm dependants. The cohort aged 25–29 years in 1965 would thus be subject to the effects of both the growing incidence of caring and the increased tendency to return to work after family formation.

FUTURE EMPLOYMENT PLANS

In both 1965 and 1980 non-employed women were asked about the possibility of their return to work. The wording of the questions was different. In 1965 the question was prefaced by the statement, 'It is very important for the Government to know whether women who are not now in paid employment will eventually go back to work.' The question itself was: 'Is it practically certain that at some future date you yourself will go back to work?' Where the answer was not 'yes' interviewers used probing techniques to establish whether women, even though not certain, thought it likely they would return, or whether they thought it unlikely or could not say at that time. Under the circumstances existing in 1965, this question was of major importance, and much effort was used to devise the best wording and techniques to identify women's future work intentions. In 1980, under different circumstances, the question was simpler: 'Do you think you will ever do a paid job (again) in the future?' The effects of variations in question wording can be quite considerable, but it is reasonable to assume that both forms of this question would produce reliable evidence of women's future intentions to engage in paid employment. In any event, the differences between carers and others in each of the years 1965 and 1980 are not in dispute, whether or not the difference between the two surveys may have been influenced by question wording. In Table 7.7 we attempt to minimise this possible effect by combining for 1965 those practically certain with those likely to return to work and those uncertain with those unlikely. Between-year comparisons are made using the first of these groups for 1965 and those who stated that they were 'likely to return' in the 1980 survey.

Table 7.7 shows that the general changes in women's employment patterns are exhibited by both carers and others, with a considerably higher proportion of each group envisaging a return to paid employment in 1980 than in 1965. The percentage of non-employed carers who expected to return was considerably lower than that of other non-employed women in both surveys. The table also shows that in every age group in both surveys (except those aged 55–59 in 1965 and those aged 16–34 in 1980) the percentage of carers who expected to return to work is lower than that of others. This shows that the overall difference is not a consequence of the different age structures of carers and others in either year. The different patterns in evidence can possibly be explained by the comparatively small numbers of carers in some age groups in 1980. Nevertheless, the decline with increasing age in the percentages who expected to return is apparent in both surveys.

Some ideas of the firmness of the intention to return to work can be gained by examining the percentages who expected to return within the next year. In both surveys, non-employed carers were less likely than other non-employed women to expect to return in the forthcoming year (5 per cent compared with 8 per cent). In 1980, 70 per cent of carers and 59 per cent of others who were not employed at the time of the survey were seeking part-time work. (This question was not asked in 1965, when part-time work had not reached the importance it had in 1980.)

In 1980, 30 per cent of carers and 35 per cent of others were seeking work in occupations defined in Chapter 4 as 'better than average' in terms of earning potential. Returning carers in 1980 appear to have had more difficulty than others in finding suitable work. Forty-four per cent had been trying for six months or more, compared with 29 per cent of others. There was virtually no difference between the experiences of carers and of others who were looking for jobs in 1980. Approximately nine-tenths of each group said they were having difficulty in finding the kind of work they wanted. However, this difficulty could reflect the prevailing employment situation, as few people would have found job-seeking easy in 1980. By contrast, in 1965 82 per cent of potential returners expected to be able to obtain

TABLE 7.7 *Possibility of return to work by non-working carers and others by age group, 1965 and 1980 (%)*

	Total	*16–24*	*25–29*	*30–34*	*35–39*	*40–44*	*45–59*	*50–54*	*55–59*
1965 non-working carers under 60									
Possibility of return:									
Practically certain or likely	22		52		32	20	17	10	10
Uncertain or unlikely	78		48		68	80	83	90	90
Bases	371		48		60	64	59	70	76
1965 non-working others under 60									
Possibility of return:									
Practically certain or likely	36	60	54	48	37	28	41	13	7
Uncertain or unlikely	64	40	46	52	63	72	59	87	93
Bases	266	289	453	395	335	317	300	280	293
1980 non-working carers									
Likelihood of taking job:									
Likely	42		74		53	63	28	28	8
Not likely	38		7		21	21	48	54	83
Don't know, not stated	20		19		26	16	25	17	8
Bases	297		76		38	38	40	46	59
1980 non-working others									
Likelihood of taking job:									
Likely	59	55	79	74	63	66	41	30	20
Not likely	19	4	5	8	11	18	27	52	69
Don't know, not stated	22	41	16	18	26	16	32	18	11
Bases	1518	267	318	298	169	104	87	107	168

Note: for differences in form of questions in the two surveys, see text.
Sources: see Table 7.5.

the type of work they wanted. Carers looking for a job were more likely than others to rate job security as important (77 per cent compared with 62 per cent). One can only speculate as to the reason for this striking difference. It may be that carers have lost earlier jobs because of the demands of caring. There is still no legal protection for women (or men) who have to take time off because of caring responsibilities. Therefore, security is felt to be particularly desirable by those who may have experienced insecurity.

CARERS' OWN ASSESSMENT OF EFFECTS OF CARING ON EMPLOYMENT

In both 1965 and 1980 employed carers were asked whether their employment was affected by their caring responsibilities. The wording of the questions, while not identical, was not very different. In 1965 it was: 'Is your employment affected in any way by having to look after . . . ?' In 1980 it was: 'Has what work you do or the hours you work been affected by having to look after . . . ?' It is unlikely that the higher percentage in 1965 who said their employment was affected (22 per cent of employed carers, compared with 12 per cent in 1980) can be attributed to question wording. Part-timers in both years were a little more likely than full-timers to say their work was affected, but the differences are not significant. One can only hypothesise as to the reason for the fall in the percentage who said their work was affected, but a possible explanation may be that some at least of the additional carers found in 1980 were women whose employment conditions were such that they could cope with the additional responsibilities. For example, where there are alternatives, the caring role may fall to the lot of the person who is in part-time rather than full-time employment.

In both years a restriction on working hours was the most common effect mentioned. Non-employed carers were not asked a comparable question in 1965, but in 1980 23 per cent of non-employed carers said they were prevented from getting paid work by caring responsibilities. In 1965, 8 per cent of non-employed carers thought they would return to employment or would go back sooner if relieved of their caring responsibilities. Dex (1984) showed that in 6 per cent of 'final work phase' (i.e. after the birth of the last child) women gave up work to look after sick or elderly relatives.

While these findings provide evidence that in many cases carers are aware of the direct effects of caring on their work, they do not show the complete picture. The two surveys, covering as they did many aspects of women's employment, do not provide detailed evidence on the links between caring responsibilities and employment patterns. Causality must remain a matter for speculation in many cases, and the survey data can provide only statistical evidence of the differences that existed between carers and others at two different points in time.

ASSESSMENT OF EFFECTS OF CARING: SOME ASPECTS OF PRESENT JOB

Because of the different age structures of carers and others in both surveys, it has been desirable to analyse many findings by age group. This ensures that differences which are related to age rather than to caring responsibilities can be identified as such. Where full tables are not given but figures are given in the text, it can be assumed that the differences mentioned do not appear to be a consequence of different age structure. For the most part the following sections cover data from the 1980 survey only. Where comparable information from the 1965 survey is available it is given.

It has been recognised for some time by those interested in women's employment that the socio-economic group system of classifying occupations is inadequate for identifying the very large number of different jobs done by women (EOC, 1980b). It is not surprising, therefore, that in neither the 1965 survey nor the 1980 survey was it possible to detect significant differences between the socio-economic groups of the jobs done by carers and others. However, in the 1980 survey an alternative system was used. In Chapter 4 Elias has classed five occupational groups identified in that survey as having 'above-average earnings'. He showed that, by this criterion, part-time jobs available to women are on average inferior to full-time jobs. A comparison on this basis does not indicate that carers are more likely than other women to be found in the lower-paid jobs: carers employed part-time are, apparently, a little less likely.

Although there was little difference between the types of jobs done by carers and others, both surveys showed that there was a considerable difference between the numbers of hours worked. In 1965, 28 per cent of carers but only 17 per cent of others were employed for 20 hours a week or less. For 1980 the comparable figures were 35 per cent and 26 per cent. At the other end of the scale, in 1965 32 per cent of carers and 50 per cent of others were employed for 35 or more hours a week, and in 1980 the figures were 30 per cent and 39 per cent.

Overtime working did not contribute a great deal to the differences. In 1980 overtime was worked by 27 per cent of carers and 29 per cent of others. As well as working fewer hours, carers tended to take slightly less time on the journey to work. In 1965, 41 per cent of carers, compared with 35 per cent of others, had a journey of ten minutes or less, and in 1980 the figures were very similar (42 per cent and 36 per cent).

There is virtually no difference between the percentages of carers and others in 1980 who had fixed times of starting and finishing work (75 per cent and 76 per cent) or between those who said they were happy with the number of hours worked per week (71 per cent for both). Equally, 19 per cent of both carers and others said they would like to work fewer hours. It seems, therefore, that a majority of carers had been able to find jobs where the hours suited their domestic responsibilities.

A significantly higher percentage of carers than of other employees had been ten years or more in their present job (30 per cent compared with 20 per cent in 1965, 27 per cent compared with 16 per cent in 1980). This is not a consequence of the different age structure. The difference is particularly marked among those aged 45 and over. It is shown elsewhere that job security is particularly important to carers. It seems likely that when carers find a job which fits in with their domestic demands they are not tempted to leave it easily.

The percentage of carers who had received formal training for their present job from their employers was significantly lower than the percentage of others (32 per cent compared with 38 per cent). It can be said, tentatively, that carers may be impelled to take jobs for which no formal training is given and that this is particularly marked in the case of younger carers.

When asked whether they would like any further training, not just for their present jobs, 35 per cent of carers and 43 per cent of others said they would. This difference is to a great extent a consequence of the different age compositions, with older women, not surprisingly, being less likely to want further training. However, among those under 35, only 49 per cent of carers, compared with 57 per cent of others, would like further training.

In the present context, promotion in the past serves as a rough indicator of suitability for promotion and willingness to accept it at that time. It is interesting, therefore, that 48 per cent of carers, compared with 41 per cent of others, had been promoted in the past, either in their present job or in a previous job. The percentage is higher among carers in all age groups, indicating that the overall difference is not a product of different age composition.

By contrast, when asked whether they would want to be considered for promotion only 36 per cent of carers, compared with 48 per cent of others, said they would. Among those under 35 only 47 per cent of carers compared with 61 per cent of others would want promotion.

SOME ATTITUDES OF CARERS AND OTHERS TO WORK

We have shown in this chapter that carers are in many ways less favourably situated than others in respect of their present employment position. Many carers are not consciously aware of their disadvantages, but it is a common finding of many investigations into women's work that women say they are satisfied with conditions that objectively appear far from ideal.

In order to find out whether there is any evidence of less tangible disadvantages, we examined the answers given in 1980 to a number of attitude questions. A detailed analysis of these is given in Martin and Roberts (1984a, p. 60).

Many differences between carers and others were not significant or appeared to be, to some extent at least, related to age differences. There are a few points which are worth comment.

Employed carers were more likely to feel that they needed to work for money, that they could not cope with work and home and that they were under stress. They were less likely to have a positive attitude to employment, but, somewhat contradictorily, they were less likely to feel that they did not enjoy their jobs. The two factors, however, measure different aspects of job satisfaction: the former relates to employment in general, the latter to a particular situation.

The positive attitude to paid work is much higher among both groups of employees than among non-employees. The percentage with a high stress level is higher among non-employed carers than among other non-workers. These attitudes, taken in conjunction with some described in the previous section (the greater tendency of carers to stay in one job for a long time, their comparative unwillingness to undertake further training or to accept promotion) seem to indicate a more passive approach to employment by carers than by others. If they have found jobs which fit in with their caring responsibilities they extract what job satisfaction they can, but appear reluctant to take steps which might disturb the equilibrium they have achieved at present. Training might make additional demands both on their energy and their time and might lead to a change of job. Promotion might entail extra responsibilities and involve greater mobility which would make it harder to cope with work and home. One is left with the feeling that, whether they themselves are aware of it or not, many carers are prevented from achieving their full potential because of the effects of their responsibilities.

POSSIBLE EFFECTS OF POPULATION CHANGES ON CARING

The changing age structure of the population is causing concern among those responsible for the provision of services for the elderly. The likely increase in the numbers of old people in the coming decades is demonstrated in Table 7.8, adapted from Craig (1983).

TABLE 7.8 *The elderly population of England and Wales, 1971–2021 (millions)*

Population at mid-year	*Estimates based on population census*		*Mid-1981 based projections*			
	1971	*1981*	*1991*	*2001*	*2011*	*2021*
Age group 65–74 years						
Women	2.4	2.6	2.5	2.3	2.4	2.8
Men	1.8	2.0	2.0	1.9	2.0	2.3
Persons	4.2	4.6	4.5	4.2	4.5	5.1
Age group 75–84 years						
Women	1.3	1.6	1.7	1.7	1.6	1.8
Men	0.6	0.8	1.0	1.1	1.0	1.2
Persons	1.9	2.4	2.8	2.8	2.6	2.9
Age group 85 years or over						
Women	0.3	0.4	0.6	0.7	0.8	0.8
Men	0.1	0.1	0.2	0.3	0.3	0.4
Persons	0.4	0.5	0.8	1.0	1.1	1.1
Total persons						
75 years and over	2.3	2.9	3.5	3.8	3.7	4.1
85 years and over	0.4	0.5	0.8	1.0	1.1	1.1

Source: Craig (1983).

The population aged 75 years and over is likely to increase by 21 per cent over the decade mid-1981 to mid-1991, and by 7 per cent in the succeeding decade. The likely increase in the population aged 85 years and over is even greater: 46 per cent from 1981 to 1991 and 25 per cent from 1991 to 2001. The population of pensionable age as a percentage of working age (the 'dependency ratio') is estimated to increase from 8 per cent in 1971 and 9 per cent in 1981 to 9.4 per cent in 1991.

The findings of many surveys confirm what might seem obvious, that the incidence of serious physical disability is a major problem among those aged 85 and over. One survey (Hunt, 1978) found that 21 per cent were bedfast or housebound, compared with 2 per cent of those aged 65–74 years. People of 85 years and over were also much less likely to be able to perform such domestic tasks as cooking, cleaning, hanging curtains and so on. The probable increase in the numbers of people in this age group will therefore necessitate an increase in the number of persons providing help.

In the 1965 survey it was found that 6.5 per cent of women aged 16–64 years were caring for persons aged 75 years and over. At that time official statistics show there were 2.1 million persons of that age in the population as a whole. In the 1980 survey the age of dependants was not recorded. However, in that year there were 2.8 million persons aged 75 and over in the population, so it seems that between 8 per cent and 9 per cent of women would be caring for persons of this age. This appears to indicate that a major part of the increase in the percentage of carers from 11 per cent in 1965 to 14 per cent in 1980 can be accounted for by the increase in the elderly population.

Future projections can only be tentative, but it seems reasonable to assume that similar increases in the percentages of women carers can be expected over the next decade.

VALUE OF THE SERVICES PROVIDED BY CARERS

The findings described in this chapter and in many of the studies cited show that many carers exercise their role at considerable financial expense to themselves (by working shorter hours, taking less well paid jobs, refusing promotion). Some idea of the financial saving to the community of the services provided by voluntary carers can be obtained from a study carried out by Tinker (1984) of innovatory schemes introduced by some local authorities to assist elderly people living at home. Tinker estimated the cost of *paid* 'home carers', 'home care assistants' and 'neighbourly helps'. These people, mostly women, provided the same kinds of personal and domestic help which relatives or friends might give if they were available. The average annual costs per elderly person helped in 1981–82 were

home carer	£2466
home care assistant	£1106
neighbourly help	£346

These figures give some indication of the value in cash terms of the services provided by carers as defined by the two surveys. They provide a strong case for adequate financial recognition of the services provided by voluntary carers.

SUMMARY AND CONCLUSIONS

There are six major findings which arise from this analysis of carers in the two surveys:

1. The percentage of carers rose from 11 per cent of all women in 1965 to 14 per cent in 1980. Increases in the percentages occurred among employed and non-employed women and in almost all age groups.
2. The percentage of part-time employment among carers had increased, paralleling a similar increase among all women.
3. Carers were more likely than others to work part-time and therefore to suffer the disadvantages of part-time employment. However, there is no evidence that carers who work part-time are in an inferior position to other part-time workers in either survey.
4. In both 1965 and 1980 the percentage of non-employed carers who expected to return to employment was lower than the percentage of non-employed women without such responsibilities.
5. Carers interviewed in 1980 were more likely to show evidence of stress than non-carers.
6. Predicted changes in the age composition of the general population are likely to lead to an increase in the percentage of women responsible for looking after elderly people.

8 Women's Working Lives: A Comparison of Women in the United States and Great Britain

Shirley Dex and Lois B. Shaw

INTRODUCTION

Similar trends in women's employment are visible in Britain and the USA over the post-Second World War period. In both countries women's participation rates have increased, and yet there are differences in employment policies, in legislation and in the economic structures of Britain and the USA. By comparing British and US women's experiences we can provide some insight into the reasons why some of women's labour market experiences and changes have been occurring. Such a comparison will also facilitate an investigation of the comparative effects of legislation, social policies and economic structures in a way that has potentially important policy implications.

Cross-cultural comparisons are rare. When they do occur they are often severely restricted because of the lack of comparable data and the use of nationally specific definitions. The availability of data on women's work histories from the 1980 Women and Employment Survey (WES) offered the unique opportunity for a detailed comparison between British and American women's experiences. Work history data have been available for some time in the USA from the women's cohorts of the National Longitudinal Survey (NLS), but they are rare in Britain. These two data sources are not identical, but they overlap sufficiently over the period of family formation to make direct comparisons between women's experiences at this time both feasible and valuable.

Previous attempts to compare British and American women have had to rely on piecing together separate analyses of women undertaken in each country. Hakim (1979) presented comparisons of British and American women's occupational distributions and their occupational segregation using separate British and US studies. The picture that emerged suggested that both British and US women were concentrated in clerical, sales and semi-skilled work in the service industries; that is, in occupations which are disproportionately 'female'. The overrepresentation of women in these 'female' jobs was also found to have declined in both countries between 1900 and 1970, but the extent of the decline was much greater in the USA than it was in Britain.

More recent studies in Britain by Hakim (1981) and in the USA by Beller (1982a, 1982b), England (1982) and Shaw (1983a) have all found that there have been further declines in occupational segregation during the 1970s, although the recent recession has started to erode some of the improvements. It has been suggested that equal opportunities policies have been responsible for these changes, but there is some debate about this. Hakim (1979) makes the general point that in addition to individuals' motivation, 'both structural and historical factors must also contribute to an explanation of trends in the degree and pattern of occupational segregation' (p. 43).

Our comparisons aim to examine the extent to which structural, legislative and other policy differences contribute to the experiences of women in Britain and the USA between 1967 and 1980. In this chapter we offer a summary of some of our findings; the complete set of results and all of the technical details of the comparisons are available in Dex and Shaw (1986). In particular we will be comparing women's work histories over the period of their family formation and their occupational mobility experience at the same time. Women's occupations in large part determine their earnings. We will not discuss women's earnings in any detail, however, because this issue is discussed by Main in Chapter 5. The themes of women's work histories and occupational mobility recur throughout this book. The opportunity to see how the socio-legal framework of two countries influences the experience of women makes this a fascinating exercise.

THE SOCIO-LEGAL FRAMEWORK

Both Britain and the USA have passed legislation against sex discrimination in employment, although the extent of the law and its enforcement differs in the two countries. In Britain, the Equal Pay Act (1970) came into force by 1975; it stipulates that men and women are to be paid the same amount if they are in the same or broadly similar work. The Sex Discrimination Act (1975) prohibits discrimination with respect to hiring, opportunities for promotion, transfer and training, and dismissal procedures on grounds of gender or marriage. The Act precludes both direct and indirect discrimination, and it applies equally to men and women, thus making reverse discrimination generally unlawful (except in the case of women's training facilities). Indirect discrimination is said to occur where a requirement or condition is applied to a woman and which would apply to a man but is such that the proportion of women who are able to comply with the requirement is considerably smaller than the proportion of men who can comply. Individuals can take action against an employer under the provisions of these Acts. The burden of proof is on the complainant to show that discrimination has taken place.

In the USA, legislation outlawing sex discrimination has a longer history dating back to the 1964 Civil Rights Act (Title VII). This Act has since been amended in 1972 and subsequently by a series of Titles which have extended its range and coverage. Enforcement of Title VII is a function of the Equal Employment Opportunity (EEOC). The EEOC investigates charges of unlawful employment practices, and if it determines that there is reasonable cause to believe that discrimination has occurred, attempts to resolve the problem through conciliation are made. If conciliation fails, either the employee or the EEOC may bring suit against the employer. Therefore, unlike the situation in Britain, the individual often has the backing of a government agency in pursuing a claim. Well-publicised settlements involving thousands of employees, such as the American Telephone and Telegraph case (Wallace, 1976), have undoubtedly caused many large companies to revise their employment practices. Another notable difference between Britain and the USA is that the USA, unlike Britain, has introduced affirmative action provisions in the Executive Orders 11246 (1965) and 11375 (1967), administered by the OFCC (Office of Federal Contract Compliance). These provisions require certain firms to set goals and timetables for increasing the employment of all minority workers, including women, in the various levels of the organisation. Firms who have or want federal contracts are obliged to adopt these practices. The combination of affirmative action and the greater frequency of sex discrimination cases make the USA a more aggressive pursuer of equal opportunities for women than Britain.

There are also some important differences in the social policies of Britain and the USA with respect to child-care and maternity leave. Britain and the USA are alike in so far as they both have *ad hoc* provisions for child-care. There is evidence in Britain that child-care provision is inadequate to meet the demand for it.[1] There are no uniform government-sponsored schemes for child-care in either country, and a wide variety of provisions exist which include private day nurseries, co-operative day nurseries, employer's nurseries, paid childminders, relatives or friends. In the USA the government's involvement in child-care has been part of a poverty policy since 1962, and it has been aimed at very low income families. Provision varies widely from place to place and is generally limited to single, widowed or divorced mothers.

A further difference between the two countries is that since 1954, working parents in the USA have received tax concessions for expenses incurred for child-care. Until 1976 child-care costs were a deductible expense in computing income subject to taxation; the maximum deductible amount in 1975 was $4800 for families with incomes up to $18 000. (Beyond $18 000 the deductible amount gradually decreased and beyond $26 000 no deductions could be taken). Depending on the family's tax bracket, up to as much as 25 per cent of child-care expenses might have been recovered in lower taxes, but most families probably recovered no more than 20 per cent of their child-care expenses in this way, and lower-income families much less. In 1976 the deduction for child-care expenses was replaced by a tax credit of 20 per cent of working parents' total child-care and housekeeping costs up to a maximum of $400 for one child and $800 for two or more children. Under both the deduction and tax credit schemes, low-income families that owe little or no income tax can obviously derive little benefit. Since 1981 tax law in the US has permitted employers to make child-care provision tax-deductible, although it is too early yet to see the effects of this new provision.

Britain has a national scheme for maternity leave which American women do not have. The Employment Protection Act (1975) gives British women the right to maternity pay and protection from unfair dismissal and the right to reinstatement, the latter having been modified in 1980. Further details of the statutory minimum provisions and the qualifying criteria are contained in Daniel (1981) and in Chapter 6 above. In sum, the qualifying criteria are fairly restrictive, and large numbers of British women fail to qualify, particularly part-time workers. Although the USA does not have any legal requirements concerning maternity leave, some employers do provide either paid or unpaid leave. In 1978 about 20 per cent of employed women in the NLS young women's sample reported that their employers provided paid maternity leave; another 25 per cent said that unpaid leave was available.

In summary, the difference between the two countries in the treatment of child-care expenses and maternity leave may not be as great as would at first be supposed. Although some women in the USA receive partial reimbursement of child-care expenses through the income tax system, the amounts involved are typically small and rarely cover more than 20 per cent of the costs. British women have the advantage of maternity leave provisions, but many women do not meet the requirements of receiving benefits; on the other hand, nearly one-half of young employed women in the USA work for employers who either provide paid or unpaid maternity leave as a fringe benefit. However, the USA is clearly ahead of Britain in the length of time that equal opportunities legislation has been in effect and in its more aggressive enforcement of anti-discrimination laws. Our analysis of women's experiences will illustrate the effects of the differing legal framework and economic structures of our two countries.

THE TWO SURVEYS

The information available from these two surveys permitted a series of direct comparisons between British and American women's experiences. Direct comparisons of this kind are rare. There are some differences between the surveys, however. Most notably the WES collected information in 1980 about British women's past experiences on the basis of their memory recall. The potential inaccuracies of such a method have been checked as far as possible against other information collected in the survey, and the researchers involved were satisfied that the work history data were of a high quality.[2] The NLS is a genuine longitudinal survey which has interviewed the two cohorts of American women repeatedly since 1967/8. The potential problems for our comparison which would have arisen from the difference in the two surveys were scrutinised, and the conclusion was reached that the findings reflect genuine differences in British and American women's experiences. A full discussion of these problems and the nature of the two surveys can be found in Dex and Shaw (1986).

In order to make direct comparisons between British and American women, two cohorts of British women were drawn out of the WES data to match the American women by age. We will refer to these cohorts as *younger* women or *older* women, the definitions of each being as follows:

younger women were aged 14–24 years on January 1st 1968;
older women were aged 30–44 years in May 1966.

The numbers of women in each group are set out in Table 8.1. The US sample sizes are based on the numbers remaining in the survey by 1980, when the WES survey was undertaken. The USA contains an oversampling of black Americans, which means that in the analysis blacks are weighted by the inverse of their probability of falling into the sample. Other details about the comparisons and the ways in which British and US data were made equivalent are described alongside a discussion of the relevant findings.

TABLE 8.1 *Sample sizes of the two surveys for this analysis*

	Younger	*Older*
British (WES)	1423	1705
USA (NLS)	3509	3538

WORKING PATTERNS

If we examine women's employment in 1979/80 we see that British women in their forties and fifties were somewhat more likely to be employed than their American counterparts, but the differences are not large. The figures are displayed in Table 8.2. Among the younger women in their late twenties and early thirties, however, American women were much more likely to be employed than British women; the difference between the employment rates in the two countries was about 20 per cent for women in their late twenties and early thirties. The employment histories of the cohorts of women in the two countries over the twelve-year period 1967/8–1979/80 are displayed in Figures 8.1 and 8.2, and these illustrate that older British women had

TABLE 8.2 *Percentage of women employed at dates of NLS interviews*[1]

Age	*British*[2]	*US*
26–30	45.3	65.0
31–35	54.5	63.5
43–47	67.7	63.1
48–52	61.0	57.9
53.56	53.1	50.1

[1]January–March 1980 for young women; April–June for older women.
[2]Younger British women, February 1980; older British women, May 1979.

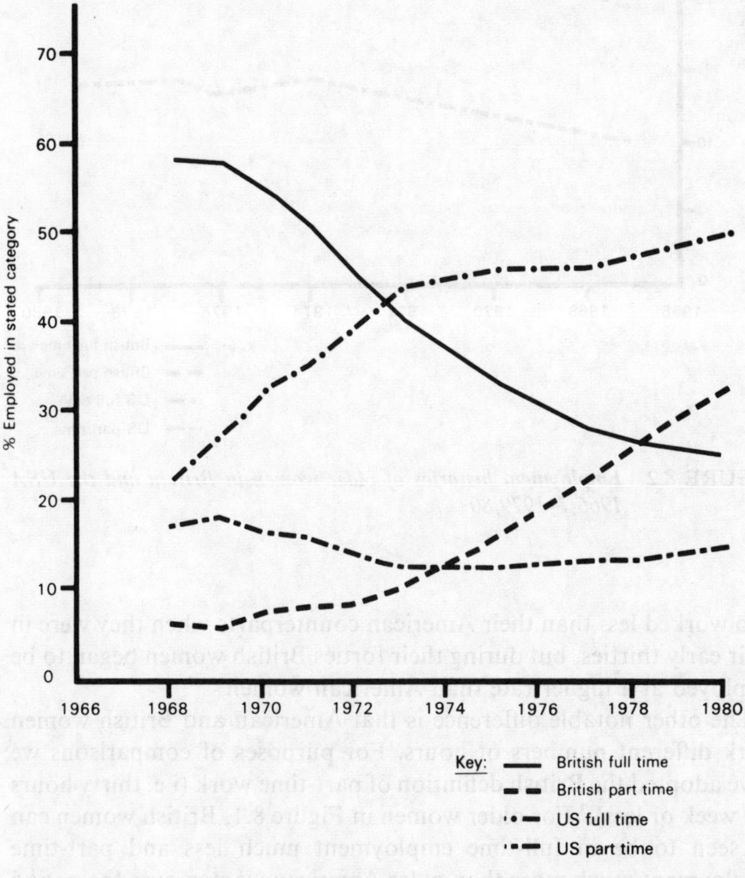

FIGURE 8.1 *Employment histories of younger women in Britain and the USA, 1966/7–1979/80*

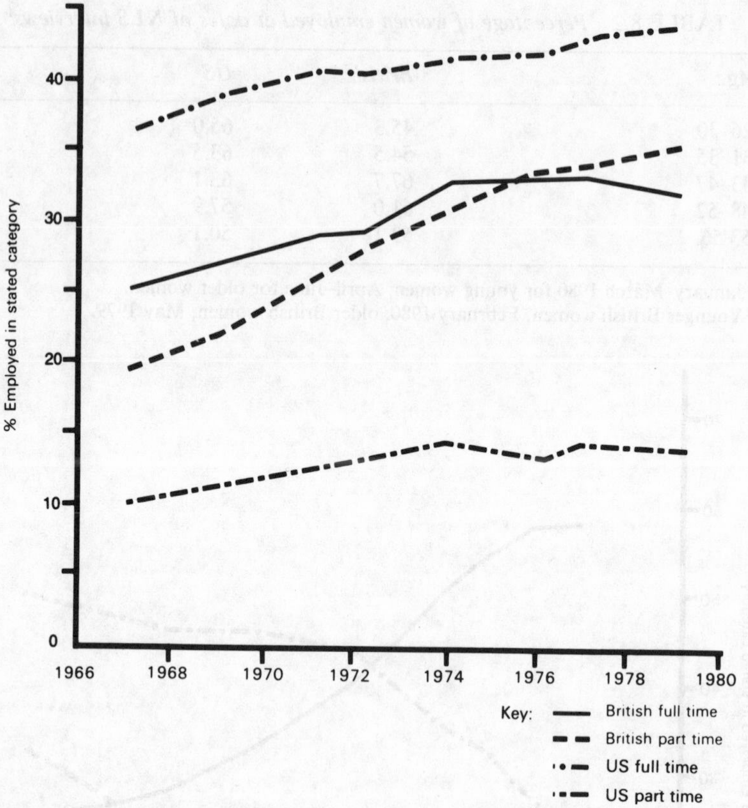

FIGURE 8.2 *Employment histories of older women in Britain and the USA 1966/7–1979/80*

also worked less than their American counterparts when they were in their early thirties, but during their forties British women began to be employed at a higher rate than American women.

The other notable difference is that American and British women work different numbers of hours. For purposes of comparisons we have adopted the British definition of part-time work (i.e. thirty hours per week or less).[3] For older women in Figure 8.1, British women can be seen to be in full-time employment much less and part-time employment much more than older American women over the period 1966–1979. The picture from the younger women's comparisons in Figure 8.2 is slightly different. We see there that younger British women were a markedly declining proportion of full-time workers but an increasing proportion of part-time workers over the period. We know from other sources that this pattern is established by school-leavers taking full-time jobs until they get married and first become pregnant in Britain.[4] British women then return to part-time employment after childbirth. Younger American women, on the other hand, work part-time more in their younger years, usually in conjunction with continuing their education. Certainly, younger American women work part-time more than British women at this age, although the positions are reversed later. American women's full-time employment increases as they get older and as they finish their education.

A summary of the total employment experience of women in the two countries was obtained by calculating their total time spent in employment as a proportion of the twelve-year period. Overall, younger women in the two countries were employed for approximately the same percentage of weeks over these years, i.e. 54 per cent. This similarity conceals differences within the younger women's cohort. British women who were in their late twenties in 1980 had worked approximately 60 per cent of the weeks during the twelve-year period compared with 54 per cent for American women. This difference reflects the much higher rate of employment of British women before the age of 20 which is not fully offset by higher rates of employment of American women when they reached their mid to late twenties. The fact that American women continue their education to a later age than British women is an important variable. The employment situation is reversed for women in their early thirties. British women had been employed for 49 per cent of the previous twelve-years, while American women had worked for 54 per cent. Older British women (in their forties and fifties in 1980) had been employed for about 57 per cent of the previous thirteen years as compared with 52 per cent for American women. More than half of the employment time of older British women was spent in part-time jobs.[5]

From the figures we have presented it is obvious that in both countries women's primary responsibilities for raising children strongly influence their employment. Three major employment patterns during the childbearing years can be distinguished: some women do not return to paid work until childbearing age is completed; some work at least part of the time between their first and last birth; and others never return. The figures are displayed in Table 8.3. Among other British women who had children, by far the most common pattern was to remain at home from the time the first child was born

TABLE 8.3 *Work patterns after childbirth up to 1980 (all women with children by 1980, %)*[1]

Work pattern	*Younger women British*	*Younger women US*	*Older women British*	*Older women US*
Never returned since first child	27.4	16.9	11.3	7.9
Returned after completing all childbirth[2]	40.3	37.0	59.5	45.9
Worked between births	31.5	46.1	28.4	44.8
Never worked	0.8	0.0	0.8	1.4
Total per cent	100	100	100	100
Sample size	1191	2247	1492	3036

[1] 1979 for older US women.
[2] Includes women who have had only one birth and have returned to work since this birth.

until childbearing was completed. On the other hand, older American women were almost as likely to undertake paid work between births as to wait until their families were completed before returning to employment.

Although returning after the completion of family formation is still the most common pattern among younger British women, a trend towards re-entering employment between births appears to be developing in Britain as well as in the USA. Since the childbearing period is not yet completed for many younger women, comparison between the two countries and between the younger and older cohorts must be tentative. We have counted women with only one birth as 'returning after all births'; if they have another birth, these women will then be counted as 'being employed between births'. Therefore, among younger women this category can be expected to increase in the future. It appears likely that by the time younger British women reach their forties and fifties, they will be more likely to have been employed between births than their older counterparts. Among younger American women, returning to employment between births has already become the most common pattern of economic activity, and by the end of their childbearing years a substantial majority of American women will have followed this pattern.

We are also able to compare the duration of time these women spent out of employment over their first break from employment for childbirth. A decision arises over whether to include women who have never returned after childbirth in this calculation. In the full report of this work we calculated both sets of figures. Here we will only describe the samples of women who had returned to employment after childbirth at least once. The duration of the not-working period in which we are interested is calculated from the date of the first birth to the date of the first return. The British and American distributions were quite different.

The mean length of time out of the labour force for older women who had returned to employment at least once after childbirth was 8.5 years in Britain and 7.7 years in the USA. For the younger women the same duration was 4.3 years in Britain compared with 1.6 years in the USA. American women therefore have on average a much earlier return to employment. The distributions of these durations are displayed in Figure 8.3. The major difference in the distributions, irrespective of whether we compare the younger or older women, is that in the USA many more women return to employment during their first year after childbirth. In the older group approximately one-quarter of the US women returned to employment within a year, compared with approximately one-eighth of British women. In the younger groups the figures have increased, almost doubled in both countries, but the gap between them is still very large. Of the younger US women who have returned to employment approximately 57 per cent had done so during the first year after childbirth, whereas in Britain the equivalent figure was approximately 30 per cent.

The fact that the younger generation has changed in the same direction in both countries, moving towards swifter returns to employment, suggests that the process occurring is the same in both the USA and in Britain, and perhaps that the gap between them means that US women are further along the road than British women in becoming continuously economically active. Between US and British women the gap is not caused through British women having significantly larger families. There is an average age difference of 30 years between the younger and older cohorts which might suggest that Britain is thirty years behind the USA, but we suspect that it is not a linear process, in which case the catching up could take a shorter time. The process will, of course, be constrained by child-care provisions.

An analysis of the determinants of this duration of not working across the first break from employment for childbirth using multiple regression analysis served to quantify the effects of a number of the influences on this duration. In particular, the effects of maternity leave on British women was examined. Women who took maternity

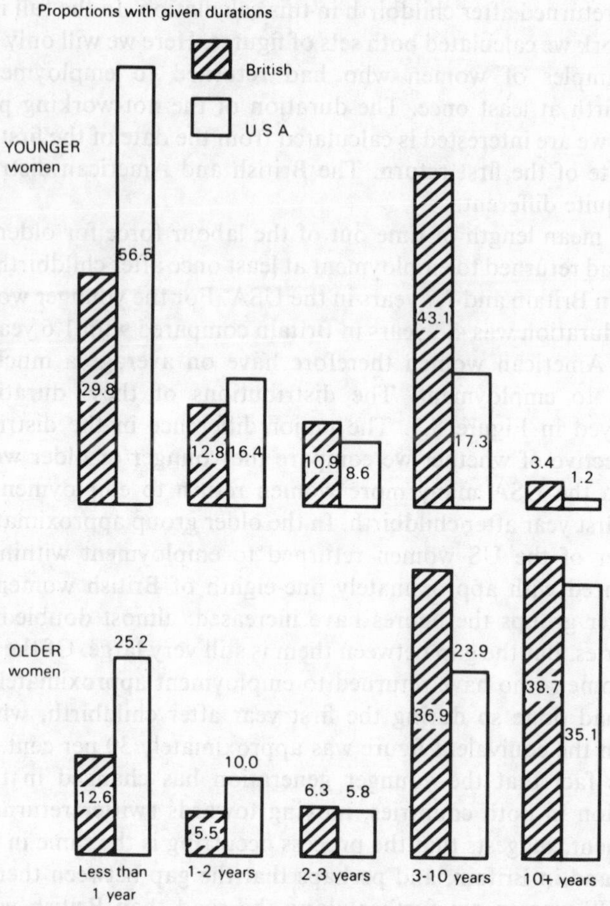

FIGURE 8.3 *Distribution of durations of time not working between first childbirth and first return to work*

leave were found to bring forward their return to employment by approximately four years in the case of the older women, and one year for the younger women. (Older women were not in a position to benefit from the statutory maternity leave provisions and relatively few of them took maternity leave). While the size of this effect was large and significant, it still leaves a gap between the average American women and British women who took maternity leave, other things being equal. Whatever the determinants of American women's shorter duration of time not working at this time, they are not balanced out by British maternity leave provisions.

CHILD-CARE

In the light of these differences in the durations of non-employment over the family formation phase, it is interesting to compare the child-care provisions used by working women in the two countries. The kinds of care used for pre-school children are set out in Table 8.4. The most striking difference between the two countries in both pre-school and school-aged child-care is in the role played by husbands. In

TABLE 8.4 *Percentage of working women using specified kind of child-care for pre-school children[1] (multiple coding of kinds of care)*

Type of Provisions used	*Younger women British*	*Younger women US*	*Older women British*	*Older women US*
Works at home (no external care)	8.2	—[2]	11.1	—[2]
Takes children to work	3.1	5.7	1.6	4.2
Only works in school hours or term	—	3.7	—	4.0
Child cares for self	—	—	—	—
Husband	51.0	16.8	36.0	17.0
Child's older brother or sister	3.1	3.5	3.3	18.7
Other relative	27.6	25.4	41.0	23.9
Person employed in informant's home	4.1	9.4	1.6	12.6
Child-minder, friend or neighbour	21.4	27.2	16.3	15.0
Day nursery/creche, soc. services, etc.	6.1	2.6	3.3	0.6
Private nursery, playgroup, etc.	5.1	14.2	3.3	8.2
Other	—	4.2	—	6.9
Total	129.7	112.7	117.2	111.1
Sample size	98	644	61	45

Notes:
[1]Asked in 1978 for US young women; 1977 for US older women.
[2]Not asked in US included in other.

Britain the care by husbands was the most common kind of care, involving half of the households of young working women and over one-third of the households of older working women who had pre-school children. In contrast, only about one-sixth of American husbands care for pre-school children while their wives are at work. Care provided by other relatives is also somewhat more common in Britain, except that older brothers and sisters provide considerable child-care for older American women workers. American women are more likely than their British counterparts to hire someone to come into the home or to send the child to a private nursery school or playgroup. Differences between child-care arrangements in the two countries persist after children enter school. Although the British husband's role in child-care is reduced when children reach school age, one-quarter to one-third of British husbands still provide care for school-aged children while the mother does paid work.

These differences in child-care arrangements are partly due to differing hours of work in the two countries. Husbands can provide child-care during their wives' part-time employment in Britain (this is not necessarily shift-work), but for women who work full-time, other child-care arrangements will usually be required. Women who work full-time are also more likely than part-time workers to be able to pay for child-care. In part these differences in child-care might be influenced by the tax incentives given to American women with respect to child-care, but in view of the small percentage of expenses reimbursed, this effect is probably not large.

We can now go on to examine some of the consequences both of the duration of time spent not working at childbirth, and the different jobs British and American women hold at this time.

OCCUPATIONAL MOBILITY

Women's occupations are important in that they determine to a significant extent the pay an individual woman receives as well as her employment prospects over the lifetime. Women's occupational changes over their family formation period are particularly interesting since it is the break from employment for childbirth which has been thought to be largely responsible for women's occupational downgrading and for limiting women's advancement. In Britain, many women also make a status transition from full-time to part-time employment over the family formation phase.

By comparing British and American women's experience at this time we hope to begin to answer some of the questions raised by other analyses. If a large proportion of women returning to employment in Britain return to part-time jobs, is this a major cause of occupational downward mobility? If a large part of women's downward mobility in Britain is associated with the take up of part-time employment, is this relationship similar in the USA? If downward occupational mobility over the period of family formation in the USA is not related to part-time employment in the same way as in Britain, then important policy implications can be drawn in Britain concerning women's occupational mobility.

Studies of occupational mobility in both the USA and Britain have found that women fail to make occupational status gains in comparison with men because of discontinuities in their employment to some extent. The studies also show, however, that the differences between men's and women's employment histories are only a part of the explanation of the status or wage gap between them, and that women also receive lower returns on their human capital.[6] Other studies have documented and quantified the extent of downward occupational mobility, particularly in Britain, and have located its occurrence across the break from employment for childbirth.[7] Our comparisons between British and US women allow us to evaluate the explanatory value of the various factors which are thought to influence occupational mobility across breaks from employment for childbirth. We can also see the effects of different policy provisions in the two countries.

We have the details of the younger women's occupations in their last jobs before and their first jobs after childbirth. The distributions of these occupations for the younger women are displayed in Table 8.5. The US occupations were reclassified to match the twelve occupational categories used in the British survey.[8] In part the distributions reflect some of the features of the British and US occupational structures for women. US women can be seen to be in clerical work to a greater extent, but in semi-skilled factory, sales and sometimes unskilled work to a lesser extent than British women of the same age. US women also have higher proportions as a whole than British women in the higher grade non-manual occupations (professional, teaching, nursing, and intermediate non-manual occupations).

Some notable changes occur across childbirth from these figures. Both countries experience a decline in the proportion in clerical work, although the fall is far more dramatic in the case of British women. The proportion in semi-skilled factory work in Britain also falls after

TABLE 8.5 *Younger women: occupational distributions of women at key points in their life-cycle (%)*

Occupation	*Last job before first child* *British*	*US*	*First job after first child* *British*	*US*
Professional	0.6	0.7	0.5	0.9
Teacher	4.7	7.0	4.3	6.7
Nurse	6.8	7.8	6.9	7.9
Intermediate non-manual	2.7	3.3	2.6	4.1
Clerical	34.1	38.3	19.2	33.1
Sales	13.9	6.5	12.8	8.7
Skilled	9.0	5.3	7.1	7.3
Child-care	0.5	4.6	3.1	3.2
Semi-skilled factory	20.5	10.6	17.8	10.8
Semi-skilled domestic	2.7	8.7	12.8	8.8
Other semi-skilled	3.8	5.3	4.3	6.8
Unskilled	0.7	2.0	8.7	1.6
Total	100	100	100	100
n=	854	1421	859	1421
Not available	16		1	

Sample: women with at least one child who have returned to work after childbirth.

childbirth, although in the USA there is no change. The US changes can be summarised as being a fall in clerical work, which is largely balanced by an increase in semi-skilled jobs (including sales). For the British women, the large fall in clerical work and semi-skilled factory work is taken up by large increases in semi-skilled domestic and unskilled work.

The examination of these summary tables suggests that British women experience a lot of occupational change over their family formation phase, whereas for US women the changes are not so great. We would be wrong to draw this conclusion, however, and a more detailed examination of transitions made at this time illustrates that the reverse is the case. American women tend to have more mobility than British women over this break from employment. The occupational mobility that is exhibited by American women at this time tends to balance out between the categories to a greater extent than with British women. For example, there is a greater flow out of clerical work for US women, but also a greater flow into clerical work than is the case for British women. There is least movement out of the higher grade non-manual jobs at this time in Britain and in the USA.

British women experience less downward occupational mobility than US women at the top of the occupational hierarchy, with the exception of nursing, but from clerical work downwards, US women experience less downward mobility and more upward occupational mobility than British women. In fact American women experience considerable amounts of upward mobility over this period and far more than British women, irrespective of their origin occupation. The conclusion from this comparison is that US women do not maintain their occupational position over the family formation phase by experiencing less mobility than British women, but by women in lower-level jobs experiencing less downward occupational mobility than British women and more upward mobility. These lower-level jobs are the ones which most women have, of course.

We can compare the older cohorts of British and US women before and after childbirth using their last job before childbirth and their most recent job at the interview. A summary of the distributions of these occupations is displayed in Table 8.6. The major occupational categories are the same both before and after childbirth, and they are similar to those found in the examination of younger women. In Britain, the most recent jobs of these older women show a decline in the proportion of clerical work and an increase in semi-skilled domestic and unskilled work. There is also an increase in the total proportion in all of the higher-grade non-manual occupations, which amounts to a rise of 6 per cent altogether. In the USA the fall in clerical work is more than balanced by an increase in the higher-level jobs.

The fact that we have found similar changes to be occurring to different generations of women in each country at approximately the same point in their life-cycle suggests that the occupational structures in the British and American economies have become accommodated to women's life-cycle employment patterns; in particular, to women's discontinuous employment over their family formation phase. These structures are slightly different from each other in Britain and the USA, however. Older British women exhibit the same pattern of downward occupational mobility at this time as their younger counterparts, and the experience of downward mobility is again greater for older British women than it is for American women. We will now go on to examine the determinants of downward occupational mobility

TABLE 8.6 *Older women: comparison of last occupation group before first birth and most recent occupation group (%)*

Occupation group	*Before first birth* British	US	*Most recent job* British	US
Professional	0.1	0.5	0.2	0.6
Teacher	3.0	5.1	4.2	5.8
Nurse	4.0	4.5	6.0	5.2
Intermediate non-manual	1.2	2.5	4.0	9.0
Clerical	29.4	40.8	21.3	32.6
Sales	11.5	7.2	12.0	8.4
Skilled	8.3	4.6	5.8	8.2
Child-care	0.6	0.6	2.5	1.3
Semi-skilled factory	27.8	14.8	15.0	10.9
Semi-skilled domestic	5.3	8.9	12.6	8.1
Other semi-skilled	6.2	9.4	3.7	6.8
Unskilled	2.6	1.1	12.7	2.3
Base (=100%)	1283	2171	1311	2171
Not available	28			

Sample: Women with at least one child who have ever worked after childbirth

at this time for the younger women's cohort. We were unable to perform this exercise for the older women.

We examine whether a woman's experience of downward occupational mobility between her last job before childbirth and her first job after childbirth was related to her occupation before childbirth, her time out of employment, and whether she returned to a part-time job after childbirth. Using multiple regression analysis we were able to quantify the importance of these factors on the experiences of occupational mobility across childbirth. Since the dependent variable that we are seeking to explain is dichotomous, taking the value of one if the woman experienced downward mobility and zero if she did not, the appropriate estimation technique is logit.[9] For purposes of comparison, a regression using ordinary least squares (OLS) was also carried out. A list of variables included with their definitions is provided in Table 8.7.

The definition of what counted as downward occupational mobility

TABLE 8.7 *List of variables in the regression*

DOWN –	Dichotomous dependent variable = 1 if woman experiences downward occupational mobility between last job before childbirth and first job after. Definition of downward mobility is in the text.
PART –	If job of first return after childbirth is part time, variable = 1, zero if full time.
TIME –	Time spent not working between date of birth of first child and first return to work, to nearest year.
OCC1 –	Occupational dummy variable = 1 of last job before first birth was either professional or teacher.
OCC2 –	Occupational dummy variable = 1 if last job before first birth was nurse.
OCC3 –	Occupational dummy variable = 1 if last job before first birth was intermediate non-manual.
OCC4 –	Occupational dummy variable = 1 if last job before first birth was clerical.
OCC5 –	Occupational dummy variable = 1 if last job before first birth was skilled.
	Excluded occupational dummy = semi-skilled factory
RACE –	Dummy variable = 1 if respondent black. Applies to US sample only.

at this time is partly dependent upon our occupational categories. A ranking of occupations according to the average earnings of working women in the occupation at the time provided a scale which approximately followed the order in which we have listed these categories in earlier tables. Downward occupational mobility is then a move to a lower occupation in the list. More precisely, our scale is as follows:

1. Teachers
2. Nurses
3. Intermediate non-manual
4. Clerical
5. Skilled
6. Semi-skilled factory
7. All other semi-skilled, sales, child-care and unskilled

There can be no downward mobility from the bottom category, so that we are left with six categories from which this experience can take place. This gave us five occupational dummy variables, with the excluded category being semi-skilled factory work.

A list of regression results for the British and US samples of younger women are contained in Table 8.8. The logit coefficients have been adjusted to yield 'OLS equivalent' coefficients in the usual way using the mean of the dependent variable. The likelihood of experiencing downward mobility at this time is increased if the first return job is part-time. The amount of the increase is approximately 31 per cent for British women and 18 per cent for Americans. Taking a part-time job has serious consequences in both Britain and the USA, although, as we know, it is British women who take this option on the whole, and the effect is considerably greater in Britain. Every additional year spent out of employment before the first return also increases the likelihood of experiencing downward occupational mobility on one's return by approximately 3 per cent for both British women and American women.

British and US women differ slightly in the effects of their previous occupations. Teachers and nurses are unlikely to experience downward occupational mobility at this time in Britain, a result which is confirmed by an examination of the transitions by occupation which

TABLE 8.8 *Regression results on the determinants of downward occupational mobility across the first break for childbirth (younger woman)*

Independent variables	*British*		*USA*	
	OLS	*logit*[1]	*OLS*	*logit*[2]
PART	0.254 (6.4)[3]	0.306 (6.1)	0.167 (5.8)	0.176 (5.7)
TIME	0.026 (5.2)	0.028 (4.9)	0.029 (4.5)	0.028 (4.2)
OCC1	−0.196 (2.5)	−0.263 (2.5)	0.025 (0.5)	0.023 (0.4)
OCC2	−0.110 (1.6)	−0.128 (1.5)	−0.134 (2.4)	−0.199 (2.6)
OCC3	0.037 (0.4)	0.043 (0.4)	0.270 (4.0)	0.238 (3.5)
OCC4	0.028 (0.6)	0.030 (0.6)	−0.001 (0.0)	−0.004 (0.1)
OCC5	0.10 (0.2)	0.013 (0.2)	0.053 (0.8)	0.048 (0.7)
RACE	—	—	0.098 (2.9)	0.108 (3.0)
CONSTANT	0.143 (3.2)	0.416 (7.1)	0.131 (3.5)	0.346 (8.1)
R^2	0.130	—	0.088	—
−2 (log likelihood ratio)		918.9		1082.5
n	679	679	1024	1024

Notes
[1] Adjusted by $p(1-p)$. Mean $p = 0.410$.
[2] Adjusted by $p(1-p)$. Mean $p = 0.263$.
[3] t values in parentheses.

took place over this period. The likelihoods of downward occupational mobility from the other occupations are insignificant and similar to semi-skilled factory work in Britain. US women are least likely to experience downward mobility at this time if they were in nursing before childbirth, and they were most likely to experience downward mobility from an intermediate non-manual occupation. Clerical and skilled workers have insignificant results in the USA in comparison with semi-skilled factory workers, as is the case in Britain. The constant terms for the two countries are slightly different because British women clearly have a higher probability of experiencing downward occupational mobility over childbirth than American women. Other things being equal, US women even have a small negative probability of downward mobility. When the occupational dummy variables are used to adjust the constant terms we can note that semi-skilled factory workers' experiences are quite different in Britain and the USA, other things being equal, as are teachers' and nurses' experiences, but the other occupations are closer together.

This set of variables together explains only a fairly small amount of the variation in women's experiences of occupational mobility across childbirth, but they are all highly significant. We might have expected that the higher one's occupation to start with, the more likely one would be to experience downward occupational mobility, but these results show that there is no necessary relationship of this kind. In Britain it is rather the reverse, and the higher one's occupation the greater one's likelihood of keeping it. This analysis is not able to examine any changes in occupational status that may have taken place within an occupational category, so that we only have part of the story here. There may be considerably more experiences of downward occupational mobility than we are capturing (for example, part-time teaching jobs are mostly offered at the bottom of the income scale). Part of the unexplained differences between British and US women are likely to be because of the differences in equal opportunities legislation and policies which favour US women.

CONCLUSIONS

This comparison of British and American women over their period of family formation has revealed that the pattern of women's experiences is quite different in the two countries. American women have been moving towards taking very little time off for childbirth, returning to employment within one year of the first childbirth to a full-time job and paying for child-care, partly out of their full-time earnings and partly with the help of tax concessions for child-care. They experience relatively little occupational downward mobility at this time, and even experience some upward occupational mobility. British women, by contrast, take a longer time off paid work, although the trend has been to reduce this duration; they return to part-time jobs and rely on husbands or relatives for child-care. British women experience far more downward occupational mobility as a result.

We have been examining the younger cohorts while they are still in the middle of, or have recently completed, their family formation phase. The older cohort are further on from their family formation phase. It is interesting to note, therefore, that the results for the older women show a similar picture of losses and gains in occupational status over their family formation as that seen at its beginning in the younger group. One way of interpreting the difference between these generations is that the older women are further along the path which involves a recovery of any loss of occupational status caused by childbirth. In this respect, US women are also in a better position than British women.

The gap between British and American women's experiences is large and has not narrowed significantly between the generations. The most striking difference is the movement of British women out of clerical, skilled and factory jobs into less skilled and lower-paid jobs after they have children, whereas women in the USA actually show a slight improvement in occupational status during this period. We have also shown that both higher levels of part-time employment and the longer period away from employment contribute to the greater downward occupational mobility of British women. Now we must consider what contributes to more part-time employment and longer breaks from employment. Probably both demand and supply factors are important; labour demand and supply may in turn be influenced by legislation.

On the supply side, the lack of affordable child-care may lock British women into longer durations out of employment and into part-time jobs when they return. Tax deductions or credits for child-care have made it somewhat easier for American women to pay for child-care and take full-time jobs. On the demand side, there appear to be more higher-grade non-manual and clerical jobs open to American women than to British women. It is possible that the earlier enactment and more aggressive enforcement of equal opportunities laws in the USA have contributed to this difference. Increasing the number of women in managerial and administrative jobs has probably been one of the major successes of this legislation. However, there is little reason to believe that equal opportunities legislation has created much clerical employment. Rather, demand in traditionally female clerical occupations has increased throughout the 1960s and 1970s in the USA at well above the rate of growth in employment in the economy as a whole. We presume that the rate of increase of clerical work in the USA is faster than any increase that has occurred in Britain.

In the future, maternity leave provisions in Britain may go some way towards helping women to maintain their occupational status across childbirth. Our results also suggest that if women's position in the British labour market is to change, one part of the change must be better child-care provision than exists at present. In addition, improving women's status after childbearing may depend on renewed growth in clerical and other better-paying female occupations, and on the progress in opening non-traditional fields to women.

NOTES

1. See Bone (1977) and EOC (1978).
2. See Martin and Roberts (1984a, 1984b).
3. The exact hours of employment were available from the NLS data at all the interviews, so that the British definition of part-time employment could be used on the NLS data. In the WES data, the exact hours of employment were only available from the 1980 main interview schedule. The work history information contained details about whether women were working full- or part-time in the past, but the women were permitted to assess the definition of part-time employment for themselves.
4. See Dex (1984a).
5. Although a comparable figure could not be calculated for American women it appears from the yearly cross-sectional data that probably only 20–25 per cent of American women's employment was part-time during these years.
6. See Sandell and Shapiro (1978) and Corcoran (1979) for US studies, Greenhalgh and Stewart (1982), Stewart and Greenhalgh (1984) and Elias (1983) for British studies.
7. See Dex (1984b), Martin and Roberts (1984a), Joshi (1984) and Elias in this volume.
8. For the full details of this reclassification see Dex and Shaw (1986).
9. See Pindyck and Rubinfeld (1976) for a description of logit analysis.

9 Women and Paid Work: Prospects for Equality

Peter Elias and Kate Purcell

INTRODUCTION

> The principle which regulates the existing social relations between the two sexes—the legal subjection of one sex to the other—is wrong in itself and now one of the chief hindrances to human improvement; and ... it ought to be replaced by a principle of perfect equality, admitting no power or privilege, on the one side, nor disability on the other. (John Stuart Mill, 1869)

Since these words were first written over a century ago, women's legal status and rights relative to men's have undergone considerable improvement. Few would now take exception to the contention in the first part of the quote cited above, yet the elimination of privileges and perceived disabilities is a complex objective, especially when there is disagreement about what constitutes both privileges and disabilities. The concepts of equality and equality of opportunity are difficult to define, and even among individuals, organisations and governments aspiring to pursue these elusive ideals, there is considerable variation in both the goals aimed for and the means perceived as appropriate to achieve them. However, it is indisputable that Mills's 'perfect equality' is far from having been realised.

The contributors to this book have drawn on detailed materials from a wide variety of sources to yield what must be, for many women and men, a depressingly familiar picture. Women in paid work, particularly those who work part-time, are too often relegated to jobs which fail to capitalise on their education, training, experience and potential. The resulting inefficient use of human resources is directly related to the inequitable division of non-paid work; not only are women the major providers of care for children and the elderly, but they also administer and manage most other aspects of domestic life. The assumption that this entails a complementary and desirable asymmetry within households and communities which capitalises on the different qualities, characteristics and preferences of men and women is not borne out by the evidence we have assembled.

This chapter reviews and complements the evidence, examining the implications of these and other findings for the future of paid employment – the 'public sphere' of adult life – and for individuals, households and families – the 'private sphere'. Within each of these areas, we study past trends, review current research findings, and discuss possible developments over the latter half of the decade, outlining obstacles to, and scope for, further improvement. Finally, we examine the existing legislation which regulates the relationship between these two areas of social and economic interaction, and assess the prospects for increasing equality of opportunity in paid employment through changes in the legal framework.

THE PUBLIC SPHERE

The current situation

At the time of writing, there are over three million people in Britain who are registered as unemployed. It is important to take account of the fact that many people, including some women themselves, see male unemployment as a considerably more pressing social and economic problem than gender inequality. Indeed, popular commentary often suggests that married women's increased economic activity over the last twenty years has been a cause of male unemployment. A brief examination of recent and current employment and unemployment statistics will reveal that this is a misguided analysis for at least two reasons. First, we cannot rely upon official unemployment statistics to yield information about the relative male and female shares of job loss or unemployment. The official count of persons 'claiming unemployment benefit' understates female unemployment, since many older married women who are not entitled to unemployment benefit are, by definition, excluded. Undoubtedly the collapse of full-time employment in many sectors of manufacturing industry has had a pronounced impact upon male unemployment, but the impact on females has been equally if not more dramatic in some areas and industries (Coyle, 1984; Martin and Wallace, 1984). Given the extent of occupational segregation by sex (Hakim, 1979, 1981) and the different rates of pay for 'men's' and 'women's' work, there are unlikely to be many male applicants for the jobs which most women do.

Second, consideration must be given to the nature of women's participation in paid work. Broad trends in employment indicate little about the nature of jobs in terms of their pay, prospects for promotion, hours of work and stability. Table 9.1 illustrates these trends, showing that the growth of female employment over this period has essentially been a growth of part-time employment. While there has been some growth in self-employment for both males and females in recent years, the predominant feature of the labour market over the last decade and a half is the decline in full-time jobs and the rise in part-time working.

Table 9.2 shows some of the major occupational shifts that accompanied these employment changes of the previous decade. This table shows extracts of information from a comprehensive review of occupational trends over a thirteen-year period (Elias and Wilson, 1986), using a broad grouping of occupations in twenty categories.

TABLE 9.1 *The changing structure of employment, 1971–90 (millions)*

Category	*1971 level*	*Change between 1971–76*	*1976–81*	*1981–84*	*1984–90*	*1990 level*
Employees	22.1	0.4	−0.6	−0.7	−0.2	21.0
males	13.7	−0.3	−0.8	−0.7	−0.6	11.2
females	8.4	0.7	0.2	—	0.4	9.8
full-time	18.7	−0.5	−0.9	−1.1	−1.1	15.2
part-time	3.4	0.9	0.3	0.4	0.8	5.8
Self-employed	2.0	−0.1	0.2	0.4	0.3	2.8
males	1.6	−0.1	0.2	0.2	0.2	2.1
females	0.4	—	—	0.2	0.1	0.7
Total employment	24.1	0.3	−0.4	−0.3	0.1	23.8
males	15.3	−0.4	−0.6	−0.5	−0.4	13.3
females	8.8	0.7	0.2	0.2	0.5	10.5

Sources: Employment Gazette, various issues and historical supplement; *IER Review of Economy and Employment*, 1985, Vol. 1.

TABLE 9.2 *Major shifts in employment by occupational groups*

Occupational category		*1971 level (mills.)*	*% of male or female employment*	*1984 level (mills.)*	*% of male or female employment*	*Change 1971–84 level (mills.)*	*% Increase in male or female employmnt*
Males							
'Gainers'	Managers and administrators	0.6	8.6	0.7	5.0	0.1	21.5
	Other professions	0.7	4.6	0.9	6.6	0.2	18.0
	Engineers, scientists	0.4	2.9	0.6	4.5	0.2	28.3
'Losers'	Other operatives	3.8	24.5	2.8	20.3	−1.0	−17.6
	Other occupations	0.9	6.0	0.5	4.0	−0.4	−38.1
	Clerical occupations	1.0	6.2	0.7	5.3	−0.3	−19.1
Females							
'Gainers'	Health, welfare professions	0.5	6.0	0.8	8.5	0.3	46.8
	Clerical occupations	1.8	19.9	1.9	19.3	0.1	11.5
	Other personal service occupations	.4	16.0	1.6	16.3	0.2	10.9
	Other operatives	1.2	13.8	0.8	8.0	−0.3	−26.0
	Skilled operatives	0.4	4.9	0.3	2.5	−0.1	−31.5
	Other craft occupations	0.1	0.7	—	0.3	−0.1	−46.2

Source: IER Review of Economy and Employment, Vol. 2, Tables A5–A9.

For men and women, the three major growing occupational groups ('gainers') and the three declining occupational groups ('losers') are shown in Table 9.2. For men, the three occupational categories which exhibited the strongest growth in the period 1971–84 were 'managers and administrators', 'other professions' (a group which includes accountants, financial analysts, stockbrokers, economists, lawyers, etc.) and the professional scientific group 'engineers and scientists'. These three high-level occupational groups provided about half a million extra jobs for men, offset by major declines in the low-skilled manual 'other operatives' and the unskilled labourer group 'other occupations'. Together with clerical occupations, male employment declined by 1.7 million in these three occupational categories. By contrast, female employment expanded rapidly in health and welfare occupations (predominantly nursing), clerical occupations and the low-skilled, low-paid 'other personal service' occupations. These gains were offset by losses in craft, skilled and semi-skilled operative jobs.

The implications of these changes are clear. Male employment while contracting overall, has expanded in areas of relatively highly paid, high-status, full-time jobs. Conversely, female employment has expanded in line with the growth of service sector employment generally and part-time employment in particular. However, Beechey and Perkins (1987) show the importance of looking at the number of hours worked by employees relative to the numbers employed. They make the point that the numbers of women in employment have risen substantially in recent years, but the total hours worked by women may have actually decreased. Townsend (1986) makes essentially the same point in relation to the comparison of women's economic activity rates among EEC countries. He reflects that the female share of the labour force in the UK is amongst the highest in the EEC, but if part-time female employment was converted to 'full-time equivalents', the UK share of employment would drop to the EEC average. Thus, women's *share* of employment has not increased as dramatically as the activity statistics imply. The associated occupational/industrial trends yield no support for the popular idea that women gained paid employment at the expense of men. For many young women, particularly those who left school in the late 1970s and early 1980s without gaining qualifications, their job prospects were as bad, if not worse, than those of young men. For these women, the concept of a 'return' to work after a period of family formation may be particularly inappropriate. While more women are gaining access to higher-status jobs, these remain a very small proportion of the female workforce, and there is evidence that such 'highly qualified' women tend to become concentrated in female-dominated 'ghettos' within their chosen occupation and/or to form a flexible (and disposable) secondary workforce within it (Crompton and Sanderson, 1986).

Women and part-time employment

According to the preliminary results of the 1985 Labour Force Survey, 45 per cent of all women in employment and 55 per cent of married women work part-time (*Employment Gazette*, May 1986, p. 137). Part-timers tend to be concentrated in particular sectors, but the proportions vary dramatically between sectors. In the textiles and clothing industries, for example, about 20 per cent of all women employed in this sector work part-time. In miscellaneous services (hotels, clubs, restaurants, pubs, etc.) this proportion is closer to two-thirds of all female employees.

Robinson (1984, p. 59) has provided a minimal definition of part-time work as 'regular . . . work carried out during working hours shorter than normal', which begs far more questions than it answers and leads to variations, as she further discusses, between what is regarded as part-time in different countries. The 1980 Workplace Industrial Relations Survey defined part-time employees as those working fewer than thirty hours per week, whereas the Census of Employment uses the marginally broader definition of those working thirty hours or less. The Women and Employment Survey asked women to classify themselves as full-time or part-time and then asked the usual number of hours they worked per week and also asked about the arrangement of hours worked on a 'typical working day'. The findings illustrate the enormous variety of working hours and arrangements subsumed within 'part-time' and indeed within 'full-time' employment (Martin and Roberts, 1984a, pp. 34–8). Elias (1983), using a similarly self-rated classification, found that most women who classified themselves as part-time worked around twenty hours per week and most classifying themselves as full-time worked around forty hours, but patterns varied between different occupational and sectoral groups, and a considerable minority of both full- and part-time employees were dispersed over an overlapping range of weekly hours. This illustrates the fact that the labelling of jobs as full- or part-time can be, for political or administrative reasons, an ideological rather than descriptive classification which may be less closely correlated with hours worked than with terms and conditions of employment. According to the evidence of the 1980 Women and Employment Survey, part-time female employees appeared to be more likely to be segregated in low-status, low-paid occupations, and in all industrial and occupational groups to be in 'women only' jobs where they are unlikely to be given training, have terms and conditions of employment inferior to those of full-time employees, have little opportunity to acquire transferable skills or promotion, and are less likely to belong to trade unions than women in full-time employment.

The evidence for Britain, as several of the chapters in this book discuss, is unequivocal that women returning to part-time employment are likely to have experienced downward occupational mobility and skill downgrading relative to jobs they held before leaving the workforce to bear children. Approximately two-thirds of mothers initially return to part-time employment, but part-time employment is associated with varied employment careers, with women moving between full- and part-time work in both directions, rather than necessarily using part-time employment as a 'stepping stone' to full-time employment (Dex, 1984a). Part-timers are more likely to work in smaller establishments, but so are all female employees; Elias and Main (1982) report that 48 per cent of all female part-time employees included in the 1975 National Training Survey were employed in establishments of less than twenty-five employees, compared with 29 per cent of full-time females and 21 per cent full-time males. Part-time employees were more frequently found by Craig *et al.* (1985) to be employed in low-paying firms.

The future outlook

In an attempt to assess future job prospects for men and women, we draw upon recent work by the Institute for Employment Research, relating recent trends in public expenditure, world trade, productivity growth and investment to develop a forecast of employment by industry. Combining this forecast with information on past trends in occupations and part-time versus full-time working yields a projection of the likely distribution of paid work to the end of this decade. This projection is included with the historical trends portrayed in Table 9.1. The two right-hand columns show that a modest recovery in employment is forecast for the period 1984–90. The decline in male employment will probably slow down, while the recent growth in female employment may accelerate somewhat. Again, this growth is linked to a further major rise in part-time working, a link which derives from the forecast employment growth in insurance, professional business services, the National Health Service and miscellaneous services.

In terms of the occupational distributions of employment, high-status, male-dominated 'industrial' occupations will continue to expand. Clerical occupations will decline, mainly due to major productivity gains associated with recent technological advances. The health professions, particularly nursing, will probably provide an additional 150 000 jobs between 1984 and 1990. The only other occupations in which there will conceivably be significant increases in employment are skilled and unskilled personal service occupations (in catering, cleaning, hairdressing and the like). From this analysis of trends in employment, coupled with the findings presented in the earlier chapters of this book, we suggest that 'market forces' will operate in such a way as to increase the extent to which men's and women's jobs are 'segmented'. The continued decline in full-time, well-paid jobs, coupled with the expansion of less secure, part-time jobs, is likely to increase the pressures which propel women into low-status, low-paid employment.

THE PRIVATE SPHERE

The domestic division of labour and women's employment

The material discussed by Hunt in the introductory chapter indicates clearly that the complementary woman-in-the-home/man-in-the-labour-market model of family life is unlikely to have been a widespread pattern of household composition at any stage in twentieth-century Britain. It certainly is not representative of current practice, given that in 1986 women formed 42 per cent of the labour force, and over half of married women were engaged in paid employment. As Main discussed in Chapter 2, most women spend a considerable proportion of their adult lives in paid employment. Yet this stereotype represents a powerful cultural image of an idealised relationship between the sexes, and between the private sphere of the family and the public sphere of employment: an image which implicitly underlies contemporary social organisation. This has three main effects, which interact to reinforce one another. First, in practical terms, most domestic and non-paid work is delegated to women. Second, it is assumed that women are likely to have such extraneous responsibilities, which will inhibit their capacity and motivation to carry out responsible paid work wholeheartedly and make them a poor investment from the employer's point of view. Third, most secure, well-paid employment has been organised in terms of full-time jobs, which are not easily compatible with responsible parenting and household maintenance. The concepts of breadwinner and the family wage, allied to the reality of men's considerably higher average earning capacity, have reinforced this asymmetry in the past. Many male-dominated occupations make explicit demands on the labour and time of the job-holder's wife (Finch, 1983) and make additional out-of-work demands upon the holder himself – what Coser (1974) referred to as 'greedy occupations'. But as Delphy (1976, p. 81) has observed, in virtually all paid employment 'a "normal" day's work is that of a person who does not have to do his own domestic work'. Behind the concept of 'a normal day's work' lurks the shadowy and increasingly inappropriate concept of 'normal' family life, which also underlies the organisation of education, the health and welfare services, and commerce. Furthermore, the existing tax and social security systems serve to reinforce gender division and women's dependency (Abel Smith, 1983; Land, 1983). The cumulative outcome of these pressures is so powerful that, as Rimmer's evidence in Chapter 3 indicates, single parents are effectively forced to make the choice between taking on the traditional 'father' role of breadwinner, or the 'mother' role of carer: they are virtually precluded from being both.

Within two-parent families, the most common solution to the conflicting demands of responsible parenthood and employment is for the wife to work part-time, with paid working hours which enable her to minimise the conflicting demands from the public and private spheres. Dex and Puttick's exploration of the choices and constraints facing a couple who decide to have children indicates that the logical outcome of the British *laissez faire* approach to parental leave and child-care is to lock the male into full-time employment and the female into paid part-time work which complements but does not conflict overmuch with her parental role. The extent of women's participation in the labour market is obviously closely related to the constraints which most of them experience, for part of their working lives at least, relating to their family responsibilities. Child-care and responsibility for school-age children was the most frequent reason given by women interviewed in the 1965 survey who worked part-time (Hunt, 1968, Vol. 2, p. 52, Table B12a), and a clear correlation still exists between women's paid working hours and employment arrangements and whether or not they have dependent children (Martin and Roberts, 1984a, p. 37). Nevertheless, in periods when demand for labour has been high, policies and practices, at both legislative and local institutional levels, have been introduced to attract women into the labour market and to maximise the participation of those at the most labour-intensive phases of the family life-cycle. The relationship between the demands for labour, social policy and welfare measures and women's economic activity can be observed with particular clarity during and immediately after the Second World War (Riley, 1983; Summerfield, 1984). Furthermore, the evidence of both national surveys and other research on women's aspirations and attitudes to employment makes it clear that women 'fit in' employment around their child-care and domestic responsibilities less by choice than because there are not accessible or acceptable alternative ways of organising their dual workloads (Purcell, 1978).

Employers' labour force strategies

The most recent empirical evidence available (Craig *et al.*, 1984; Beechey and Perkins, 1987) suggests that employers' labour force strategies, allied to the changing labour supply conditions generated by unemployment levels, means that patterns of part-time employment and the relationship between full-time and part-time labour are undergoing considerable change. The major stimulus for this is employers' pursuit of increasing labour flexibility and the systematic use of new tactics to minimise labour costs and maximise productivity. Until the mid-1970s, most evidence suggested that part-time manufacturing employment was decreasing: Beechey and Perkins talk about finding themselves 'researching an absence' in some sectors of engineering where part-time employment had virtually disappeared by the time they carried out their field work, compared to prior patterns of 'supply-led' shifts in the 1960s, where women could unofficially 'name their hours'. 'Twilight shifts' for young mothers are far less common in manufacturing than they were ten years ago. Yet Townsend (1986) expects that the 1984 Census of Employment figures will almost certainly confirm that part-time employment is still the leading feature of national employment growth. As we indicated in the previous section, this is almost certainly due in large part to public and private sector services, but there are some grounds for anticipating increased part-time working in manufacturing if the prescriptive advice currently being directed at employers is anything to go by (cf. Nollen, 1982; Syrett,1983; Atkinson, 1984; Lee, 1985; Kendall, 1985). The attraction to employers of part-time female job holders, according to Bruegel (1983, p. 159), is precisely their assumed lesser attachment to the labour market and hence their flexibility and dispensability.

Discussions about part-time employment generally start from the two assumptions that there are some jobs which are by nature part-time jobs and that the supply of labour, i.e. married women, have particular characteristics which cause them to prefer and be more suited to part-time rather than full-time employment, principally their assumed domestic responsibilities. Of the first assumption, it is certainly the case that some tasks, such as those carried out by school dinner staff, do not apparently lend themselves to organisation into full-time jobs, but as Beechey and Perkins (1985, 1987) have pointed out, where there is such shortfall in tasks carried out by men, they have tended to be organised differently, in a package with additional tasks to fill the full-time hours: for example, school janitors and hospital porters. Of the second assumption, Craig *et al.* (1984) have pointed out that their study of six industries indicates wide variations in women's working time arrangements, with some industries being characterised by full-time female employment, shiftworking, and women working what are generally regarded as unsocial hours, whereas in others, women's absence was explained by their alleged generic unwillingness to work full-time or on shiftwork. They conclude that, 'to a large extent the traditions and expectations within a given work environment determined the patterns of working-time women found acceptable' (p. 77). Similarly, Robinson and Wallace (1984) and Robinson (1985) argue that *demand* for part-time employees, rather than employers' response to the *supply* of part-time employees, is now the major determinant of hours worked and the organisation of paid employment. It is true that women themselves often express preference for part-time employment. However, different patterns of employment in other developed countries and even within the UK, amongst different localities and across occupations, suggests that this is likely to reflect lack of alternative child-care provision and the organisation of education hours, as well as the so-called 'traditional' sexual division of labour in the home and the community.

Nevertheless, it is certainly the case that gender stereotypes, and the custom and practice of the sexual division of labour in the home and in the workplace, are intrinsically related to gender segregation and the segmentation of workforces both within establishments and the workforce as a whole. Craig *et al.* (1982, p. 84), assessing the relationship between the sexual division of labour and objective skill and task differences in the work that women and men in industry are typically employed on, conclude that 'jobs are not feminised because they are deskilled but deskilled because they are feminised'. The whole question of task definition, allocation, organisation and evaluation in workplaces is saturated with assumptions about gender, as Cockburn (1986) in particular has recently demonstrated. Beechey and Perkins (1985, 1987) argue that in some areas of employment, particularly public sector services with a 'caring' component, jobs have been constructed as part-time precisely because they have been seen as 'women's jobs', assumed to be best done by mature women who are mothers, and therefore organised in such a way as to take account of these women's presumed domestic commitments. The classic examples of this are women in the home help services. In other sectors Beechey and Perkins also found that where job requirements implicitly contained assumptions about gendered skill stereotypes – gentleness, caring, neatness, patience – they were more likely to be constructed by employers as part-time jobs. This is a rather different approach from the response to labour *shortage* which appears to have stimulated the growth of part-time employment during the war and throughout the 1950s and 1960s, when employers courted female labour by providing shifts and part-time working hours to fit in with women's working preferences. Both Beechey and Perkins and Craig *et al.* report a reduction in the provision of jobs with arrangements tailored to fit employees rather than employers' preferences throughout the 1970s. Where new part-time work had been created, the hours were clearly designed to fit in with employer or customer demand and not to minimise the 'dual role' conflict. It is clear that the factors which determine the level and distribution of part-time work are not necessarily congruent with those which determine female economic activity rates.

Given the extent of job 'labelling' and gender segregation at the workplace, it comes as no surprise that the difference between men's and women's earnings clearly *cannot* be attributed solely to differences in the training and qualifications acquired by women and men, or to the fact that women take breaks from employment associated with childbirth and family formation, as Main showed in Chapter 5. In his counterfactual example, if women 'behaved like men' in terms of their work histories, by working full-time throughout their working lives, this would only decrease the gap between men's and women's earnings by a factor of between one-third and one-half. Nor need the childbearing/childrearing phase be associated with downward occupational mobility and lifetime cost to the women concerned, as Elias's and Dex and Shaw's chapters indicate is clearly the case for most British women. Dex and Shaw's analysis of a similar cohort group of American women indicates that they had experienced on average a slight improvement in occupational status during their family-building phase.

We conclude, therefore, that the prospect for equality in paid work looks particularly bleak for most women. The combination of the shift towards those sectors of the economy in which jobs are constructed as part-time, coupled with the strategic move by employers towards greater 'flexibility' in employment practices, allied to increasingly *laissez-faire* caring arrangements for children and the elderly, suggests that many more jobs for women will be part-time jobs in the low-skilled low-paid sectors of the economy.

EMPLOYMENT LEGISLATION

The case for intervention

If, as we have argued, the persistence of inequalities of opportunity between men and women derive principally from gendered intra-household dependency relationships – the fact that most women continue to be ultimately financially dependent upon men, and both men and society as a whole depend upon women to carry out the bulk of caring and domestic work – what are the prospects for future progress? It may appear to be unrealistically radical and Utopian to begin from a position which stresses the necessity for reappraisal of the relationship between organisation of work in the house and work outside it, but this seems to us to be basic and inescapable. David and New (1986, p. 10) point out that 'the relations between the sexes are not just relations between adult men and women, or between male and female children, but relations between men and women and children of either sex'. It is the *political* question of how far such relations should be organised which underlies the promotion and denial of equal opportunities at every level of the life-cycle.

Both the private and public spheres and the relationship between them have already undergone considerable change in the last two decades. On one hand, women have argued that to be undergoing a period of transition, between being defined primarily in terms of their relationships to being held responsible for their own identities (Fields, 1985). This trend is reflected in married women's increased economic activity, the introduction of sex discrimination and equal opportunity legislation and other legislative and policy moves away from married women's dependency, such as recent British changes in the law pertaining to divorce and social security provision. On the other hand, increasing levels of unemployment deriving from economic restructuring and recession have made both governments and employers less enthusiastic about actively promoting equal opportunities for women. In addition, the present British government is on record as regarding women's employment as a threat to social stability and children's welfare, favouring fiscal and welfare policies which are designed to foster the woman-in-the-home/man-in-the-labour-market model of family life, both as an institution and economic unit.

There is a fundamental incompatibility between women's dependency and equality of opportunity. There is a fundamental incompatibility between equality of opportunity and being given special treatment in a way which reinforces the idea that childrearing and housekeeping are essentially women's responsibility. In an earlier work which addresses these incompatibilities, Rapoport and Rapoport (1976) identify four levels at which changes are required in order to achieve a more just and efficient division of labour: the societal, the institutional, the interpersonal and the personal. At a societal level, the legislation and policies that determine how employment, social welfare, education and public administration are organised are obviously crucial. At an institutional level, policies and practice in schools, places of employment, local recreational facilities and government agencies, both influence and constrain equality of opportunity. At an interpersonal level, people treat one another according to the norms and values which they have come to take for granted, according to their upbringing and experience. Gender roles and stereotypes are a central component of the way in which people relate to one another, in both formal and informal situations. At a personal level, each individual's identity – who they think they are and what they think their capabilities are – is inextricably linked to their gender identity, their perceptions of gender roles, and their experience of the sexual division of labour.

Although change at any one of these levels will have reverberations throughout the others, we feel that the most effective impetus for change is likely to come from the societal level, as has already been the case with equal pay and sex discrimination legislation in Britain. The limitations encountered so far are related to the limitations of the particular legislation (Bruegel, 1983; Gregory, 1982). We need to consider recent modifications and further proposed changes in such legislation to see if they have the potential to make substantial progress.

The case for intervention in the labour market rests upon the assumption that, left to themselves, employers and employees cannot resolve the tensions between the need for flexible contracts of employment, the sexual division of non-paid work, and the maximisation of women's labour potential. On this issue we have no qualms. The existing segregation of paid work into low status, low-paid part-time 'women's jobs' and generally more secure, better-paid, full-time, male-dominated occupations is derived from the operations of short-term market forces in a value-loaded context where women are systematically disadvantaged. Employers require to be convinced of the advantages of employing women at various levels of responsibility within their organisations and encouraging them to develop their full potential: they also require to be convinced of the social value of greater paternal participation in child-care. Without the backing of the law, few employers are likely to be sufficiently enlightened to take this radical change of perspective. Equally, the pretence that employees, particularly women employees, can organise for effective campaigning on the issues reinforcing job segregation has a hollow ring. Many women who work part-time are employed in small organisations, which limits the scope for union organisation and effective action. This factor, together with the competing demands upon their time which constrain many women in paid work, makes the possibility of large-scale collective action improbable (Purcell, 1979). Male employees are more often on record as opposing rather than facilitating the extension of equal opportunities in employment (Coote and Kellner, 1980). We conclude, therefore, that there must be significant further legal reforms if the relative position of women in paid work is to be enhanced. Other countries in Europe have already moved further down the road towards equality of opportunity than the UK, and there are proposals in the pipeline which, if implemented across the EEC, would force the British government to enact more progressive legislation.

The impact of EEC membership

Much of the most recent pressure for reform of legislation which affects men's and women's terms and conditions of employment has come from this country's membership of the European Community (Alexander, 1985). The medium-term Community programme on equal opportunities for women, submitted to Council in December 1985, advocates measures designed to effect considerable progress by 1990 (*European Industrial Relations Review*, 1986). The 1983 Equal Pay (Amendment) Regulations, which came into force on 1 January 1984, sought to bring the UK into line with other countries in the European Community in terms of a person's legal rights in pursuit of a claim for equal pay. Before the Equal Pay Act was amended, British women could only claim equal pay with male workers if they were doing exactly the same or similar jobs, or if two jobs had been rated as equal under a job evaluation scheme. Under the new regulations, a woman may pursue an equal pay claim 'where she is employed on work which . . . is in terms of demands made upon her (for instance, under such headings as effort, skill and decision) of equal value to that of a man in the same employment' (Section 1 (2) (c)). the number of equal value claims that have been made since the amendment came into force is small, and given the daunting procedural difficulties facing a claimant, it is not surprising to find that only a very few have so far been resolved (*Industrial Relations Review and Report*, 1985). Nonetheless, the implications for occupational segregation are enormous, as the most famous case, that of Hayward v. Cammell Laird Shipbuilders Ltd, illustrates. Ms Hayward, a cook, compared her job to those of male painter, joiner and insulation engineer. An expert report was commissioned and five factors or types of demand – physical, environmental, planning and decision-making, skill and knowledge, and responsibility – were assessed for each of the jobs cited. The jobs were assessed to be of equal value, but the employer appealed against this decision and refused to pay Ms Hayward the same basic wage and overtime rates as her comparators on the grounds that her terms and conditions of employment were alleged to be already more favourable than theirs. Ms Hayward has subsequently been unable to have this assertion declared invalid, and the appeal which she has lodged against the decision has yet to be heard.

If her appeal is allowed, the case provides a precedent which challenges the entire gendered evaluation of the relative worth of 'male' and 'female' skills (cf. Phillips and Taylor, 1980). There is already some indication that the 1984 equal value amendments to the Equal Pay Act has promoted a new awareness of the desirability to scrutinise taken-for-granted assumptions underlying payment systems and job evaluation schemes. Some unions have actively pursued claims on behalf of their female members, and others have used the implications of the amendment as a bargaining lever in negotiations with management. A number of equal value claims have been withdrawn following voluntary agreements between the parties. While there tend to be differing interpretations of how successful such agreements have been in terms of the amended Act, there can be little doubt that they represent an advance on prior practice and would not have been reached without its existence.

Current EEC proposals

Pressure for the removal of other obstacles towards equal treatment in paid employment have also derived from membership of the European Community. Two draft directives which are currently particularly relevant in this respect are those concerned with part-time work and parental leave. Under the former, part-time workers must be offered *pro rata* employment benefits (e.g. holidays, sick pay and pension arrangements) relative to those of their full-time counterparts. The directive also proposes that the process of internal recruitment from part-time to full-time jobs (and *vice versa*) should be used to promote routes back into full-time employment. Such personnel policies can hardly be deemed radical in terms of their potential to improve the status of women in low-paid part-time jobs, but they were judged to be 'inflationary' by the present British government, which has, so far, succeeded in blocking the implementation of this directive on a Community-wide basis.

Under the directive on parental leave, UK employers would be required to give parents a minimum amount of leave from paid employment of three months per worker per child following the end of maternity leave, to be divided equally between mother and father.

Thus, in a two-parent family where both parents are at work, there would be a total entitlement of six months' full-time leave. With the agreement of parent and employer the three months' leave available to each parent could be taken part-time and extended proportionately. All other EEC countries now have some form of parental leave or proposal for such. A 1985 House of Lords report noted concern about the possible increase in industry's wage and salary bill, but a study commissioned by the EOC (Holtermann, 1986) shows that such a scheme would increase the total wage and salary bill by less than 0.01 per cent. The potential benefits to employers were not estimated, relating as they do to less quantifiable advantages such as continuity of employment of female employees and less 'sick leave' taken by women with very young children, but it should be noted that the implementation of parental leave would also have an impact upon unemployment. In West Germany it was estimated that after the introduction of parental leave in 1986, one-year contracts would be given to 200 000 people currently unemployed. Other potential benefits to the Community as a whole are equally difficult to quantify, but if Cohen and Clarke (1986) are correct in their assertion that lack of alternative child-care does not prevent women from taking paid work, but merely restricts them to low-level, flexible employment, then it is likely that the capacity to take parental leave legitimately would lead fewer women to underachieve in terms of the jobs they feel able to commit themselves to doing. All nine other EEC countries already provide some form of parental leave for all or substantial parts of their workforces. Moss (1987) has indicated that the employment rate among mothers with young children in the United Kingdom is very low and that employed mothers work shorter hours compared with France, Italy, Belgium and Denmark. The British situation, he argues, is becoming 'increasingly atypical of industrialised societies'.

It is our opinion that these two areas, the status of part-time jobs within employing establishments and the issue of parental leave, represent the areas where there is an urgent need for legislative action. We do not delude ourselves by thinking that reform in these areas can bring about a rapid transformation in terms of the existing inequitable distribution of paid and non-paid work in our society, a distribution which is strongly rooted in terms of gender-based social roles and expectations and existing male-dominated power relationships in the workplace, at home and in the political arena. What parental leave does is to move the focus somewhat from facilitating the *mother's* employment and career to presenting *parenthood* as carrying responsibilities. Thus, the societal change has implications for the institutional, interpersonal and personal levels, so that employers and employees of both sexes are presented with the recognition of the need to modify employment practices to accommodate parental responsibilities.

We see this as not simply shifting part of the burden and occupationally disruptive aspects of child-care and domestic maintenance to fathers, but of enabling fathers to share more closely in the experience of early parenthood, to the benefit of parents and children. Recent research has established that fathers are increasingly participating more actively in childrearing and would welcome measures to facilitate their further involvement (Bell *et al.*, 1983). An indication of how such legal provision can gradually change attitudes and practices is given by examining the extent to which parental leave has been taken by fathers in countries where it has been established for some time. For example, in Sweden, where a paid parental leave scheme was introduced in 1974 and further extended in 1978 and 1979, mothers initially took the bulk of leave allowed, but fathers have been increasingly taking up their allowance (Moss, 1986, pp. 24–6). The Swedish parental leave measures, backed up by extensive and growing child-care services, are among the most comprehensive in Europe. Parental leave of 180 days immediately after the birth, plus 180 days which can be taken at any time before the child's eighth birthday, can be taken by either parent or can be shared between them in any way. Most parents take the entire leave allowance soon after the child's birth. A study carried out by Swedish researchers found that the largest proportion of fathers appear to take leave between the child's fifth and ninth month. For 270 of the days taken, the parent receives 90 per cent of her normal salary, and for the remaining 90 days a flat-rate allowance, the equivalent of about £5 per day, is paid. In addition to the above parental leave, Swedish fathers are entitled to ten days' paternity leave to assist at the time of birth. Most parents are entitled to 60 days' paid leave for family reasons for each child, to cover for sickness of the child or those who normally care for him or her, or for other legitimate reasons. Since 1979, parents of children under 8 have the right to reduce their normal working day by two hours. It has been estimated that the working hours lost and the cost of all these parental leave measures in Sweden in 1981 was considerably lower than those of sick leave. The social advantages, in terms of responsibile parenting and the facilitation of women's increased continuity of employment and exercise of skills, are qualitative rather than quantifiable. Perhaps the most valuable impact is the extent to which such measures and practices shift the balance of caring and co-operation and begin to break down the boundaries between employment and family development.

Moss (1986, p. 20) concedes that there are always likely to be tensions and difficulty in combining employment and parenthood, but argues forcefully that these can be minimised by child-care policies and provision which enable mothers to maintain continuity of employment and encourages fathers to play a more conspicuous role in childrearing. These include flexible initiatives such as the possibility of temporary part-time working for parents at particular stages of family-building, parental leave, the availability of high-quality child-care outside the family and, related to this, improvement in the socially valued image of child-care.

OTHER MEASURES TO FACILITATE EQUALITY

Child-care policies

The other main contributory factor which requires to be reassessed and developed is the provision of child-care outside the home – the extent to which it is seen as a private or public concern. As Cohen and Clarke (1986) have pointed out, the advantages of adequate pre-school and after-school child-care extend beyond facilitating parental employment, to facilitating parents' (and particularly mothers') participation in public and community life generally. They stress that it must be recognised that there is no direct causal relationship between the provision of public daycare and the incidence of women's economic activity. Of the full-time employed mothers of pre-school children in the 1980 Women and Employment Survey, only a minority paid for child-care outside the family, and most of these used childminders (Martin and Roberts, 1984a, pp. 38–40). Thus, most of the child-care which enables mothers to participate in the labour market consists of private arrangements with family and friends, supplemented by unqualified, low-paid carers in the community, who may or may not be registered as such. The provision of after-school care on schooldays and school holidays is similarly informal, unregulated and frequently inadequate, in terms of the needs of both parents and children (Simpson, 1978).

The provision of full-time places for the under fives in maintained nursery schools and primary schools in England and Wales has declined significantly since the late 1970s, and although childminders often provide an excellent service, there is disquieting evidence that the use of unregistered, untrained and irresponsible childminders is the only alternative available to many low-paid women (Jackson and Jackson, 1979). Moss (1986) advocates the creation of a coherent and comprehensive infrastructure to develop and maintain high-quality, accessible child-care services, administered by one or more government departments and local authorities working together. Rather than one preferred system of pre-school care, he suggests the retention of the current variety, enabling parental choice, but recommends an increase in publicly funded nurseries and nursery schools and more official monitoring of the provision, registration and supervision of non-statutory services. He believes that the incidence of unregistered private services would decline in the face of more widely available, high-quality publicly funded alternatives. Staffing, training and a more flexible and integrated approach to child-care and education in the locality as a whole would raise the status of child-care as an occupation and reinforce the legitimacy of all parents' participation in employment and public life.

Mottershead (1986) extends this debate to argue for an integration of care and education, and David and New (1986) advocate the provision of children's community centres modelled on the school rather than the day nursery. They have reservations about the obvious facilitating factor of workplace nurseries on the grounds that these ultimately suffer from the 'tied cottage' syndrome. They argue powerfully for a universally available integrated system of public provision of family support from infancy to adolescence to supplement and facilitate joint parenting, which would be reinforced by uniformly shorter working hours for all employees. We find their arguments persuasive. The costs of implementing such programmes are less than might be supposed if the benefits, including the creation of jobs which would be necessitated, are taken into account (Simpson, 1986; Land and Puttick, 1986). A less radical, but perhaps more immediately realisable, example of admirable publicly funded pre-school child-care is given by the French system, where the proportion of women in employment is broadly similar to that in Britain, but the proportion of women who are enabled to work in full-time employment is considerably higher (Walters, 1986).

Fiscal policies

The other most obvious approach to funding alternative systems of child-care is to encourage private provisions and parental choice by tax allowance, as is, to a limited extent, the case in the USA (cf. Dex and Shaw in this volume). As Land and Puttick (1986, p. 70) have pointed out, 'the [British] tax system operates on the assumption that childcare and domestic work are done in return for maintenance, not a wage'. It is, however, the case that recent proposals to reform the structure of personal taxation could have much wider and more serious repercussions for equality of opportunity. Under the present system of personal taxation, husbands receive a married man's allowance (that part of taxable income which is taxed at a zero rate) which is over half as large again as a single person's allowance. Married women with employee earnings receive an allowance equal to the single person's allowance. If the wife's earnings exceed her allowance, she pays tax at a rate determined by both her and her husband's income. This system, based upon the aggregation of a couple's income, must have a positive impact in terms of encouraging married women to participate in paid work at least up to a point where the couple cease to receive a tax-free income from her earnings.

Proposals to replace this system with single but transferable allowances could act to accentuate the domestic division of labour. With such a system, it is always in a couple's interest for the person who is likely to have a variable income to transfer all of their tax allowance to the person who has the variable income. This raises the question of whether such a system will act as a disincentive for a woman who wants to return to work following a period of family formation, but faces an immediate tax on her employment at a rate equal to the highest marginal rate paid by her husband. In Chapter 3 Rimmer exposed the inadequacies of the current tax and social security systems which encourage a woman to work part-time if her husband works full-time, yet discourage her initial work effort with a massive 100 per cent tax rate if her husband is unemployed. This punitive measure, reinforced by women's concentration in part-time and low-paid occupations, is the dominant cause of the increasing polarisation into two-earner and no-earner households discussed by Pahl (1984). The proposed 'transferable allowance' system of taxation may have a similar disincentive effect (Symons and Walker, 1986), but will impinge upon many more women, particularly those who have been out of paid work for some time and not just those whose husbands are unemployed.

CONCLUSION

Progress or regression

Legislation can undermine the mechanisms which perpetuate patterns of gender inequality on two levels: it can improve women's *access* to the labour market and occupational opportunities, and it can seek to ensure the equal treatment of women and men *in* employment. Without progress on the former dimension, equal pay, sex discrimination and employment protection legislation, however sophisticated and comprehensive, can only make limited inroads to the underlying problem of women's dependency. Without progress in the latter, women are increasingly likely to be segregated in a secondary labour market (Dex, 1987). As we stressed earlier, the continued decline in full-time, well-paid jobs, coupled with the expansion in part-time employment in the service industries and employers' growing preoccupation with the pursuit of flexibility, are likely to reinforce current trends. There is evidence that the hours of work and conditions of employment of part-time workers, notably where privatisation of public industries and services has taken place, are particularly vulnerable to restructuring, reorganisation and cost-cutting exercises (Coyle, 1985; Beechey, 1986). As Armstrong (1982, p. 35) concluded, 'Once women are confined to labour intensive processes, they will then be disproportionately exposed to their employers' attempts to minimise wage costs'. Without a major change to the system of tax and social security, to current arrangements regarding maternity, paternity and parental leave, to the provision of complementary child-care and to working hours (most immediately, the integration of part-time and full-time working as alternative and interchangeable lifetime employment strategies), then most women, unlike men, will continue to be faced with a choice between parenthood and a career. The majority of women will continue to underinvest in training, underachieve in their paid work, have discontinuous employment and re-enter the job market following family formation to a part-time, often 'dead-end' job. Employers have every incentive to increase the provision of such jobs not only at the margin of their workforce, given the greater flexibility that part-time working affords them, the relative lack of union interest in, and capacity to recruit, part-time workers, and the abundant supply of women willing to accept such jobs to increase their families' disposable income. Part-time workers have considerably less rights than full-timers, particularly with reference to employment protection and maternity leave provisions (Incomes Data Services, 1985). The British government, in direct contravention of the directive on voluntary part-time work, has recently advocated a reduction in current rights for employees working less than twenty hours per week, so that they become an even more economical 'flexible' proposition for employers. The impact of the recession has undoubtedly been to move the promotion of equal opportunities lower down the political agenda in Europe as a whole. Where opportunities for training and career advancement are becoming scarcer, it is possible that women have been losing ground.

On the other hand, there are positive indications. Women's confinement to the private sphere and lack of equal legitimacy in the public sphere is currently being seriously challenged by the ramifications of two recent European Court judgments. The Marshall case led to the amendment of the Sex Discrimination Bill of 1986, which gives women the right to retire at the same age as men in similar occupations. The Drake case, cited by Hunt in Chapter 1, highlighted Britain's failure to conform to EEC standards in the provision of invalid care allowance, which will henceforth be paid to married women carers, backdated to December 1984, the date of the implementation of the European Community equal treatment draft directive. The equal value amendment to the Equal Pay Act, as discussed, has enormous potential to break down gender segregation in employment, particularly if it is reinforced by the proposed parental leave directive's encouragement to fathers to regard part-time working positively, and employers to facilitate the movement between full-time and part-time employment. The EOC's *Code of Practice* (1985a), backed by the government, the Confederation of British Industry (CBI) and the Trades Union Congress (TUC) has been well received by employers and their organisations, and if it were universally adhered to, would represent major progress.

The composition of the labour force has undergone considerable change in the last decade, and projections suggest that if present trends continue, women will comprise almost half the labour force in the 1990s. There has also been a recent dramatic increase in the numbers of women setting up their own business (McLoughlin, 1985), although the majority of these are self-employed without employees and thus more likely to represent additions to the highly vulnerable flexible workforce than incipient captains of industry. Similarly, women have made substantial inroads into management and the professions (*The Economist*, 23 August 1986), but they are more prevalent at the lower levels, and among the flexible part-time niches of these occupations (Crompton and Sanderson, 1986).

Part-time employment, overtime working, temporary and casual employment, flexitime and annual hourly contracts, job splitting, job sharing and the use of short-term contractual labour are all different ways of managing the relationships between labour costs and productivity, but they also have implications for managing the relationship between employment and family life. The evidence we have reviewed indicates quite clearly that the growing demand for more flexible forms of labour utilisation by employers will reduce the prospect for equality of opportunity unless it is counterbalanced by measures to promote a better gender balance in the supply of persons willing to engage in flexible working arrangements. Given a breakdown in the occupational segregation which irrationally evaluates what have traditionally evolved as female jobs and male jobs differently, accompanied by measures which promote equal opportunities in employment through a smoother integration of parenting and employment, the selection at different stages of life from a cafeteria of possible working arrangements could provide the infrastructure for a more just, more efficient society. A change of government, or a change of priorities and strategies more closely aligned to the European Community programme, could lead to the implementation of such measures. But we are forced to conclude that the likelihood of a major change of perspective in the near future is, given the current economic situation, unlikely. There is a danger that women in the 1990s will be worse off than they are now, unless the erosion of such protection as was provided by their legal status as dependants is compensated by adequate opportunities to become potentially independent and equal to men. The provision of an equal opportunities framework has led governments and employers to become complacent, unwilling to face up to the very real barriers to equality which remain. Inequalities at the personal, interpersonal and institutional level will continue to be resisted unless further changes are promoted at a societal level. After all, over 90 per cent of individuals become parents at some stage in their lives. Policy measures at the societal level which promote flexible working arrangements for both women *and* men, such that they constitute a normal phase of the life-cycle mix of paid and unpaid work would, over time, have a positive influence upon personal, interpersonal and institutional gender relationships.

The measures advocated in this chapter can be divided into those which require major legislative initiatives, but which would be relatively low-cost, for example implementation of the parental leave and part-time work directives, and those which do not require extensive legislation but which, in the short term, would call upon public funds to a greater extent, for example the provision of nurseries and after-school activities. There is considerable political resistance to both categories of measure and, at a time of high unemployment, they are particularly vulnerable, in so far as even those who favour their introduction may find it difficult to promote them as priorities in the face of competing claims on public time and money. The message which must get through to politicians, at both national and local levels, is that such measures will almost certainly be cost-effective and promote a more efficient use of this country's human resources as well as promoting a more egalitarian society.

References

Abel-Smith, B. (1983) 'Sex Equality and Social Security', in J. Lewis (ed.) *Women's Welfare, Women's Rights* (London: Croom Helm).

Alexander, M. (1985) 'The Contribution of the European Economic Community to Equality Between Women and Men', *Equal Opportunities International*, 4, 4, pp. 28–31.

Appelbaum, E. (1981) *Back to Work. Determinants of Women's Successful Re-entry* (Boston, Mass: Auburn House).

Armstrong, P. (1982) 'If Its Only Women, It Doesn't Matter So Much', in J. West (ed.) *Work, Women and the Labour Market* (London: Routledge & Kegan Paul).

Atkinson, J. (1984) 'Manpower Strategies for Flexible Organisations', *Personnel Management*, August.

Beechey, V.(1986) 'Women's Employment in Contemporary Britain', in V. Beechey and E. Whitelegg (eds) *Women in Britain Today* (Milton Keynes: Open University Press).

Beechey, V. and Perkins, T. (1985) 'Conceptualising Part-time Work', in B. Roberts, R. Finnegan and D. Gallie (eds) *New Approaches to Economic Life* (Manchester: Manchester University Press).

—— (1987) *A Matter of Hours* (Cambridge: Polity Press).

Bell, C., McKee, L. and Priestley, K. (1983) *Fathers, Childbirth and Work* (Manchester: Equal Opportunities Commission).

Beller, A. (1982a) 'Occupational Segregation by Sex: Determinants and Changes', *Journal of Human Resources*, 17, 3, pp. 371–92.

—— (1982b) 'Trends in Occupational Segregation by Sex', Working Papers in Population Studies No. PS 8203, School of Social Sciences, University of Illinois at Urbana-Champaign.

Beveridge, W. (1942) *Social Insurance and Allied Services*, Cmnd 6404 (London: HMSO).

Black, C. (1915) (ed.) *Married Women's Work*, reprinted with an introduction by Ellen F. Mappen, 1983 (London: Virago).

Blinder, A. S. (1976) 'On Dogmatism in Human Capital Theory', *Journal of Human Resources*, 11, 1, pp. 8–22.

Bone, M. (1977) *Pre-school and the Need for Day-care* (London: HMSO).

Braybon, G. (1981) *Women Workers in the First World War* (London: Croom Helm).

Briggs, A. (1983) *Who Cares?* (London: Association of Carers).

Britton, M. (1979) 'Birth Intervals', *Population Trends*, 18 (London: HMSO).

—— (1980) 'Recent Trends in Births', *Population Trends*, 20 (London: HMSO).

Bruegel, I. (1983) 'Women's Employment, Legislation and the Labour Market', in J. Lewis (ed.) *Women's Welfare, Women's Rights* (London: Croom Helm).

Central Statistical Office (1983) *Social Trends*, 14 (London: HMSO).

Charlesworth, Wilkin and Durie (1983) *Carers and Services*, University of Manchester Psychogeriatric Unit (unpublished report).

Clark, G. (1982) 'Recent Developments in Working Patterns', *Employment Gazette*, July, pp. 284–8.

Cleary, J and Shepperdson, B. (1981) *The Ffynon Fathers*, Supplementary Papers No 2, Medical Sociology Research Centre, University of Swansea.

Cockburn, C. (1986) 'Women and Technology: Opportunity is Not Enough', in K. Purcell, S. Wood, A. Watson and S. Allen (eds) *The Changing Experience of Employment* (London: Macmillan).

Cohen B. and Clarke, K. (1986) *Childcare and Equal Opportunities: Some Policy Perspectives* (Manchester: Equal Opportunities Commission/ HMSO).

Coote, A. and Kellner, P. (1980) 'Hear This, Brother: Women Workers and Union Power', Report 1 (London: New Statesman).

Corcoran, M. E. (1979) 'Work Experience, Labor Force Withdrawals and Women's Wages: Empirical Results Using the 1976 Panel of Income Dynamics', in C. B. Lloyd *et al.* (1979), *Women in the Labor Market* (New York: Colombia University Press).

Corcoran, M. E., Duncan, G. J. and Ponza, M. (1983) 'A Longitudinal Analysis of White Women's Wages', *Journal of Human Resources*, 18, 4, pp. 499–520.

Coser, L. (1974) *Greedy Institutions* (New York: Free Press).

Coyle, A. (1984) *Redundant Women* (London: The Women's Press).

—— (1985) 'Going Private: The Implications of Privatisations for Women's Work', *Feminist Review*, 21, pp. 5–23.

Cragg, A. and Dawson, T. (1984) *Unemployed Women: A Study of Attitudes and Experiences*, Department of Employment, Research Paper 47 (London: HMSO).

Craig, J. (1983) 'The Growth of the Elderly Population', *Population Trends*, 32 (London: HMSO).

Craig, C., Rubery, J., Tarling R. and Wilkinson, F. (1982) *Industrial Organisation, Labour Market Structure and Low Pay* (Cambridge: Cambridge University Press).

Craig, C., Garnsey, E. and Rubery, J. (1984) *Payment Structures and Smaller Firms: Women's Employment in Segregated Labour Markets*, Department of Employment, Research Paper 48 (London: HMSO).

—— (1985) 'Labour Market Segmentation and Women's Employment: A Case-study from the United Kingdom', *International Labour Review*, 124, 3.

Crompton, R. and Sanderson, K. (1986) 'Credentials and Careers: Some Implications of the Increase in Professional Qualifications amongst Women', *Sociology*, 20, 1, pp. 25–42.

Daniel, W. W. (1980) *Maternity Rights – the Experience of Women* (London: Policy Studies Institute).

—— (1981) 'Employers' Experiences of Maternity Rights Legislation', *Employment Gazette*, July, pp. 296–301.

David, M. and New, C. (1986) 'Feminist Perspectives on Childcare Policy', in B. Cohen and K. Clarke (eds) *op. cit.*

Davidson, M. J. and Cooper, C. L. (1984) (eds) *Working Women: An International Survey* (London: Wiley).

Delphy, C. (1976) 'Continuities and Discontinuities in Marriage and Divorce', in D. L. Barker and S. Allen (eds) *Sexual Divisions and Society: Process and Change* (London: Tavistock).

Dex, S. (1983) 'Women's Work Histories – Part II', Report to the Department of Employment (unpublished).

—— (1984a) *Women's Work Histories; An Analysis of the Women and Employment Survey*, Department of Employment, Research Paper 46 (London: HMSO).

—— (1984b) 'Women's Occupational Profiles. Evidence from the 1980 Women and Employment Survey', *Employment Gazette*, December, pp. 545–9.

—— (1987) *Women's Occupational Mobility: A Lifetime's Perspective* (London: Macmillan).

Dex, S. and Perry, S. M. (1984) 'Women's Employment Changes in the 1980s', *Employment Gazette*, April, pp. 151–164.

Dex, S. and Shaw, L. B. (1986) *British and American Women at Work: Do Equal Opportunities Policies Matter?* (London: Macmillan).

Dolton, P. J. and Makepeace, G. H. 'Sample Selection and Male–Female Earnings Differentials in the Graduate Labour Market', Department of Economics, University of Hull (mimeo).

Elias, P. (1983) 'Occupational Mobility and Part-Time Work', paper given at conference on Women and Social Class, University of Surrey, 1983.

—— (1984) 'The Changing Pattern of Employment and Earnings Among Married Couples', *EOC Research Bulletin*, 8.

Elias, P. and Main, B. (1982) *Women's Working Lives: Evidence from the National Training Survey* (Coventry: Institute for Employment Research, University of Warwick).

Elias, P. and Wilson, R. A. (1986) 'Development in the Occupational Structure of Employment', in R. M. Lindley, P. Elias and R. A. Wilson (eds) *Review of the Economy and Employment*, Vol. 2 (Coventry: University of Warwick, Institute for Employment Research).

England, P. (1982) 'The Failure of Human Capital Theory to Explain Occupational Sex Segregation', *Journal of Human Resources*, 17, 3, pp. 358–70.

Equal Opportunities Commission (1978) *I Want to Work .... But What about the Kids?* (Manchester: EOC).

—— (1980a) *The Experience of Caring for Elderly and Handicapped Dependents* (Manchester: EOC).

—— (1980b) *EOC Research Bulletin*, 4 (Manchester: EOC).

—— *Behind Closed Doors* (Manchester: EOC).

—— (1982) *Caring for the Elderly and Handicapped* (Manchester: EOC).

—— (1985a) *Code of Practice* (Manchester: HMSO).

—— (1985b) *Model of Equality* (Manchester: EOC).

—— (1986) *Tenth Annual Report, 1985* (Manchester: EOC).
European Industrial Relations Review (1986) 'EEC: Equal Opportunities for Women: Medium-term Programme 1986–1990', *EIRR*, 148, May.
European Information Bulletin No. 1 (1985) (Sheffield: Trade Union Division of the Commission of the European Communities).
Ferguson, S. and Fitzgerald, H. (1954) *History of the Second World War: UK Civil Series, Studies in the Social Services* (London: HMSO and Longmans Green).
Fields, R. M. (1985) *The Future of Women* (Bayside, New York: General Hall, Inc.).
Finer, M. (1974) *Report of the Committee on One Parent Families*, Cmnd 5629 (London: HMSO).
Finch, J. (1983) *Married to the Job* (London: Allen & Unwin).
Finch, J. and Groves, D. (1983) *A Labour of Love* (London: Routledge & Kegan Paul.
Fry, V. (1984) 'Inequality in Family Earnings', *Fiscal Studies*, 5, 3, pp. 54–61.
Gershuny, J. (1982) 'Household Tasks and the Use of Time', in S. Wallman (ed.) *Living in South London* (London: Gower).
Gershuny, J. and Thomas, G. S. (1982) *Changing Patterns of Time Use 1961–1974/5* (University of Sussex: Science Policy Research Unit).
Greenhalgh, C. (1979) 'Male Labour Force Particiption in Great Britain', *Scottish Journal of Political Economy*, 26, 3, pp. 275–86.
Greenhalgh, C. and Stewart M. (1982 'The Training and Experience Dividend', *Employment Gazette*, August, pp. 329–40.
Gregory, J. (1982) 'Equal Pay and Sex Discrimination: Why Women Are Giving up the Fight', *Feminist Review*, 10, pp. 75–89.
Gustaffson, S. (1980) 'Lifetime Patterns of Labour Force Participation', Swedish Centre for Working Life, Stockholm, working paper.
Hakim, C. (1979) *Occupational Segregation*, Department of Employment, Research Paper No. 9 (London: HMSO).
—— (1981) 'Job Segregation: Trends in the 1970s', *Employment Gazette*, December, pp. 521–9.
Harris, A. I. (1968) *Social Welfare for the Elderly* (London: HMSO).
—— (1971) *Survey of the Handicapped and Impaired* (London: HMSO).
Heckman, J. (1979) 'Sample Selection Bias as a specification Error', *Econometrica*, 47, 1, pp. 153–61.
HMSO (1942) *Social Insurance and Allied Services*, Cmnd 6404 (London: HMSO).
—— (1944) *Statistics Relating to War Effort in the United Kingdom*, Cmnd 6564 (London: HMSO).
—— (1974) *Report of the Committee on One Parent Families*, Cmnd 5629 (London: HMSO).
—— (1980) *The Taxation of Husband and Wife*, Cmnd 8093 (London: HMSO).
—— (1986) *The Reform of Personal Taxation*, Cmnd 9576 (London: HMSO).
Holtermann, S. (1986) *The Costs of Implementing Parental Leave in Britain*, report prepared for the Equal Opportunities Commission, May.
House of Lords (1985) *Parental Leave and Leave for Family Reasons* (London: HMSO)

Hunt, A. (1968) *A Survey of Women's Employment* (London: HMSO).
—— (1970) *The Home Help Service in England and Wales* (London: HMSO).
—— (1975) *Management Attitudes and Practices Towards Women at Work* (London: HMSO).
—— (1978) *The Elderly at Home* (London: HMSO).
Incomes Data Services (1980) *Maternity Cover and Child Care*, IDS Study No. 230.
—— (1985) 'Part-timers, Temporary Workers and Job Starters', IDS Employment Handbook 31.
Industrial Relations Review and Report (1985) 'Equal Value: Where Are We Now?', *IRRR*, 356, pp. 2–8, November.
Institute for Employment Research (1985) *Review of the Economy and Employment*, 1 (Coventry: University of Warwick, IER).
Jackson, B. and Jackson, S. (1981) *Childminder* (Harmondsworth: Penguin).
Joseph, G. (1983) *Women at Work, the British Experience* (Oxford: Philip Allan).
Joshi, H. E. (1982) 'The Effect of Children on Women's Propensity to Earn Pension Rights', London School of Hygiene, Centre of Population Studies, working paper (April).
—— (1984) *Women's Participation in Paid Work: Further Analysis of the Women and Employment Survey*, Department of Employment Research Paper No. 45 (London: HMSO).
—— (1985a) *A Multiple Regression Analysis of Women's Participation in Paid Work* (London: Centre for Economic Policy Research).
—— (1985b) 'Gender Inequality in the Labour Market and the Domestic Division of Labour', *Cambridge Journal of Economics*.
Joshi, H. E. and Owen, S. (1981) 'Female Labour Supply in Post-war Britain: A Cohort Approach', London School of Economics, Centre for Labour Economics, Discussion Paper No.79.
Joshi, H., Layard, R. and Owen, S. (1984) 'Why Are More Women Working in Britain', *Journal of Labour Economics*, special issue, September.
Kendall, S. (1985) 'Changing Patterns of Work', *Industrial Society*, March.
Kiernan, I. and Diamond, I. (1983) 'The Age at Which Child Bearing Starts – a Longitudinal Study', *Population Studies*, 37, 3, pp. 363–81.
Land, H. (1983) 'Who Still Cares for the Family? Recent Developments in Income Maintenance, Taxation and Family Law', in J. Lewis (ed.) *Women's Welfare, Women's Rights* (London: Croom Helm).
Land, H. and Puttick, E. (1986) 'Paying for Childcare', in B. Cohen and K. Clarke (eds) *op. cit.*
Layard, R., Barton, M. and Zabalza, A. (1980) 'Married Women's Participation and Hours', *Economica*, 47, 1, pp. 51–72.
Lebo, D. (1984) 'On The Road to Emancipation', in *Cairo Today*, November 1984 (Cairo: International Business Associates).
Lee, R. A. (1985) 'Controlling Hours of Work', *Personnel Review*, 14, 3.
Lewenhak, S. (1977) *Women and Trade Unions* (London: Ernest Benn).
McIntosh, A. (1980) 'Women at Work: A Survey of Employers', *Employment Gazette*, November, pp. 1142–9.
McKee, L. (1980) 'Fathers and Childbirth – Just Hold my Hand', *Health Visitor*, 53, September, pp. 368–72.

—— (1982) 'Fathers' Participation in Infant Care: A Critique', in McKee and O'Brien.

McKee, L. and O'Brien, M. (1982) *The Father Figure* (London: Tavistock).

McLoughlin, J. (1985) 'How the Policy Didn't Work Out and Women Got the Jobs', *The Guardian*, 5 August.

Maddala, G. S. (1983) *Limited-dependent and Qualitative Variables in Econometrics* (Cambridge: Cambridge University Press).

Main, B. (1984) 'Earnings, Expected Earnings and Unemployment among School Leavers', University of Edinburgh, Department of Economics, mimeo.

Main, B. and Elias, P. (1987) 'Women Returning to Paid Employment', *International Review of Applied Economics* 1, 1, pp. 86–108.

Martin, J. and Roberts, C. (1984a) *Women and Employment: A Lifetime Perspective* (London: HMSO).

—— (1984b) *Women and Employment: Technical Report* (London: Office of Population Censuses and Surveys/Department of Employment).

—— (1984c) 'Women's Employment in the 1980's Evidence from the Women and Employment Survey', *Employment Gazette*, May, pp.199–209.

Martin, J. and Wallace, J. (1984) *Working Women in Recession* (Oxford: Oxford University Press).

Marwick, A. (1977) *Women at War 1914–1918* (London: Fontana).

Mill, J. S. (1869) *On The Subjection of Women*, reprinted 1919 (London: Dent).

Mincer, J. (1974) *Schooling, Experience, and Earnings* (New York: Columbia University Press).

Mincer, J. and Polachek, S. (1974) 'Family Investment in Human Capital: Earnings of Women', *Journal of Political Economy*, 82, 2, Part 2, S76–S108.

—— (1978) 'Women's Earnings Re-examined', *Journal of Human Resources*, 13, 1, pp. 118–33.

Mincer, J. and Ofek, H. (1982) 'Interrupted Work Careers: Depreciation and Restoration of Human Capital', *Journal of Human Resources*, 17, 1, pp. 3–24.

Moss, P. (1980) 'Parents at Work', in P. Moss and N. Fonda (eds) *Work and the Family* (London: Temple Smith).

—— (1986) 'Some Principles For a Childcare Service for Working Parents', in B. Cohen and K. Clarke (eds).

—— (1987). Private communication to Peter Elias, 25 September.

Mottershead, P. (1986) 'Resource Implications of Childcare Policy: A Discussion Paper', in B. Cohen and K. Clarke (eds).

Moylan, S., Millar J. and Davies, P (1984) *For Richer, For Poorer?*, DHSS cohort study of unemployed men, Research Report No. 11, Social Science Branch (London: HMSO).

Ni Bhrolchain, M. (1983) 'Birth Spacing and Women's Work: Some British Evidence', Centre for Population Studies Research Paper CPS 83, London School of Hygiene and Tropical Medicine.

Nixon, J. (1981) *Fatherless Families on FIS* (London: HMSO).

Nollen, S. D. (1982) *New Work Schedules in Practice: Managing Time in a Changing Society* (New York: Van Nostrand & Reinold).

OECD (1980) *Women and Employment* (Paris: OECD).

Olmsted, B. (1983) 'Changing Times: the Use of Reduced Work Time Options in the United States', *International Labour Review*,122, 4, pp. 479–92.
OPCS (1984a) *OPCS Monitor*, LFS 84/1, Labour Force Survey.
—— (1984) *OPCS Monitor*, GHS 84/1.
—— (1985) *OPCS Montitor*, FMI 85/3.
Owen, S. and Joshi, H. (1984) 'How Long is A Piece of Elastic?, Discussion Paper 8414 (Cardiff: University College).
Pahl, R. E. (1984) *Divisions of Labour* (Oxford: Blackwell).
Phillips, A. and Taylor, B. (1980) 'Sex and Skill: Notes Towards a Feminist Economics', *Feminist Review*, 6, pp.79–88.
Piachaud, D. (1982) *Family Incomes Since the War* (London: Study Commission on the Family).
Pindyck, R. S. and Rubinfeld, D. L. (1976) *Econometric Models and Economic Forecasts* (London: McGraw-Hill).
Purcell, K. (1978) 'Working Women, Women's Work and the Occupational Sociology of Being a Woman', *Women's Studies International Quarterly*, 1, 2, pp. 153–63.
—— (1979) 'Militancy and Acquiescence amongst Women Workers', in S. Burman (ed.) *Fit Work for Women* (London: Croom Helm).
Rapoport, R. and Rapoport, R. N. (1976) *Dual Career Families Re-examined* (Oxford: Martin Robertson).
Riley, D. (1983) *War in the Nursery* (London: Virago).
Rimmer, L. (1984) *The Changing Family*, working paper no. 4 (London: National Consumer Council).
Rimmer, L. and Popay, J. (1982) *Employment Trends and the Family* (London: HMSO).
Roberts, E. (1984) *A Woman's Place: An Oral History of Working Class Women 1900–1940* (Oxford: Blackwell).
Robinson, O. (1984) 'Part-time Employment and Industrial Relations Developments in the EEC', *Industrial Relations Journal*, 15,1, pp. 58–67.
—— (1985) 'The Changing Labour Market: The Phenomenon in Part-time Employment in Britain', *National Westminster Bank Quarterly Review*, November, pp. 19–29.
Robinson, O. and Wallace, J. (1984) *Part-time Employment and Sex Discrimination Legislation in Great Britain*, Department of Employment, Research Paper 43 (London: HMSO).
Rossiter, C. and Wicks, M. (1982) *Crisis or Challenge?* (London: Study Commission on the Family).
Rowland, V. (1981) 'The Impact of Current Maternity Leave Legislation', Report to Joint EOC/SSRC Committee, unpublished.
Sandell, H. and Shapiro, D. (1978) 'The Theory of Human Capital and the Earnings of Women: A Re-examination of the Evidence', *Journal of Human Resources*, 13, 1, pp. 103–17.
Shaw, L. B. (1983a) 'Human Capital Depreciation: Important or Unimportant for Women's Wages?', Center for Human Resource, The Ohio State University, mimeographed.
—— (ed.) (1983b) *Unplanned Careers: The Working Lives of Middle-aged Women* (Massachusetts: D. C. Heath).
—— (1983c) 'Does Working Part-time Contribute to Women's Occupational

Segregation', paper presented to the annual meeting of the Mid-West Economics Association, St. Louis, Missouri, mimeo.

Simpson, R. (1978) *Daycare For School-Age Children* (Manchester: Equal Opportunities Commission).

—— (1986) 'The Cost of Childcare Services', in B. Cohen and K. Clarke (eds).

Smee, C. and Stern, J. (1978) *The Unemployed in a Period of High Unemployment*, Government Economic Service Working Paper 11 (London: DHSS Economic Advisors Office).

Smith, J. P. (ed.) (1980) *Female Labor Supply: Theory and Estimation* (Princeton, New Jersey: Princeton University Press).

Smith, V. (1986) 'The Circular Trap: Women and Part-time Work', *Berkeley Journal of Sociology*, 28, 1, pp. 1–17.

Snell, M., Glucklich, P. and Povall, M. (1981) *Equal Pay and Opportunities*, Department of Employment Research Paper 20 (London: HMSO).

Stewart, M. (1983) 'On Least Squares Estimation When the Dependent Variable is Grouped', *Review of Economic Studies*, 50, pp. 737–53.

Stewart, M. B. and Greenhalgh, C. A. (1982) 'Work History Patterns and the Occupational Attainment of Women', Warwick Economic Research Paper No. 212, University of Warwick.

Stewart, M. and Greenhalgh C. (1984) 'Work History Patterns and Occupational Attainment of Women', *Economic Journal*, 94, 375, pp. 493–519.

Summerfield, P. (1984) *Women Workers in the Second World War: Production and Patriarchy in Conflict* (London: Croom Helm).

Symons, E. and Walker, I. (1986) 'Transferable Allowances: Some Questions Answered' (London: Institute for Fiscal Studies) (mimeo).

Syrett, M. (1983) *Employing Jobsharers, Part-time and Temporary Staff* (London: Institute of Personnel Management).

Thomas, G. (1944) *Women at Work. The Attitude of Working Women Towards Post-war Employment and Some Related Problems* (London: Central Office of Information).

—— (1948) *Women and Industry* (London: Central Office of Information).

Tinker, A. (1984) *Staying at Home: Helping Elderly People* (London: HMSO).

Titmuss, R. M. (1958) *Essays on 'The Welfare State'* (London: Allen & Unwin, reprinted 1976).

Townsend, A. (1986) 'Spatial Aspects of the Growth of Part-time Employment in Britain', *Regional Studies*, 20, 4, pp. 313–30.

Wallace, P. A. (1976) *Equal Employment Opportunity and the A T & T Case* (Cambridge, Massachusetts: MIT Press).

Walters, P. (1986) 'The Financing of Childcare Services in France', in B. Cohen and K. Clarke (eds).

Werner, B. (1983) 'Family Size and Age at Childbirth: Trends and Projections', *Population Trends*, 33, pp. 4–13.

—— (1984) 'Fertility and Family Background: Some Illustrations from the OPCS Longitudinal Study', *Population Trends*, 35, pp. 5–10.

Whitehorn, K. (1984) *The Observer*, 7 October.

Wilson, E. (1977) *Women and the Welfare State* (London: Tavistock).

Women's Advisory Committee of the TUC (1965) *Women Workers 1965*, report at the Annual Conference of Unions Catering for Women Workers (London: TUC).

Zabalza, A. and Arrufat, J. (1985) 'The Extent of Sex Discrimination in Great Britain', in A. Zabalza, and Z. Tzannatos, *Women and Equal Pay* (Cambridge: Cambridge University Press).

Zabalza, A. and Tzannatos, Z. (1985) 'The Effect of Britain's Anti-discriminatory Legislation on Relative Pay and Employment', *Economic Journal*, 95, 379, pp. 679–99.

Index